KLIM

KLIM

Michael Klim

With Nicole Jeffery

hachette
AUSTRALIA

hachette AUSTRALIA

Published in Australia and New Zealand in 2024
by Hachette Australia
(an imprint of Hachette Australia Pty Limited)
Gadigal Country, Level 17, 207 Kent Street, Sydney, NSW 2000
www.hachette.com.au

Hachette Australia acknowledges and pays our respects to the past, present and future Traditional Owners and Custodians of Country throughout Australia and recognises the continuation of cultural, spiritual and educational practices of Aboriginal and Torres Strait Islander peoples. Our head office is located on the lands of the Gadigal people of the Eora Nation.

NATIONAL LIBRARY OF AUSTRALIA

A catalogue record for this book is available from the National Library of Australia

ISBN: 978 0 7336 5161 8 (paperback)

Cover design by Adam Stuart Williams
Cover photography courtesy of © Simon Upton
Picture section photography courtesy of the author's collection unless otherwise specified
Typeset in Sabon LT Std by Kirby Jones
Printed and bound in Australia by McPherson's Printing Group

MIX
Paper from responsible sources
FSC
www.fsc.org
FSC® C001695

The paper this book is printed on is certified against the Forest Stewardship Council® Standards. McPherson's Printing Group holds FSC® chain of custody certification SA-COC-005379. FSC® promotes environmentally responsible, socially beneficial and economically viable management of the world's forests

To my beloved partner Michelle, my wonderful parents Ewa and Wojtek, my dear sister Anna, and my amazing kids Stella, Rocco and Frankie. Your endless support and love have been my greatest strength through the years. Thank you for always being there for me.

CONTENTS

Foreword

by Gary Hall Jr.

Swimmer and Olympian

This book is crap.

The temptation to indulge a villain reputation is too great at times. I was one of those kids who always cheered for the antihero.

I grew up watching professional wrestling in the 80s. Guys like Randy 'Macho Man' Savage flexed and growled through gritted teeth, hurling spittle-laced, incoherent trash talk toward equally bombastic opponents. Boxing had the outrageous antics of the legendary promoter Don King. Sport is entertainment. The ratings for these shenanigans dwarfed the viewership of swimming at the time. Swimming needed pizazz and showmanship. It needed character. And rivalry.

Then, unwittingly, after deboarding the flight into Sydney for the 2000 Olympic Games, I had an opportunity to play such a role. I wouldn't have chosen it. I didn't deserve it. But there it was on the front page of every Australian publication, 'Smash Them Like Guitars'. It was stamped on my chest before I got my passport stamp. The Aussie press had unfairly branded me the Ugly American.

For many years, I received a nod and a wink of acknowledgement from the members of that famous Sydney relay team. They knew; I'm not a total fucking prick. And ugly? No way.

I'd like to thank Klimmy for shedding some light on the infamous 'Smash Them Like Guitars' quote that manipulatively served as a rivalry powder keg in the lead-up to the 2000 Sydney Games. It effectively ignited the passions of Australian Swimming and the Australian public.

I did suffer consequences from that media branding. It took six years and six Olympic medals before I could sign a single swim sponsor. Apparently, sponsors dislike Ugly Americans as much as Australians do.

So with this disclosure that we've been behind-the-scenes mates, forever linked in Australia's greatest Olympic swimming moment, I'd like to drop the act and retract what I said about this book being crap.

There are great athletes and there are great people. Michael Klim is both. He was so difficult – and at times impossible – to beat in the pool. His perseverance, in and out of the water, inspires me. This book will inspire you. The raw honesty is disarming. His resilience in the face of adversity secures his placement in the upper tier of champions.

I'm proud to call him a friend.

Preface

I was first approached to tell the story of my life when I retired from swimming in 2007, but it felt premature at that stage. I'd spent most of my life in the cocoon of high performance sport and I didn't feel like I had enough life experience to produce anything more than a vanity project.

Over the years, I've received other proposals to write a memoir, but again I hesitated. I still didn't think I had something significant to say. In my mind, I'd just moved from one thing to another and had never taken the time to look back and consider what it all meant.

My perspective changed in 2020, as I'm sure it did for many other people. But it wasn't just the COVID-19 pandemic that encouraged me to re-examine my life and my priorities. 2020 was also the year I was diagnosed with the autoimmune disease Chronic Inflammatory Demyelinating Polyneuropathy (CIDP).

I was still in the process of receiving a diagnosis when the pandemic hit, borders closed and lockdowns began. It was a perfect storm. My symptoms worsened, I couldn't access specialist medical care from my home in Bali, and travelling to and from Australia became extremely difficult. I was cut off not only from appropriate medical treatment, but also from most of my family and friends at a time when I needed their support more than ever. The pandemic also severely impacted my business life, so I was under substantial financial stress too.

I went through the darkest period of my life from 2020 to 2022, when it felt like my whole life was crashing down around me. My physical capacity was draining away, I thought I might never be able to walk again, and I lost myself. That personal crisis could have cost me everything I love.

It was only through the love and care of my family and close friends, plus professional counselling, that I was able to pull out of my tailspin and find my way back. It has taken a huge amount of work and personal growth for me to get to a place where I can reflect honestly on my life and look forward with hope.

This book has come out of the terrifying period in which I was forced to confront my own mortality. As an elite athlete, I'd gotten used to feeling superhuman. My athleticism had formed my identity and I now had to rediscover who I was without a large slab of it. That's a work in progress. I'm not there yet, but I'm getting closer.

My diagnosis forced me to confront not only the future, but the past and the demons I had carried for many years.

I'm not sure which part was more difficult, but I'm laying it all out here now.

Writing this book has become part of the healing process. It has helped me to accept my new 'normal'. I hope that it resonates with others who are facing similar challenges.

Finally, I want to share my story in the hope that it will raise both public awareness and financial support for research into CIDP, which is one of the lesser-known autoimmune disorders but can be utterly life-changing for sufferers, as it has been for me.

Through the Klim Foundation, which my partner Michelle and I established this year, we are championing the search for new treatments and possibly a cure for CIDP, as well as providing greater support for sufferers. I want those who follow me on this unwanted journey to have an easier time and better outcomes. I want something good to come from my experience.

It's one thing to conquer the world, but another to make the world a better place. For many years, I pursued the first ambition with all the passion and drive I possessed. Now I'm going in the other direction. I invite you to come along with me for the ride.

PART 1
CHAMPION

CHAPTER 1

Smashing Guitars

I am standing on the blocks, waiting for the gun. I've been here a thousand times before, but never like this. In this moment, there are 34,000 eyeballs on me, 10 million watching through their television screens in Australia, and countless millions around the globe. But all I can see is my lane, and all I can hear is a thick silence. An eerie hush descends as we all strain to hear the starting signal.

Despite all those watchers, the three teammates standing behind me and my competitors beside me, in that moment I am alone. Swimming is often seen as a solitary sport – all those laps, hours daily when we are submerged, in water and in our own heads. But in reality, as an elite swimmer, I am rarely alone. I have coaches, training partners, teammates, managers, medical staff, sports scientists. There is a team around me, at training and in competition, that guides and advises, treats and supports. The team is with me every step of the way, until now. Once I stand on the blocks, no-one else can help. It's all up to me.

Before the gun fires, all things are possible. I could win or lose, return in triumph or despair, become immortal or forgettable. The hours, days, months, years of preparation will add up to victory, or come to nought.

It's an extreme place, and that leads to extreme emotions. Sometimes I love this moment; sometimes I hate it. My feelings are different every time. I've felt hope and fear and desire and desperation on the blocks, depending on how prepared I am for the race and the weight of expectation I carry. Ultimately, it's a place where you can't hide. Whatever you have inside yourself at that moment will come out in the race and will determine your fate.

But on this night, my mind is clear and I feel free – which is strange because things have not exactly gone to plan in the last 30 minutes.

The men's 4 x 100m freestyle relay final is the last event on the first night of the Sydney Olympic Games. It is my first swim of the Games. The team coaches agreed to rest Ian Thorpe and me from the morning heats – Thorpey because he also has the 400m freestyle to swim today and me because I'm the fastest swimmer and, by convention, it's my privilege to decide whether I want the hit-out or not. I don't. My final training hit-out yesterday was exactly as I wanted it to be. I'm ready.

In my absence, the Australian team has qualified second fastest for the final, behind the US team. They will be in lane 4 and we will be in lane 5. There's been quite a build-up to this race. The United States has never lost this relay at the Olympics, but there's been speculation that our young Australian team could challenge them with the aid of our home advantage in Sydney. A couple of weeks earlier, the US anchorman Gary Hall Jnr had written an Olympic diary entry for the online edition of US-based magazine *Sports Illustrated* in which he said:

> I like Australia. In truth, I like Australians. The country is beautiful, and the people are admirable. Good humour and genuine kindness seem a predominant characteristic. My biased opinion is that we'll smash them like guitars – but the logic in that remote area of my brain says it won't be so easy for the US to dominate the waters this time …

I don't know Gary that well at this stage, but he's a showman: loud, expressive, confident. At his home Olympics in Atlanta four years earlier, he came out shadow-boxing for his showdown with the great Russian sprinter Alex Popov, now my training partner at the Australian Institute of Sport (AIS) in Canberra. Gary thinks of himself as an entertainer, not just a sportsman, and he has a sponsorship with Gibson Guitars, so he reaches for a colourful phrase to liven up his diary: 'smash them like guitars'. It will play well to his audience.

Unfortunately, in the early days of the internet, his audience now includes Australia – and he has just given the Australian media the perfect ammunition to turn this race into a grudge match. It also plays perfectly into the Australian psyche. We're already underdogs, and that's the position in which we're most comfortable, an underrated team ready to rise to the occasion. Now our fiercest opponent has given us extra motivation to prove the world wrong.

Gary's words reach the local media while we are in our pre-Olympic training camp in Melbourne. Our relay team has already formed a bond, had meetings to discuss our approach to this race, led by our teammate Brett Hawke. He isn't a member of the relay – he's more a 50m specialist – but he has knowledge we need. Hawkey went to college in the United States – to Auburn University, a famed sprint school that has produced generations of Olympic medallists – so he knows how the Americans approach relays and why they are so successful. His message is that we need to do more than just prepare technically, by practising our changeovers and working out our team order and strategy. We also need to build trust between us to bind ourselves into one unit and truly believe we can win. We have meetings at our hotel, where we sit around and talk about tactics and the American approach to racing, but the most important meeting is at the MSAC pool, during a training session. We come together right on the pool deck, gathering our group, including our coaches. It is a statement of intent, in front of the rest of the Australian team.

I already have a good bond with the other guys. I regularly room with Thorpey at major championships; I live and train with Todd Pearson and Adam Pine at the AIS; I have been on multiple teams with Hawkey and our elder statesman Chris Fydler, who's already announced he will retire after these Games. Ash Callus is a rookie and we don't know him that well, but he seems unflappable. He carries himself well for someone who hasn't been in this position before. Between us, we settle on a strategy. The US team is confident of beating us ('smash them like guitars'), so we will try to use that sense of superiority against them, to take them out of their comfort zone. We will change the traditional racing order – second fastest, third fastest, fourth fastest, with the fastest as anchor. Instead, we will swim fastest to slowest. The plan is that our fastest swimmer (me) will establish a lead on the first leg and make the Americans chase us. Their second, third and fourth swimmers will want to reassert their authority quickly, so will burn energy to regain the lead on the first lap. We will let them do that. We will save our energy down the first lap and then surge on the second lap to retake the lead when they are starting to hurt toward the end of each leg. That's the theory anyway, but now it's all down to the execution.

Fydes, Todd, Ash and Adam Pine have been selected to swim the morning heat and qualify the team for the final. That was settled during the Melbourne camp, so they've had weeks to prepare for their part. Fydes' place in the final team is secure so the other three are fighting for one place in the final four. They need to bond together while they are competing with each other. It's a tricky balance to maintain, but necessary for them to perform on the first morning of the competition.

When it comes down to it, they all perform their parts perfectly. It's a close-run thing between the three contenders for the final spot, but despite his inexperience Ash swims the fastest in the heats and he earns the last spot, by 0.01 seconds from Piney. Todd and Piney have been integral to the team, but they will watch from the grandstand. The final team is announced in our Australian team meeting before the evening finals session. We will swim in reverse order, as planned – Klim, Fydler, Callus, Thorpe. We must declare our team an hour before the competition starts, so the Americans will get their first look at our strategy then, but they won't see the full picture because Thorpey hasn't shown his true ability in the 100m yet. To them, he's still a bit of an unknown quantity as a sprinter.

He heads to the pool before us because he has the 400m freestyle first. Fydes, Ash and I get on the shuttle together a bit later. Arriving too early at the pool tends to suck out your energy. We need every ounce we have for the task we have set ourselves. By the time we arrive, Thorpey is about to race, but I don't go out to the main pool to watch him live. I'd love to, but if you are exposed to the crowd's energy too early, it can overstimulate and drain you. I watch my roommate win Australia's first gold medal on a TV screen out the back. I'm happy for him, but I keep calm and focus on my warm-up. Ash and Fydes do the same, and we regroup afterwards. From now on, we will stay tight. We know Thorpey will join us later. Winning a gold medal is just the beginning. He has to do broadcast and mixed zone interviews, the medal ceremony and snatch a bit of warm-down time so he can get his lactic acid out and be ready to swim again, all in an hour. We're expecting him to join us in the marshalling room.

It's quiet at the warm-down pool now. The pool is usually a hive of activity during a session, with swimmers warming up and down, coaches running along the deck with stopwatches, managers wrangling us, but now it has emptied out. Apart from our support staff, everyone has gone into the grandstand so they can watch the big showdown.

One of our team managers, Jan Talbot, has been assigned to escort us to the call room. I'm happy it's Jan – she always has good energy about her. She tells us it's time to go. As we walk to marshalling, she's checking on Thorpey's progress on the walkie-talkie. Everything feels under control. We're ready for battle.

We're not the first to arrive in the waiting room, nor the last. The Americans arrive last. The race is only minutes away now. We're in a small room crowded with big testosterone-filled guys, all preparing themselves for the contest. All the other teams have their four swimmers ready, but we are still only three. Jan is checking again. Still no Thorpey. The marshals are now lining us up in order to walk out to the pool. And we're still three. Now the other teams are looking sideways at us. Where is he? Jan tells us he's having trouble getting into his suit, but he'll be here in a minute.

We know he has a problem with his suit, but we don't know the extent of it. In fact, he has ripped the zip of his fresh, dry racing suit while getting into it for the relay. Two years earlier, that wouldn't have been a problem because we all wore briefs for racing. But a technological revolution has taken place in swimsuit design since the World Championships in Perth. The swimwear manufacturers have created fabrics that slip through the water more easily than our skin. Now we cover up in full-length bodysuits. The downside is that they are so tight that it takes at least ten minutes to get into them – and that's when they are dry. No-one in their right mind would try to get into a wet suit. But Thorpey's one dry suit is now an expensive rag on the floor. His suits are personally designed for him, so he can't borrow one from a teammate. Unless he wears training briefs, he has no alternative but to try to get back into the wet suit he wore for the 400m. Most other swimmers are wearing neck-to-ankle suits with no arms, but his suit has full-length arms, and that makes it worse. Soon there are six people around him, each helping him to wrestle into an uncooperative skin-tight suit as carefully and as quickly as possible because there is no backup plan. Thorpey decides there are too many helpers and orders everyone out except Piney, who finally gets him into the suit.

In the call room, we play for time, sitting still while the other teams stand and get into line. Now every team is focused on the man who isn't there. Ash and Fydes still look calm, and that keeps me calm too. If these guys are chilled about it, I have to keep it together. Then there is no more time. The marshals are sending us out. We walk out to the arena and I look up at the massive spectator grandstand, trying to spot my parents, but I can't see them in the sea of faces. We stand behind our lane and begin our final preparation. We're still three. They begin the introductions with lane 1. We're still three. They get to the Americans in lane 4. We're still three. I have my head down, waiting for our introduction. Then I hear 'Hey, guys!' and he's finally here. Thorpey's wearing just his suit and his runners, and carrying a towel. He looks a bit flustered, but he's here, just in time for us to link hands and raise our arms to the crowd. They respond with an almighty roar. It's the loudest noise I've ever heard in a swimming pool. It rolls around over and through us, and it penetrates our bones. It's like an atomic blast from the 17,500-strong crowd.

The wave of sound passes and Thorpey plops himself in the chair behind our lane. The chair is usually reserved for the first swimmer, so they can rest their legs for a minute before the start. But I can see he needs a moment to centre himself so I let it go and work around him.

The benefit of this mini-drama is that none of us has had time to think about the race – or, more importantly, overthink the race. Thorpey's late arrival is the perfect distraction. As I shrug off my tracksuit and take a moment for myself, I register that I feel amazing, the freshest I have ever been before a race.

The whistle goes and the first swimmers step up to the blocks. My mouth is dry so I take a mouthful of water from the pool before I step up. I have Lorenzo Vismara of Italy to my left and Anthony Ervin of the United States to my right. Anthony is super young and talented, but I'm not focused on him. We haven't studied the American team that much. This isn't about them, it's about us.

We all step onto the blocks and I look straight down my lane. I feel so clear-headed. Everything is in balance, my body is primed, my emotions are charged. I'm not thinking about anything but the start.

The gun goes and ... pandemonium. I'm below the water now, doing my nine butterfly kicks before I break the surface at 15m. I can only hear white noise, but the energy of the crowd is electrifying. I launch through the surface and take my first stroke. It's pure. I catch the water like it's solid and propel myself forward. By 30m, I feel like I am skimming across the water. Everything feels automatic, quick but in control. I take my first breath at 25m, and a second breath as we approach the far wall. I'm in the lead at the turn. I stay under water to let the waves in my wake roll over me before surfacing again. I pick up my rhythm and the field starts to fall away. This is where the effort can start to tell, so I'm breathing every four strokes now to suck in oxygen, but I feel strong, like I'm on a wave and surfing. I can't see anybody, but I can feel Anthony somewhere near my thigh or my knee. That gives me the confidence to keep pushing. For the last 15m I bring my dolphin kick in again for the finish. I'm driving to the wall as if I will go straight through it. As I touch, I know it's been a fast swim. Fydes dives in and I look up to the scoreboard. For an instant I think I see 48.1 but then the splits vanish. I'm not sure what I've seen, but I know that Alex's world record is 48.21 seconds. I jump out of the pool and walk over to Thorpey. I can't help asking, 'Did I just break the world record?' 'Yes,' he confirms.

I look across at Alex, who is still to swim for the Russian team, but we don't make eye contact.

Fydes is doing well against Neil Walker. The plan is unfolding as it was designed to do. He lets Walker lead down the first lap and he goes past him on the way back. Ash is now on the blocks ready to hit the water. I'm yelling at Thorpey, knowing his anchor leg will be crucial, that we have a chance to win now. As he gets ready to step up to the block, I'm in his ear, trying to motivate him, but he doesn't need it. He's 17 years old and he has just won an Olympic gold medal. He shoots me a stern look that says, 'Don't ever shout at me like that again.' Noted. I turn to the pool and start yelling at Ash instead. The emotions I was keeping under control for my own swim are now bouncing around the arena. Ash has got us a slight lead against Jason Lezak. Thorpey dives in, a heartbeat ahead of Gary Hall. My own heart feels like it is about to break through my chest.

We had done a trial run with Thorpey anchoring our relay at the Pan Pacs a year before, and we'd won then, but this is the Olympics, he's still 17 and he's backing up after a world record in the 400m freestyle. So this is a gamble, even though it's based on solid training and competition data and our faith in his already demonstrated ability to rise to the occasion. We know he doesn't have Gary's top-end speed, but we also know that he will come home hard.

Gary dashes to the lead and at the turn he has half a body-length on Thorpey. With 25m to go, Thorpey is holding but he's not gaining much. Then the balance begins to shift.

Gary is tiring and Thorpey is gaining. With 15m to go, it still seems that the gap is too big. But Thorpey is charging now, eating into the lead with every stroke. His famous feet are churning up the water like an outboard motor. The three of us are leaning over the top of the block, desperately calling him home and trying not to get in the way of the officials. Three strokes out, he draws even and I know we've got this. In the last metres, momentum is everything and it is all with Thorpey. His timing is perfect. He reaches out and stops the clock at 3 minutes, 13.67 seconds, a world record, but even he isn't paying attention to the details now. I reach down and yank him out of the pool and we four hug and lift our arms in triumph and roar with delight, not that we can hear anything because the crowd is in an even higher orbit. They have lifted the roof off the Sydney International Aquatic Centre. Thorpey says we should play air guitars and we do. The crowd loves it, although it's not really our style. We start to settle down and the first person who comes to congratulate us is Gary. He's been painted as the villain, but he gets out of the pool, walks straight over and shakes our hands. That moment of sportsmanship lodges in my brain and will lead to a friendship further down the line.

It's not the first time Gary has been generous, and not the first time he and I have been connected by a guitar. But we'll get to that story later.

As this is the last race of the night, our medal ceremony is almost immediately afterwards. We have only a few minutes to collect ourselves, don our tracksuits and Australian flags and walk to the podium, with the US team and the Brazilians, who are even more excited than us to have won the bronze medal. Often the crowd is leaving while the last medals are being presented, but not tonight. The huge grandstand to the western side of the pool stretches almost to the heavens and it seems that everyone has stayed to celebrate with us. At the Olympics, the medals are presented by International Olympic Committee members, who nominate which ceremonies they want to do before the Games begin. Australia's IOC member Kevan Gosper has selected ours and presents us with the gold medals. We sing the anthem, congratulate the other medallists and then start a lap of honour. I break ranks almost immediately when I spot my parents at the front of the crowd and climb up into the photographers' stand to kiss them. I turn to go back to the pool deck, but then I hear a voice calling me that I would recognise anywhere. My sister Anna has joined my parents, so I turn back to hug her as well. I catch up with the team and we continue the tour. Prime Minister John Howard and his wife Janette are madly waving a flag at us. We come to the Australian team, and our coaches and some of the legends who have acted as mentors for us, Dawn Fraser and John Konrads among them. We get back to the warm-down pool and Greg Norman is there to congratulate us.

Then there are media interviews, a press conference, drug-testing, warm-downs and massages. It's a blur, but one moment stands out. After the press conference, the Australian team's media manager Ian Hanson leads us out onto a terrace overlooking the Olympic Boulevard, saying:

'Come over here, have a look at this.' By then it is almost midnight, but there is a sea of people in Olympic Park, hundreds of thousands, as far as the eye can see. We're spotted and it's bedlam. They are cheering and screaming and clapping and waving. It's a surreal scene. I wonder if this is what it feels like to be a rock star. Not bad for an immigrant kid they called Lumpy.

CHAPTER 2

Beginnings

In the 1970s, times are pretty tough in Poland. The country is struggling economically behind the Iron Curtain and under a communist system that has limited options for a natural entrepreneur like my father. The Solidarity trade union, which will be born in the Baltic Sea shipyards of Gdansk and Gdynia under Lech Wałęsa, and will eventually end communist rule in Poland, is still a few years away, but the protest movement is growing on the docks.

A wave of strikes, demonstrations and riots occurs in Gdynia and Gdansk just before Christmas 1970, sparked by a sharp rise in food prices, and a dozen or more Polish workers are killed in Gdynia by police and soldiers putting down the rebellion. The turmoil leads to a change of party leadership, but the unrest continues on and off through the 1970s and gains pace in the 1980s. As a Gdynia native, my father Wojtek gravitates naturally toward trade as his occupation. After finishing school, he completes a master's degree in the economics of international trade in nearby Sopot, then gets a job in a state-owned trade company. About that time, he and my mother Ewa start dating. Their families have lived in the same apartment building for 20 years. Her family is from Warsaw, but they moved to Gdynia when she was seven. She studies pharmacy at university, but then switches to become an engineer in food technology. They marry in 1972.

By 1974, my father's expertise and further postgraduate study of foreign trade have earned him a six-month posting to the Polish-Lebanese company in Beirut for management training. He's supposed to follow up with a five-year posting there from 1975, but a civil war breaks out in Lebanon and his posting is cancelled. My sister is born in December 1975 and I am born in August 1977, in my father's hometown of Gdynia. Shortly afterwards, my father is appointed as a trade attaché to the Polish consulate in India.

People assume my first memories are of grey Poland in the communist era, but the exact opposite is true. My earliest memories are of the heat and colour of Bombay, now Mumbai, where we live a relatively privileged expat life in a wealthy enclave, with a nanny, a housekeeper and a driver. The expat community is very social so lots of parties take place. As recent arrivals from northern Europe, we're not used to the heat. We spend all our spare time trying to cool off at the Breach Candy Club, which boasts one of the biggest salt-water pools in the world, on land adjacent to the Arabian Sea. Anna and I spend many hours there, playing in the water and having swimming lessons. That's where we first learn to swim under the expert tutelage of

Mrs Bathena, who will become a family friend for life. Only 18 months older, my sister is my pathfinder, protector and constant companion. She's always by my side. Whatever she does, I want to do, including learning to swim. The pool is the safest place for me because I am active and curious, climbing on things, falling off them, going to the hospital for stitches or, most memorably, sticking a piece of LEGO® so far up my nose that we have to go back to the hospital to get it out. Conveniently, the hospital is part of the same complex as the club.

We are in Bombay for almost five years before my father's term finishes and we return to his hometown of Gdynia, where he secures another position in a state-run trade company. Our name is Klim, but it should be Klima as it was in my grandfather's day. It means climate or weather, which might account for my emotional volatility. But there was an administrative error when my grandfather Jerzy, a construction engineer and architect, joined the Polish Army as an officer before World War II. They accidentally left the 'a' off his name on his identity card, so Klima became Klim. That was his name when he was captured by the Germans and interned in a detention camp for the five years of the war. My maternal grandfather spent the war fighting as part of the Polish underground. He was a member of the Armia Krajowa (Home Army). Afterwards, both families decided to make a new start in Gdynia, where there was the promise of work.

When we return from Bombay, we move into a comfortable three-bedroom apartment in the north of the city. It is near a forest and a cemetery so there is space to play and explore. As it turns out, it's safer outdoors than in my own apartment building.

A marble staircase winds through the centre of the building, and one day I take it into my head to slide down the banister from our third-floor apartment. But I overbalance and fall down one floor, knocking myself out. A neighbour finds me bloodied and bruised with a dislocated jaw, and carries me back up to our apartment. I wake up just as Mum opens the door and sees me. And we are back to the hospital again.

Then there is the Coke bottle incident. I am carrying too many bottles at once, and I drop them and fall on the broken glass. Hello, hospital. My parents agree to buy a dog, a black boxer we call Shot. One day, Anna and I are walking Shot next to the road and he's so strong that he pulls me into the traffic and a passing car hits him. It bowls him over but he's okay afterwards, with a few stitches. For once, I escape unscathed.

We're an active family so we join the local equivalent of Breach Candy, the Arka Gdynia sporting club, where we swim and play tennis. Dad's sporting passion is tennis, so we all play. At that point, Anna and I are both swimmers, but soon Anna will switch her sporting passion to tennis. I'm only six but I'm already a fairly good swimmer. In Bombay I've had the kind of exposure to swimming at a young age that is rare in Poland. So I'm ahead of the game here. But not at school. After the freedom of our expat life, school is a shock to the system. In India we have spoken mostly English in public, together with a bit of Hindi, so my Polish is not great. With my white-blond hair, tan from the Indian sun and imperfect Polish, I stand out. My speech is also affected by a lisp, due to a slight malformation in my mouth. I undergo minor surgery to cut away the excess skin above my front teeth, and Mum and Dad send me to a speech therapist. The lisp improves significantly but never disappears entirely. It takes time, but eventually I find my feet.

Meanwhile, Dad works for the State Foreign Trade Company as Head of Import, supplying a chain of hard currency shops, providing western products like Toblerone and Johnny Walker. On his travels, he also buys us brightly coloured western backpacks, which make us the envy of our schoolmates.

After two years, my parents buy a house near the sea between Gdynia and Sopot. Christmas is particularly magical, with heavy snow blanketing the streets. We have lots of family, including a glamorous great aunt who is a historian and married to a Frenchman. They live in Paris. She and her family visit us for Christmas and through her we have the opportunity to travel around France on holidays, visiting the castles and historic sites. When our family arrives for Christmas, Dad greets them at the door with a shot of vodka, to banish the cold, and a plate of pickled herring.

Our big celebration is on Christmas Eve. Tradition dictates that we sit down for dinner as the first star appears in the sky. The spread includes marinated fish, jellied carp, pierogi (dumplings stuffed with vegetables) and borscht (beetroot soup). Christmas Day is for visiting family and neighbours. As part of the Christmas celebrations, our neighbours put together a kind of sled train in the snow. The first sled is attached to a car, which tows all our sleds around the streets with ten kids riding, falling off, running to catch up and jumping on again. It's great fun.

One winter, Dad drives us all down to Austria for a skiing holiday. We've learned to ski on a small mountain in Poland, but this is the real thing. Anna and I are getting off the chairlift on one run when we get tangled up and Anna falls on the edge of my ski and breaks her wrist. But we still enjoy our Austrian adventure.

At home, I also take myself off on my own adventures. I ride my bike everywhere and, when the sea freezes over, we walk out onto the ice. Generally, life is good for me. I'm protected by my parents from much of the harshness and deprivation that exist under communist rule. However, one day my mother goes shopping for groceries with our food tickets and comes home with broken ribs after a man elbows her to push in front in the queue to buy food. Still, we generally don't want for much as Dad is a resourceful man. Not long after returning from Bombay, Dad announced that he had to drive to the Polish–German border and asked me to go with him. We drove through the night and picked up a Phillips television that he had arranged to have delivered to the customs station at the border. Our original set had been broken in transit from India.

Yet having too many western contacts can get you into trouble in communist Poland. We assume our phone is tapped by the secret police. Dad's job gives him access to international travel and foreign contacts. It is allowed, but he has to be careful and ensure he represents his company in the right way. Even so, he is regularly quizzed about his contacts. One of these 'interviews' lasts for two days. We bounce between the freedom of the West and the restrictions of our home country.

In 1986, we are at school one day in April when we are all unexpectedly sent home. It's the day of the Chernobyl nuclear explosion in neighbouring Ukraine. Once school resumes, we are called to the assembly hall and given a strange drink. Later we understand that it contains potassium iodide to prevent radiation sickness. The Polish Government has a stock, but not enough for the whole population. The military, essential services and schools get priority until there is enough for everyone.

Despite the best efforts of the communist regime, the Solidarity movement continues to grow in strength and power as it campaigns for workers' rights. We live through various crackdowns where curfews are imposed, arrests are made and tanks move through the streets. In 1989, Solidarity will finally help to end communist rule in Poland, but by 1987 my parents have had enough. All their parents – my grandparents – have died in the last ten years, as has my mother's brother, and we no longer have close family in Poland. They know what life is like in the West, and they can see a better life for us there. My father is offered a trade consultancy contract for 18 months in Germany through a business contact and that is our way out, but the Polish state still has its hands on him. He will have to pay a percentage of his salary to the government. He goes to Hamburg ahead of the rest of us to prepare the way. When I'm nine years old, Mum, Anna and I pack and drive to the West German border, through Poland and East Germany, where Dad meets us for the rest of the drive to Hamburg. Life is good in Germany. I can't get enough of western food – particularly the sweets. Before long, I am a chubby kid.

As a family living in our third country in eight years, we are used to establishing ourselves in a new place. We begin the process of settling into the community. Our parents' first priority is to find a pool for me and a tennis club for Anna. School is a bit more intimidating at first because we don't speak any German, but there are some other Polish kids around and we pick up the language quickly. One day, I end up in a fistfight after a group of kids makes fun of my sister. It's short: I throw one punch and the ringleader goes down. I'm more surprised than he is, but my father is called to the school to sort it out. By nature, he's a disciplinarian – that's the Polish way of raising kids – and he's concerned that I've lost my temper. From then on, he preaches to me that I must control my emotions and show respect for others.

Once again, swimming is my passport to friendship and acceptance. We join SG Hamburg swimming club, where Stefan Pfeiffer, already an Olympic medallist, is the star swimmer, and his father the coach. We can't get over how beautiful the pool and the facilities are, but then Hamburg as a whole is clean and manicured. I'm in Hamburg when I first become excited by the Olympic Games. It's 1988, the Games are in Seoul and the German swimming team is strong, led by 'The Albatross', Michael Gross, who wins the 200m butterfly gold medal. Stefan Pfeiffer wins the silver medal in the 1500m freestyle behind the great Russian Vladimir Salnikov. We also have high hopes for Gross in the 200m freestyle, but it turns into a duel between Australian Duncan Armstrong and American Matt Biondi. That's the race that fires my imagination. The German commentators are focused on the Gross–Biondi battle and don't even notice Duncan flying down 'Lucky Lane 6' to win. Their shock at the result makes for riveting television, as do the crazy antics of Duncan's coach, Laurie Lawrence. I've been taping all the swimming finals on our VHS recorder and I watch them over and over.

I'm an instinctively competitive person – there's nothing that I love more than chasing the swimmer in front of me. I've just been to Berlin for a meet, racing kids much older than my ten years, and I loved it. An idea pops into my head and fixes there. Maybe one day I could compete at the Olympic Games. I start to feel a sense of purpose about my swimming. I'm chasing that big dream, not just the feet of the swimmer in front of me.

Dad's work contract in Germany is only for 18 months but he immediately starts planning the next move. Through contacts in Australia, he applies for a business visa to immigrate, but the process is long and slow and not completed by the time his German contract finishes.

Mum and Dad hedge their bets by also applying for a Canadian visa, as my dad's brother Paul has recently settled in Toronto. The Canadian visa arrives first so that's where we go next. We don't know how long we will be in Canada, and Mum and Dad don't want to burn through our savings so they look for jobs to support us. Factory work is available, so that's what they do, working long hours to provide for us.

Dad gets a job as a storeman for a medical supplies company and learns how to drive a forklift. The manual labour leaves him lean and fit. Mum is initially working on a food production line until she uses her engineering background to solve a problem on the line and is immediately promoted to the office. At the time, Anna and I don't recognise the sacrifices they are making to find a better future for us.

We're enrolled in a small Catholic school, St Cecilia's, and we try to come to grips with kids playing ice hockey and throwing basketballs. We're living in a high-rise apartment with no real playing area so I gravitate to the car park, where I meet a kid hitting tennis balls off the wall with a hockey stick and join him. There's also a baseball diamond down the road, so I buy a glove and join the kids down there. Of course, I join a swimming club – the Etobicoke Swimming Club, which has produced generations of Olympic swimmers.

Swimming has always been my sanctuary and it will be again. But there are unseen dangers in this new world. Dad has bought a Chevy Bel Air to drive Anna and I to training and competitions. One winter morning, on our way to the Ontario Swimming Championships, we hit black ice on the road. The car skids and goes sideways. We seem to be skidding endlessly in slow motion and Dad is helpless to arrest the slide, but luckily we are stopped by a snowbank and no real harm is done. I make it safely to the competition.

When Mum and Dad are working, I take a train and a bus to reach training. Anna's switched to playing tennis now, so I travel alone – often before dawn – in the cold, 20km across a city I don't know, trusting in my fractured English to get me to the pool. By now I'm pretty adaptable and independent, and I'm dedicated to my sport. I may look different from the other kids, I may sound different, I may be in a foreign country, but at the pool I am comfortable. That has been one of the few constants in my life, and it's the one place where I know I can shine.

After nine months in Toronto, Dad comes home one day and says we are moving to Australia. His business visa has come through. I wasn't aware that this was even in the plan, and I don't know much about Australia. Kangaroos and Duncan Armstrong – that's about it. My sister Anna knows a bit more. An Australian television series called *Return to Eden* aired while we were in Poland, and Anna was obsessed with everything about it. I was too young to watch it, but she's very excited that we're going to Australia.

We arrive in Melbourne on 30 April 1989, when I am 11. Dad's new business partner picks us up from the airport and takes us straight to Pizza Hut for a meal before dropping us at a motel at the end of Brighton Road in Elwood, near the bay. Melbourne seems vast, but like a huge country town. In our motel room, I turn on the TV and there's another weird sport – big guys wearing singlets and chasing an odd-shaped ball around an oval field. We're not in Canada anymore.

CHAPTER 3

Lumpy

Our first home in Australia is in Marquis Road, Moorabbin. It's prime Melbourne working-class territory. We have a weatherboard house on a big block of land with a stand of gum trees up the back and a netball ring in the backyard, which we convert for basketball by adding a backboard. It's a huge contrast to the small apartments we had in Germany and Canada. The backyard is a great luxury and soon becomes my main playground. As we've arrived just before the winter, the key point about the house is that it's not insulated. We're colder than we were in Canada.

The house is only about 500 metres from Linton Oval, where the St Kilda VFL club trains. I end up following the crowd to the ground one day and watch Tony Lockett – Plugger – kick a bunch of goals. Before you know it, I'm a St Kilda supporter. Dad buys an old Mazda, we inherit a border collie named Sasha and we fall quickly into a very Australian lifestyle. But we're still working out the culture.

I'm at the tennis centre watching Anna play a match on a Saturday in late September when I notice an extraordinary sight. Tens of thousands of people, some dressed in yellow and brown stripes and others in navy blue and white stripes, are flooding the streets outside, all on their way to the Melbourne Cricket Ground. I'm aware of Australian football, through St Kilda, but this is something else again as the fans pack into the 'G' for the grand final between Hawthorn and Geelong. For days afterwards, it's all anyone in Melbourne can talk about – the 'Bloodbath at the G'. It's all thrilling stuff for a young Polish boy trying to figure out what Australia's all about.

I can speak reasonable English, but I'm often bamboozled by what the Australians are saying. Why does 'the pot call the kettle black'? I can't get my head around all these bizarre phrases, which makes me reluctant to express myself.

As summer arrives, while Mum and Dad are out at Southlands shopping centre, I decide to help with the garden. The gum trees in the backyard drop a lot of leaves and branches, so we are out there regularly cleaning up. It's hot and dry on this particular day, but I don't know about total fire bans yet. I gather all the leaves and twigs into a big pile and set it alight. In seconds, the flames are five metres high and heading toward the house. I panic and grab the garden hose but it's not having any effect. I yell for help and suddenly I see heads and hoses popping up over the fences around me, and our neighbours spring into action to douse the flames. By the time Mum and Dad get home, there is only scorched earth as evidence, and my very obvious remorse.

I don't get into too much trouble from them, but I learn two lessons that day about Australia: one about the danger of fire and another about the way neighbours pull together when there is trouble.

We've only been in Melbourne a few months when the Berlin Wall falls and Eastern Europe begins a dramatic transition. Poland is changing too, but it's too late for us to go back. We're committed to making a life in Australia and we can see that life can be good for us here.

Anna and I start school at University High School in Coburg. It requires an hour-long trip across Melbourne to school every day, but Mum and Dad are working in the city, I've joined the Melbourne Vicentre swimming club at the State Swimming Centre in Batman Avenue, on the edge of the city, and Anna is training at the adjacent tennis centre, so we're all going in the same direction. The pool is not as modern as those I've trained in at Hamburg and Toronto. It's old and dark, and you have to walk under the pool to get to the change rooms. But it has a lot of history and atmosphere. Gene Jackson is the head coach. He's spent time at the University of Illinois, and he brings an American approach to our training, incorporating a lot of games – sharks and minnows, gambling and Shane Gould 50s are among his favourites. The Shane Gould 50s are like a beep test. We start the first 50m on 60 seconds, the next one on 59 seconds, then 58 seconds, and go for as long as possible. Gambles give us the opportunity to get out of training if we 'win' our gamble and hit the target time we've agreed on. It's all part of nurturing a fun team environment.

Gene holds me back initially. He's careful with my training, not pushing me to do two sessions a day until he judges that I'm ready for it. He lets my talent mature at its own rate. He loves a chat, he has a weird sense of humour and he believes in swimmers being versatile and having good technique. He has me training and racing in every event from backstroke to the 200m individual medley. His habit is to put only the next training set on the whiteboard for us because he wants to keep us in the moment and focused on what we are about to do, not what is coming further down the line.

Nicole Livingstone, who made her Olympic debut in Seoul in 1988, is the squad's star swimmer, but there are other national team swimmers too. At 11, I'm short and stocky and my English is heavily accented, which makes me the perfect target for some of the older boys, who give me a rough time. They call it an initiation, although it lasts for the best part of a year. They hang me on hooks by my clothes, put me in garbage bins and throw my clothes in the shower so I have nothing dry to wear. I get my revenge in the pool, by swimming up behind them and tapping on their feet to let them know that the chubby kid is swimming faster than they are. When I qualify for my first Australian junior team, to compete at the trans-Tasman competition in New Zealand, they tell me I can't represent Australia because I can't sing the national anthem. They call me Lumpy and Chunky. I take my lumps as well as I can and Nicole, who is 18, does her best to protect me. She appoints herself as my guardian and now I have another big sister.

Eventually Dad finds out what's happening. He's waiting outside the pool for me when someone tells him that I have nothing to wear home because my clothes are all wet, and why they are wet. He comes storming into the pool, bursts through the door in the change rooms, where the culprits are hiding, orders them out and tells them this won't happen anymore, and it doesn't. But my nickname in swimming circles is Lumpy ever after.

Things get better after that and I find my place in the squad and make friends, including Naantali Marshall, who is also into surf lifesaving, which I'm keen to explore. Another of my squad mates Hamish Cameron and his brother Angus introduce me to the Torquay Surf Club, where they are members because their family has a house at Jan Juc, near a couple of famous surfing breaks, Bells Beach and Winkipop. Angus is the club captain and recruits me to compete for the club. I go on to win the cadet surf race at the Victorian state championships. Away from the surf club, the Camerons are wild boys. There's a dam on their property and one of their favourite occupations is surfing on the dam, being dragged along by a ute. I attend my first live concert at the Torquay Football Club with them. I don't have a ticket, but I'm encouraged to jump the fence so I can join the older boys to watch the Hoodoo Gurus play. I'm becoming more of an Aussie by the minute.

One of my parents drives me to training early each morning with three bags – one for food, one for swimming, one for school. After training, I walk up Elizabeth St and catch the train to University High School, where I'm primarily known as that swimming kid – the one who sometimes falls asleep at his desk after the early mornings and heavy training. After school, I take the same journey in reverse to the pool and then Mum or Dad takes me home at the end of the day. Anna is also at University High and her tennis is going well. She's being coached by Wimbledon doubles champion Peter McNamara and another former pro, John McCurdy, and training with a talented boy called Mark Philippoussis. After my training sessions finish, sometimes I go and watch her training. I like to join in with the tennis squad when they are hitting balls or running laps of the Tan, the famous riverside track around the Melbourne parklands.

At weekends, our family is either at one of my meets or one of Anna's tournaments. We get to know Melbourne and regional Victoria that way.

At 12, I'm not the best swimmer for my age in the country. I win some and lose some. There's a big kid called Sean Turner, who is the national under-13 champion, and there's a lot of buzz around him. He looks like a man already, with chest hair and everything. But things change the next year at the Australian Age Championships, when I win seven medals – mostly gold – and I realise that maybe I can really make it as a swimmer. I've always been the odd one out – the kid who looked different or couldn't speak the language – but at the pool I fit in.

Anna is also making her way up the junior ranks at national level. When she's 15, she is selected for Australia's

Junior Federation Cup team. There's just one problem: she's not an Australian citizen – none of us are – so she is not eligible to represent Australia under the tournament rules and has to decline the invitation. However, Tennis Australia steps in to facilitate our applications for Australian citizenship, with support from Australian Swimming. In April 1991, we become proud Australian citizens, attending a ceremony at the Dandenong Town Hall where we receive our certificates. I've settled so easily into Australian life that it feels completely natural. It's too late for Anna to go to the Junior Federation Cup, but just in time for me to represent the Australia junior team in the Trans-Tasman Series against New Zealand.

Anna goes on to win the Australian 16 and under championship at the end of 1991 when she is in Year 11. We're all there at the National Tennis Centre to watch her final match and we're delighted for her. It's a big achievement to be the best in a country that has such a huge tennis tradition. For us, it's confirmation that she has the talent to become a professional player one day. The private school Wesley College has already offered her a scholarship to complete Year 12 so she switches schools. Then they offer me one too and I move to Wesley in Year 10. The college has a stunning campus on St Kilda Road, and a strict uniform policy. Philippoussis is there too, in the year above me. But it is less diverse than Uni High and it's harder for me to fit in. I'm worldly and speak multiple languages, but I am committed to swimming, and training takes most of my time. My spoken English is good now, but I'm not comfortable in English classes, where I particularly hate reading aloud. I don't think it has occurred to me that if I make it as a swimmer, I will be required to speak in public.

I make friends at Wesley, mostly with the other boys who started there in Year 10. My favourite subjects are geography and art. I've already seen a lot of the world, but my geography teacher Mr Brenner shows me there's still much more to see. I also spend a lot of time working on my sketching in the art department with my favourite teacher, Mrs Stone. Art is secondary to swimming, though. All my school report cards, across four countries, are variations on one theme: 'Michael has a lot of potential, but he is very easily distracted.' That's a sentiment my swimming coaches would recognise too.

I've been going to the national junior championships since I was 12. The first year in Melbourne, 1990, I'm not that successful, courtesy of Sean Turner, but in 1991 in Sydney I start to hit my straps and break the 13 years national age record in the 50m freestyle, my first real splash in Australian swimming. I'm selected in the national junior team to compete against New Zealand in the Tri Series. The team also includes Matt Dunn, Craig Hackett, Susie O'Neill and Elli Overton, but they are all much older than me. In 1992, I break the 14 years national age record for the 50m freestyle and I start racking up titles. I'm selected again for the Tri Series. I'm still carrying my puppy fat and I'm starting to feel self-conscious about racing in front of a crowd. But it doesn't seem to stop me swimming fast.

I've also qualified to compete at the senior national championships and it's a big one: the Barcelona Olympic trials in Canberra. I'm there only for experience, my times aren't yet competitive with the senior swimmers, but it's an eye-opener. Spectators and media hang from the rafters in the temporary stands around the Australian Institute of Sport pool. Nicole qualifies for her second Olympics and another of my training partners, Toby Haenen, qualifies for his first Olympic team, also in backstroke. I'm suddenly mixing with some of the biggest stars in the sport – Duncan Armstrong, Lisa Curry, Hayley Lewis, Glen Housman, Susie O'Neill – but the highlight of the trials is Kieren Perkins' swim on the final night as he smashes the world 1500m record. I'm now so close to my dream that I can taste it.

Nicole wins her first Olympic medal in Barcelona, bronze in the 200m backstroke, and seeing that only makes me hungrier. I'm finally growing taller and I've started a basic gym programme. Between 15 and 16, my lumps start to redistribute themselves, from my stomach to my chest, arms and shoulders as I sprout up.

Around that time, Gene sits me down and tells me I have to 'listen to the lion' inside me. At first, I don't really understand what he's saying. But the next day he brings in a cassette tape of Van Morrison singing the song 'Listen to the Lion'. It strikes a chord with me. I'm a Leo in the astrological chart and I have always felt an affinity for lions. The lyrics speak to me about finding my courage. I play it regularly, and the lion becomes the symbol of my swimming career.

At the 1993 Age Nationals in Brisbane, I win five gold medals and break the 15 years 100m backstroke record. Swimming Victoria proclaims that I am 'probably Australia's best junior talent'. I'm starting to attract recognition outside my small circle. Through my parents' accountant, we have a connection to the Mazda Sports Club and they agree to provide me with a sponsored car. I'm too young to drive, so Mum drops me off at school each day in a car with my name emblazoned along the side. Around that time, Gene gives me another life lesson. He says: 'You are going places, but remember this: It's nice to be important, but it's more important to be nice.' I take that to heart too.

I attend my second senior National Championships, this time in Perth. I'm there with the Vicentre squad, but during a break in the competition I am approached by two coaches from the Australian Institute of Sport in Canberra, the head coach Russian Gennadi Touretski and Canadian sprint coach Jim Fowlie. I know them vaguely as I've been to a couple of talent-identification camps in Canberra. I don't know it, but Jim has been watching me for years. He was coaching in Toronto when we were there, and he remembers this 'little blond kid' with speed to burn. They introduce me to the Olympic champion Alex Popov and ask me whether I would like to join the AIS squad, at least part-time while I'm still at school. I'm still in Year 11 and it's a big step to leave home, but I immediately want to go.

Obviously, they will need to talk to my parents, but I'm determined. I have a lot of life experience for a 15-year-old – in five different countries – so I'm quite independent and I know this is where I need to be to make the most of my swimming. Funnily enough, Anna had also been offered an AIS scholarship, a year earlier, but she turned it down. She chose to stay home and train at the National Tennis Centre in Melbourne. But when the opportunity comes to me, I jump at it. Gennadi is demonstrably the best sprint coach in the world, having guided Alex Popov to the 50m and 100m freestyle titles at the Barcelona Olympics, while the Soviet Union was falling apart around them.

That geopolitical shift created the opportunity for Australia's head coach Don Talbot to snatch Gennadi from Russia, where the sports system, and the country, is in chaos. Don knows the Australian team is under-performing in sprinting and that sprint events make up more than half of the championship programme, so the team cannot fly unless we can develop world-class sprinters. He thinks Gennadi is just the man to shake things up. Alex has also relocated, following his coach. I know this is the right place for me.

The AIS offer is a tough one for Mum and Dad. We've only been in Australia for four years. We're all exceptionally close because with all the moving around we've mostly only had each other to rely on. They don't want to give their son to an institution to raise, but they don't want to hold me back either.

Gene encourages my move to Canberra. He's also lost Nicole to the AIS, but he accepts that it can offer me support and state-of-the-art facilities that are not available in Victoria. With heavy hearts, my parents agree to me joining the AIS in Canberra in early 1994, after I have finished Year 11 at Wesley College.

In the meantime, a momentous event occurs. We're still living in the house in Moorabbin in September of 1993 when, half a world away, at the Stade Louis II Stadium in Monaco, the International Olympic Committee president Juan Antonio Samaranch takes a sheet of paper out of an envelope and says: 'The winner is ... [dramatic pause] ... the winner is Syd-e-ney.' At 4 am in the harbour city, there is uproar. Thousands of people have gathered at Circular Quay to hear the announcement and they are in full party mode. Sydney has won the bid to host the 2000 Olympic Games and my life will be changed forever. I don't know that yet, but I do know that I and every other young swimmer in the country would give everything to be there competing for Australia.

Late in the year, I arrive at the AIS in Canberra for a training camp before joining full-time the following year. I'm eager to prove I belong there – maybe too eager. I want to impress the coaches Jim and Gennadi, and I do that, but not in the way I intended. Just days into the camp, we are practising our turns in the indoor 25m pool, which is shallow for a competition pool. I'm trying to flip fast at the turn and I miscalculate. I don't tuck in well enough and as I turn, I catch both heels on the edge of the pool and it slices them open. There's blood everywhere and I need stitches in both wounds (nurses in Bombay and Gdynia will be getting a feeling of déjà vu right about now). The upshot is that I'll be out of the water for two weeks. I can't complete the training camp and I'm scared that the coaches will reconsider offering me a scholarship.

I head back to Melbourne worried that I've ruined my big opportunity, but I'm reassured when the planning for me to join the next year goes on without a hitch. Later, Gennadi will tell me that it wasn't my swimming that impressed him at that camp, but my resilience when faced with the adversity of that situation. It gave him an insight into my character.

In early 1994, I move into the AIS Residence in Canberra, which is like a university dormitory on campus. We each have a small, sparsely furnished room, shared bathrooms, a common room where we watch movies together and hang out, and there are house parents to provide us with guidance. We eat in a large dining hall where athletes from all the sports gather. Some sports gel better than others: the swimmers tend to get on best with the rowers and basketball players. It's a short walk from the residence to the dining hall and the pool, so everything is very compact. I immediately feel comfortable. It feels like we're all on the same mission together. I'm the youngest boy, but not by much. Adam Pine has also joined the AIS from Ballina on the NSW North Coast. He is 17 and also a freestyle and butterfly sprinter, so we naturally gravitate to each other. There's a competition between the male swimmers about who has the best sound system installed in his room, and Adam is a contender for the title, so he introduces me to a range of music, including the Stone Temple Pilots, who become one of my favourite bands. The big difference between Adam and me is that he has a driver's licence and a car, so I become his wingman as we explore Canberra.

I also lack one other important status symbol for a teenager. I don't have any natural banter like the older boys. I don't know how to form friendships that way, but I'm going to have to learn. This is an intensely competitive environment and there is a lot of banter between the guys, in and out of the pool. Right now I just feel awkward when they are putting each other down in fun, and I have no comebacks when I'm the butt of a joke. Because I speak Polish at home, and I regularly have long conversations with my family while sitting in the hallway of the residence, they tease me by mocking my Polish. It takes me a while to learn not to take things so hard.

The AIS tries to get me to classes in a local school but it's on the other side of town and doesn't fit my training schedule. So instead we organise my studies through tutors at the AIS and the teachers at Wesley College, because it is the only school that is offering the International Baccalaureate. My parents, both university graduates, are adamant that they want me to complete Year 12.

Sometimes the whole swimming squad trains together, sometimes Jim and Gennadi work together, but mainly Gennadi works alone with his athletes, including Alex, Nicole and Australia's top medley swimmer, Matthew Dunn. They are all Olympians and that is what I want to be. Dunny is four years older than me, but I've grown up a lot since we first met when I was 13. We soon become good friends.

My strongest connection is with Gennadi. My Eastern European background helps me understand his attitude and approach. There are moments of awkwardness as we get to know each other, but I really want to gain his approval. Polish people can be no-nonsense and serious, so I don't need a lot of handholding. Gennadi is stern but also nurturing. My parents have also put their trust in him. They flew to Canberra to talk to him before they agreed to let me move away from home.

Gennadi soon becomes a huge figure in my life. He's not to everyone's taste because he's such a maverick, the Russian version of a mad professor. His head is in the clouds a lot of the time. His mind is brilliant, but sometimes he struggles with the normal responsibilities of life, like turning up on time – or at all. He pays no attention to convention, in swimming or in life, unless it makes sense to him. Yet I trust him completely. When it really matters, he always shows up ready to work. His knowledge of both the physical and mental side of swimming is so deep it seems limitless to me, and I just want to dive in and learn as much as possible. With him, I feel protected, except when he's driving. He is a truly terrible driver – he seems to have no spatial awareness and he's completely distracted by his thoughts or the conversation in the car. But it's worth taking my life in my hands to learn from him.

I spend hours in his office each week, watching him drawing on a whiteboard and talking to me about periodisation, or technique or the mindset of a champion. At those times, I feel like I'm in the lecture hall at the university of swimming. It can be quite a formal relationship at times, not unlike that with my father. When Dad visits, he and Gennadi both get dressed up for dinner. They seem to have a mutual understanding of how things should be done.

I'm very young, but all the AIS swimmers are young and far from home. There are a few shenanigans, but it's fairly innocent – playing touch footy in the rain, occasional nights out at the local nightclubs. In the squad, Jim and Lyn Fowlie tend to take the role of stand-in parents. They have their own kids, but they are naturally warm and hospitable and they regularly invite us over to their house for barbecues to give us a sense of normality outside of the AIS bubble. I'm still known as Lumpy, even though I don't bear much resemblance to the chubby kid I was when I arrived in Australia five years earlier. Thanks to a growth spurt in the last two years, I'm now 190cm tall and I weigh 84kg.

I've never worried much about my diet, but the AIS swimming team dietician Louise Burke, a fellow Saints supporter, makes sure our food is nutritionally designed for athletes, so I'm eating healthier than ever before. My meals are much lighter now – cereals and yoghurts for breakfast, lean meat and fish, salads, vegetables, grains, nuts. I'm being educated not only in what to eat but when to eat, so I'm now eating smaller meals more often. There's a protein station in the dining hall that is available all day and we are sent there directly after each of our two-hour training sessions to replenish our bodies with Sustagen and protein bars and electrolyte drinks. I learn that protein is most effective in helping your body repair from training in the first 30 minutes afterwards.

Experts on every facet of performance are available to us whenever we need them. There's no need to travel or search them out as we had to do in Melbourne. Dr Bruce Mason, our biomechanist, is regularly at training, filming us underwater and above the water, and preparing data for Gennadi. Dr David Pyne is our physiologist, Peter Blanch is our physiotherapist, Clark Perry is our psychologist and Helena Bryant does our admin. Most of these specialists are also attached to the Australian team so I know I am getting the best guidance possible.

I'm now tall, lean, athletic and explosive, but I'm not that strong. It will take time to build the strength I need to be a competitive international swimmer. The test of our strength is to be able to lift our body weight in chin-ups at least ten times in a row. I'm way off that when I start. My father has natural strength, but I don't. I'm going to have to work for it. The three gym sessions we are doing a week, in addition to our ten pool sessions, will help me get there.

Gennadi's training philosophy is based on speed and technique rather than volume. His mantra is: *rhythm, relaxation, range*. I'm shocked that Alex – the world's best sprinter – swims so little distance most of the time. We don't do as many laps as other squads, except when we go away on specific training camps where we might do up to three sessions a day, and sometimes we do them very slowly to focus on technique. You have to be proficient swimming slowly before you can master the same technique at top speed. We create muscle memory through the quality of the movement.

The world is opening up to me in every way. I've known Brooke Hanson, a breaststroke swimmer from Sydney, for a while now. We've been on junior teams and camps together and we start dating, even though we're living in different cities. She's a vibrant, fun girl from the Northern Beaches of Sydney, who's grown up in a swimming and surf lifesaving family. Her father Ian Hanson, a former newspaper journalist, is the media manager of the Australian swimming team. We're together for the best part of two years before we go our separate ways.

In 1994 there are two big competitions for the Australian team: the Commonwealth Games in Victoria, Canada, and the World Championships in Rome. The trials are held in March as usual and I'm hopeful that I can qualify for the Commonwealth Games team. I reach the 200m freestyle final, but I fall short of making the team. I've been training just as well as Dunny – most of the time I've been setting the pace for our 200m work – but I don't have the mental toughness yet to produce my best race when it counts. I'm happy to see Brooke qualify for her first Australian team. At just 16, she's the baby of the Commonwealth Games team. Female swimmers often mature faster than male swimmers, but still I'm disappointed I won't be going to Canada with her.

I put it at the back of my mind for now. I'm still adjusting to the new training environment at the AIS in Canberra and juggling that with my schoolwork. But when I go back to racing my peers at the Age Nationals in Perth, I can see how much I've grown. I win a record seven gold medals – the 50m, 100m and 200m freestyle, 100m backstroke, 100m and 200m butterfly, and 200m individual medley – to finish my junior career. However, I'm more excited by the fact that the whole AIS squad is going to Europe in May and June to train and race. We start with a high-altitude training camp in Font-Romeu in France. It's an established facility, over 1800m high in the Pyrenees near Andorra. There's a swimming pool, gym, sports science support and athletics track and it attracts athletes from many sports and countries around the world. I've never done altitude training before, but Gennadi has done close to 50 altitude camps so he's one of the most experienced coaches in the world with this process. I put myself in his hands. At the start, even easy swimming makes it difficult to breathe. I almost feel like I'm suffocating while I'm training, but over three weeks I adapt to the thin air and start to train well. It feels like this is what elite sport is really about. On a rest day, Piney, his girlfriend Sasha Van Hamburg (also an AIS swimmer) and I decide to walk up to the snowline, but we don't realise how high that is and we end up doing a six-hour hike up a mountain. So much for a rest day.

After three weeks at Font-Romeu, I am fitter than I've ever been and we head for competition at the Mare Nostrum series, a traditional series of meets held in June around the Mediterranean – in Barcelona, Canet-en-Roussillon on the French Riviera and in Monaco. I'm rooming with one of our most senior swimmers, Marty Roberts, and learning a lot. He's reliable, well organised and a hard worker in the training pool, but he's relaxed and good to be around on race day, so I try to emulate his approach.

Alex joins us from the Russian championships, so he's tapered and ready to swim fast. At the Monaco meeting, he's going to target the 100m freestyle world record. On the day of the race, I'm watching him prepare for the final, even though I'm in the same race and should be worrying about myself. But to be the best in the world, I need to start emulating the best in the world.

However, I soon realise Alex is one of a kind. He's 2m tall, lean as a greyhound, with a huge wingspan and this innate confidence. He arrived in Canberra in late 1992 with very little English, but he's very quickly fitted into the Australian lifestyle and swimming community. His swimming stroke, with the elegant high-elbow action, is so beautiful that other coaches and swimmers rave about it. But it is unique to him and is built on his surprising physical strength. He's quick-witted and cheeky, with a bone-dry sense of humour. He's also a strategic thinker. He never shows all his cards, even to a kid like me who he doesn't have to worry about at all for now. The Americans call him the 'Big Dog' as a nod to his alpha male status in the swimming pack. At this stage, I'm like an enthusiastic puppy running around his ankles. I'm so eager that I'm always the first swimmer into the water for a training session. Gennadi hasn't even finished writing the session on a whiteboard and I'm halfway down the pool. Later, people will tell me that Alex rolls his eyes every time I shoot off like that. Over time, we develop a bond, but it's a bit like a big brother–little brother relationship. I feel like he always has my measure.

In Monaco, he sets a new world record of 48.21 seconds in the 100m final, while I finish down the field in 51 seconds. It's been a great trip and I've learned a lot. Now I need to put it all into practice.

CHAPTER 4

Making a Mark

I settle easily into the daily routine at the AIS: swim, eat, train, eat, swim, eat, sleep, repeat. Typically, we rise around 5.30 am, even in the depths of winter, then stagger a few hundred metres from our dorms to the indoor pool, wearing our massive AIS parkas. Sometimes we look like ghosts materialising, as we emerge from the frosty darkness and fog of the Canberra winter into the light and warmth of the pool. Training starts at 6.30 am so we're on deck from 6.10 am for dry-land exercises to activate our muscles before we hit the water for two hours. Then we hurry to breakfast in the dining hall, where we see all the other athletes who have also completed their first training session of the day. After a short break, we do a weight-training session at 11 am, followed by lunch. Then it's time to rest before we work on recovery – mostly rehab or massage at the medical centre. By 4 pm we're back on the pool deck for another two-hour swimming session, followed by hot and cold water plunges to help our muscles regenerate from the work we have demanded of them. Then it's time for dinner and a bit of relaxation. We favour watching movies in the common room, or just sitting around and chatting to entertain ourselves, before we head to bed around 10 pm. Across the week, we get through ten swimming sessions, covering 40–60km, with three or four dry-land sessions added in, as well as biomechanical and physiological testing.

In many ways, I'm serving an apprenticeship, learning from the masters. I know I'm exactly where I need to be to fulfil my swimming dream because I'm improving all the time. I'm in that magical space where my physical development and training routine are all working together to make me fitter, stronger, faster. I'm doing the work to make these gains – but they are also flowing naturally as I develop into an adult. I turn 17 in August of 1994, having completed my junior swimming career with a record tally of 25 gold medals from the Australian Age Championships. Now it's time to take on the big guys.

The transition from junior to open swimmer is often fraught, but I'm reaching a stage when I feel I should be competitive at the senior level. Most of the Australian team swimmers skip the Australian Short Course Championships at Warringah Aquatic Centre in Sydney toward the end of 1994, but that creates an opportunity for youngsters like me. I win my first Australian senior titles, in the 200m freestyle and 200m individual medley. Yes, medley – Gene gave me a good grounding in all strokes, which serves me well for the rest of my career. These first titles give me just the confidence boost I need to shoot for the national team next year. I only just missed selection this year and I'm a better swimmer now. I think 1995 should be my year.

Rob Woodhouse thinks so too. He's a 1984 Olympic medallist who used to train with us at Vicentre a couple of times a week even after he retired. He's decided to set up his own sports management company and he wants to represent me. I'm not a star yet, but he has faith in my potential. Woody is already well known to me and my family, so it feels like a natural fit. He will become my guide through the commercial side of sport as I make my way up the ranks. Woody's first act is to organise a Speedo sponsorship to cover the cost of my swimsuits, clothing and equipment. It feels like everything is starting to come together.

To prepare for the 1995 national trials, we go back to Europe in February for a three-week training camp in the Sierra Nevada in Spain. It's an intense experience. Over 15 days, we swim 202km at 2300m in altitude, doing three training sessions a day with a 'rest' every third day when we only train twice a day. Our accommodation is a kilometre from the pool, so we walk to and from the pool through the snow. By the time we finish, we are super-fit and ready to compete in three World Cup meets across a week – in Paris, Italy and Sheffield in the United Kingdom.

In Paris, I claim my first international medal, finishing second in the 100m butterfly, but then I win at the next two meetings, which boosts my confidence again. Our flight home departs from Madrid and some of us have elected to stay an extra night there and go skiing for a day before we return. I'm a capable skier, and it's great to have a carefree day with my mates Piney and Brendan Roser at the end of an intense period of training and competition. We arrive at the airport the next day for our flight to find Gennadi waiting at the airport. He was supposed to fly out with the group that left the previous day, but he missed the bus to the airport then couldn't find his passport, so he wasn't allowed on the flight. He's been waiting for 24 hours so we get him onto our flight to ensure he gets back to Australia.

The national championships and selection trials are in Perth in March 1995. My best chance of making the team is in the 200m freestyle because they select up to six swimmers for the 4 x 200m freestyle relay, but the field is stacked – Kieren Perkins, Daniel Kowalski, Glen Housman and my training partner, Matt Dunn, are among the contenders.

Kieren is coming off the best year of his career. He's won the 200m, 400m and 1500m freestyle triple at the Commonwealth Games in Victoria, Canada, breaking the 800m world record on the way to the 1500m crown, then backed up to win the 400m and 1500m freestyle at the World Championships in Rome, this time breaking the 400m world record. But then he had a big break, so he isn't as fit as he normally would be. Dan is the rising distance freestyle star, having finished second to Kieren in the 1500m in Victoria and Rome, while Glen, a former world record-holder, remains a world-class swimmer. Matt has won the 200m and 400m individual medley at the Commonwealth Games and is also a handy freestyler.

The four of them combined to win the 4 x 200m freestyle gold medal in Canada. But they generally select five or six guys for the 4 x 200m freestyle relay to give the coaches options, as they will for this year's major meet, the Pan Pacific Championships in Atlanta, a rehearsal for next year's Olympic Games. The Pan Pac entry rules allow each country to enter as many individual swimmers as they like in each event, but only two per country can qualify for the A Final and one for the B Final, so if I can sneak onto that relay team, I will also be able to swim my individual events and gain some more experience at the international level. No-one is expecting much more from me than that, but I'm here to compete, not to make up the numbers. I qualify for the 200m freestyle final, which is the first step. Now I have a lane, so I have a chance. The advantage I have over the distance specialists is early speed, so I'm going to use that to get a lead during the first 100m and hope to hang on as they come at me in the last lap. When they do, I realise I'm strong enough to hold them off and I touch the wall first, stopping the clock at 1 minute 50.10 seconds, a personal best time that lifts me to No. 7 in the Australian all-time top ten. I'm excited and relieved to win. It feels like I've repaid the faith Gennadi and Jim and the AIS have placed in me. It's the upset of the meet and earns me that coveted national team selection. 'A star is born,' Gennadi tells the media. 'Australia has a very special swimmer who can go all the way to next year's Atlanta Olympics and a man who could be the star of the Games in Sydney in 2000.' With the pressure off, I also swim well in the 100m butterfly, finishing second behind my AIS teammate Scott Miller. I'm going to Atlanta to swim for the Green and Gold, but it turns into a bit of a rough introduction to championships swimming.

We're training in the main pool in Atlanta a couple of days before the Pan Pacs begin when Nicole stops me at one end of the pool and tells me Gennadi won't be here. There has been some trouble on the flight from Sydney to the United States and they've had to land the plane in Hawaii. They've arrested him and he's in jail. I'm shocked. I've never even seen Gennadi yell at anyone, let alone get physical. What I do know is that he won't be here for the biggest meet of my young career, when I really need his guidance. Without him, I struggle to stay calm and confident in this new environment. I still feel like a kid and I'm a bit starstruck around my new teammates. I might have beaten some of them in Perth, but I've put guys like Dan and Scotty and Chris Fydler on a pedestal. I'm shy around them as they banter and play jokes on each other. On the bus trips to and from the pool, I barely say a word but I take in everything that happens.

In Gennadi's absence, our head coach, Don Talbot, assigns me to Fydes' coach Greg Salter for the meeting. Fydes takes pity on me and helps out with some advice when I'm working on my turning technique to prepare for my races. But I still feel like I don't really belong here, and that's how I swim when the racing starts. My best result comes in the 100m freestyle, where I finish fifth, but I don't qualify for the A Final in either the 200m freestyle or 100m butterfly, despite setting national age records. I realise I still have a long way to go to be competitive at the highest level.

I return home to do my final exams for the International Baccalaureate at Wesley College in Melbourne. We all know that there are no guarantees with a sporting career and my parents and I understand that I need an education to fall back on, but it hasn't been easy to juggle my training load, travel for competition and distance education. I feel as if a weight has been lifted off my shoulders when I walk out of the college gates with my diploma. But there aren't any Schoolies Week celebrations for me. Instead, I'm on a plane to the United States after my last exam, to join the Australian team in camp in Florida.

I still have one last chance to make a mark on the world of swimming in 1995, at the World Short Course Championships in Rio in December. I like short course swimming. In the 25m pool, starts and turns are more important (because there are twice as many) and I have a natural explosiveness that gives me an advantage.

I arrive at the University of Florida in Gainesville for the Australian team's pre-event training camp and my roommate Daniel Kowalski welcomes me with a pizza and an NBA game on TV. A fellow Victorian, Dan is a great team man as well as a great swimmer. He regularly wins the Australian team's annual Swimmers' Swimmer award for the athlete who has contributed most to our team environment. He has been tasked with looking after the rookie, so he takes me under his wing.

After our camp, we arrive in Rio to find a stunning facility for the championships. The Brazilians have a strong swimming team led by sprinter Gustavo Borges and have built a temporary 25m pool on the sand of Copacabana Beach to showcase the sport. The weather is hot and the atmosphere is lively. It's a non-ticketed event. Anyone who is up for fun in the sun on Copacabana Beach can come on in and the Brazilian crowd is ready to party despite the stifling heat. Every half hour or so, the event organisers turn sprinklers onto the grandstands to cool everyone down. I never knew a swimming competition could be like this. The Brazilian fans are crazy.

We're staying one block back from the beach, so we walk to the pool each day, accompanied by gun-toting security guards. We're warned not to venture out unaccompanied due to the crime rate in Rio, so we don't see much beyond the beach precinct. But that's okay. I need to focus because I have a big programme, combining the 200m freestyle, 100m butterfly and three relays over four days. I no longer want to feel like a bystander in the Australian team.

The 200m freestyle is my first individual event and I finally crack the championships medal podium, finishing third. Borges takes the gold, giving the home crowd something to cheer about – not that they need it. The 100m butterfly gives the same result; I take bronze again, this time behind my AIS teammate Scotty Miller. I upgrade to silver in the 4 x 100m freestyle relay team, uniting with Brett Hawke, Richard Upton and Matt Dunn. We also get silver in the 4 x 100m medley relay, where I swim the freestyle leg.

But the highlight is the 4 x 200m freestyle, where I lead off the team of Dunn, Malcolm Allen and Kowalski and we win the gold.

I finish the meet with one gold, two silvers and two bronze medals, and some great momentum going into the Olympic year. Australian Swimming names me Male Rookie of the Year. When I get back to Canberra, Gennadi's difficulties seem to have been resolved and no-one mentions what happened, so I just carry on as normal.

CHAPTER 5

Olympic Debut

There's always an extra frisson of excitement in the air during the Olympic year. Almost every elite swimmer begins with the dream of going to the Olympic Games. My own imagination was sparked by watching the 1988 Seoul Olympics, particularly Duncan Armstrong's win in the 200m freestyle. As a small Polish boy living in Germany, I was utterly thrilled by it all and the possibility of experiencing that for myself has fuelled my dreams ever since. It is amazing to me that, just eight years later, Duncan has become my unofficial mentor and I might have the opportunity to swim for Australia at the Olympics.

Duncan was still training at the AIS when I joined in 1993–94 and because we specialised in the same event, he took an interest in me. By 1996 he has retired from swimming and is working as a TV commentator, but he's still available whenever I want a chat. We've talked a lot in the lead-up to the Olympic trials, mostly about letting my ability talk at a big meet, not containing myself, letting everything that's in my heart and mind and body come out through my performance. 'Let the animal loose', as Laurie Lawrence might say, or 'Listen to the Lion', as my old coach Gene Jackson put it. 'It's harder than it sounds,' Duncan says.

In the week before the Olympic trials in Sydney, he gives me a public vote of confidence, telling *The Australian* newspaper, 'I think Klimmy is the boy [to take up the mantle as Australia's 200m freestyle contender]. I believe he is one of the brightest prospects we have had.'

I'm still 18 and I'm facing a stacked field of big names – Perkins, Kowalski, Housman, Malcolm Allen and my training partner, Dunny. They are all older and more experienced, but I've had a good preparation and I have a taste for international competition now. I was just 14 at the previous Olympic trials in 1992, but I was there competing and I soaked up the atmosphere as Kieren Perkins broke the world 1500m record. This time I know I'm a contender, but the trials are a much bigger deal than they were when we all squeezed into the AIS pool in Canberra.

They are being held at the new Sydney International Aquatic Centre, which will host the Sydney Olympic competition in 2000. The Aquatic Centre is the biggest swimming venue in the country and it's in the middle of the future Olympic city. I'm the rising star, one of the big home hopes for 2000. There will be a lot more attention and a lot more pressure this time and my best event is on the first day. Gennadi is opening my mind to what's possible, trying to stop me from putting limits on myself. After the Pan Pacs, he challenged me: 'If you are going 1 minute 50 for 200m, why can't you go 1 minute 48?' There's no reason at all. Alex is less subtle. He's heading off to the Russian trials, which are the same week as ours, and he leaves me with this promise: 'If you don't kick their butts, I will come back and kick yours.'

The day before the trials begin, we do our normal shave-down session. To optimise our sensitivity to the water and our ability to slip through it, we shave all the hair off our bodies. It is a practice that has both physical and mental benefits. With smooth skin you can feel the water better and the ritual prepares us mentally for the competition ahead. It's often a group activity because sometimes you need help to shave those hard-to-reach spots like the middle of the back, or back of the legs, so there's a bonding element as well.

Once my body is done, I go ahead and shave my head as well. I've been watching videos of the 1992 Olympic 200m freestyle champion Yevgeny Sadovyi, so maybe that's given me the idea, and I've also got teammates who shave their heads to race. Gennadi is always talking about preparing physically and mentally to race. Shaving my head is definitely a statement of intent for me. It's a public display of my commitment. I'm here and I mean business. I'm serious about making this Olympic team and I won't let anything get in my way, including my hair. It also simplifies my pre-race preparation. I won't have to worry about wearing a swim cap. I can just put on my goggles and I'm ready to race. When I first see myself in the mirror, I'm not quite sure that this is a good look for me. To my eyes, I look sick. I'm pale from training indoors in Canberra and the planes of my face are exaggerated by the removal of my hair. Little do I know that I have created my signature look for the rest of my life.

I feel good on the first morning of the trials and head to the pool. I blast through my heat and stop the clock in 1:48.26, almost two seconds faster than my previous best, and the fastest time in the world for nearly two years. I know now that I can dominate the final: no-one else in the field has swum that fast. Yet I don't want to swim an aggressive race and risk fading out toward the end, given the quality of my opponents. I take a more conservative approach through the first 100m, before kicking away to lead by almost a body-length off the final turn. Daniel is also in excellent form and he challenges me over the final lap, but I have enough energy to hold him off and win by a tenth of a second in 1:48.94. But the time doesn't matter – I'm going to be an Olympian! It's my first and greatest sporting dream, and it's about to come true.

With my Olympic spot secure, I can relax and enjoy the racing for the rest of the week. I still have the 100m freestyle and 100m butterfly to swim. I'm not really competitive yet in the 100m freestyle. I don't have the power or self-belief to match it with the top guys, but I hope I can qualify for the relay. My butterfly is coming on well, although not as well as Scotty Miller's. He wins the final comfortably in 52.56 seconds, the second-fastest time in history. I'm almost a body-length back in a personal best of 53.52 seconds, but I'm second, which secures another swim for me at the Olympics.

It has all gone to plan for me, but that's not the case for everyone. We've all put in four years of blood, sweat and tears for the chance to represent our country at the Olympics, but only a select group will qualify. Even Australia's best swimmer, Kieren Perkins, has struggled with qualifying. He misses out in the 400m freestyle, finishing third, and is down to his last chance in the 1500m final on the last night, where he finishes second behind Dan Kowalski. It's a knife-edge for all of us.

After the final session, when the Australian Olympic team is announced live on television with considerable fanfare, the overwhelming emotion for every swimmer is relief. We've made it – our hard work has not been wasted. We have each earned a golden ticket to Atlanta.

The Australian team goes into a pre-Games camp at the University of Georgia in Athens, a university town about an hour from Atlanta. But I'm without my security blanket – Gennadi. One of the repercussions of the previous year's incident is that he has been excluded from the Australian coaching team. He will be in Atlanta privately, but I'll have limited access to him. However, I do feel as if I'm prepared for the Olympics. All my training has gone well, although I will only know for sure when I step onto the blocks on the first day of the Games.

Somewhat surprisingly, I'm going in as the top seed. No-one has bettered my time from the Australian trials.

I'm starting to feel the pressure of that. I'm supposed to be a medal favourite in four years, when I'm in the prime of my career, not now. Don Talbot warned after the Olympic trials, 'The Olympic Games is never about favourites winning. It's about being tough. The Olympic Games is a racing meet.' In a July 1996 column in *The Weekend Australian*, Duncan states, 'The Olympic Games are about three things: pressure, pressure and more pressure. If you can handle it, you're well on the way to the podium.' I'm worried that I'm not ready.

We arrive in the Olympic Village five days before the competition, but instead of excitement I feel a growing unease. I've been on two previous Australian senior teams, but it was just the swim team together, a tight little unit where I knew everyone. This is very different. There are thousands of athletes, a melting pot of people, walking, eating, running around in tracksuits, getting on and off buses. It's less a village than a city. Hordes of media occupy the grandstands and the mixed zone, watching every training session and asking athletes about winning gold medals. It's intimidating for me. Everyone apart from me seems to know what they are doing.

Because I'm competing on the first day, I don't attend the Opening Ceremony. The swimming team generally doesn't march in the Opening Ceremony as it involves spending a lot of time on your feet and we need to stay fresh for our competition. We watch on television from the village as Muhammad Ali lights the cauldron to open the Games.

When I get up the next morning, time seems to have sped up. I'm running late before I even leave the village. I miss the bus I planned to take to the pool and have to wait for the next one. My anxiety levels go up. When I eventually get to the pool, I can't find Gennadi, or even some of the familiar faces of my teammates. I notice the starting list posted in the entry way to the pool, with my name at the top. No pressure then. I'm a bundle of nervous energy, bouncing around the warm-up pool. I don't know where to put my bag so I can go through my stretching routine before I jump in the pool for warm-up, and the pool is packed, with dozens of swimmers in every lane. Eventually I find Gennadi, but now I only have time for a modified warm-up routine before I need to go to the call room. Everything is going too fast and it feels out of control.

Gennadi has told me repeatedly to be ready for anything, but I'm not. My thoughts are scattered, going in every direction, as I sit in the marshalling room, waiting for my race. I can't stop fidgeting. Daniel is with me as we're both in the sixth and final heat. Not even his presence can calm me as we walk out onto the pool deck. In theory, I know exactly what I need to do to qualify for the final, to set one of the top eight times. But I feel so rattled, like I am standing naked on the blocks.

The race passes in a blur. I forget my race plan and just react to the swimmers around me. I turn behind Daniel with 50m to go and he has too much strength for me to make up ground before the finish. I finish in third place in a time of 1:49.17. A Dutch teenager named Pieter Van Den Hoogenband wins the heat and Daniel finishes second in 1:48.92. He scrapes into the final in seventh place, but I miss out. My time is less than a second outside my best, but it's not good enough. I'm the tenth fastest in the field and I don't make the cut. I feel shellshocked as I emerge from the pool. My parents rush down to the front of the grandstand to see me as I sleepwalk across the pool deck. When my mum consoles me, I start crying and then a camera pops up to record my agony. I brush the tears from my face and put on a brave smile, but I'm shattered as I make the long, lonely walk back to the warm-up pool. I have to pass through the media broadcast and press areas to get there. They ask me questions and I answer, but a moment later I've forgotten what I said. I'm in so much emotional turmoil that my memory is shutting down. I don't ever want to remember this day, or this feeling, so I blank it all out.

Later, I will remember that Gennadi tried to prepare me for this possibility. In the dining hall before the Games began, we had a conversation in which he specifically said, 'What if you don't make the final?' but I brushed it off at the time. I didn't want to think about it then and I still don't.

Dan goes on to win a well-deserved bronze medal behind New Zealand's Danyon Loader in the final, the first of three individual medals he wins that week. His time is 1:48.25, one-hundredth of a second faster than my best, but the only thing that matters to me is that it will be four years before I will have this chance again.

However, this Olympic campaign isn't over yet. I've been selected in five events and the next one is tomorrow. I have to try to pull myself together for my next race, the 4 x 200m freestyle relay. That relay has been Australia's problem child for the last decade. We've repeatedly entered teams we think can win a medal only to fall short. And it happens again in Atlanta. Dan leads off, I swim the second leg, Malcolm Allen swims the third leg and Dunny does the anchor, but we finish fourth, one place short of the medals.

I've waited my whole life to swim at the Olympic Games and it's all going wrong. But I don't really have time to think about my misfortune. On Day 3, Alex successfully defends his 100m freestyle title against the challenge from Gary Hall Jnr. I'm still hurting, but I'm happy for him and I start to see a way through my own misery. On Day 4, I have the 4 x 100m freestyle relay, where we don't have huge ambitions, but I'm given the job of leading off the team and I respond well to that challenge, setting a personal best time of 49.87 seconds as we finish sixth in the final.

I'm starting to recover from my shock and I am in a better mindset by Day 5 when I have the 100m butterfly. Scotty Miller is the Australian favourite for that race, so I can fly under the radar a bit and focus on what I need to do to put together a good race. I swim a personal best time of 53.42 seconds in my heat to qualify seventh fastest for the final, as Scotty qualifies fastest in 52.89 seconds, an Olympic record. Next fastest is Russia's Denis Pankratov, the new world record-holder, who has turned the butterfly world on its head by swimming most of his race underwater. He is doing underwater butterfly kick for 25–30m of each lap. It's revolutionary and it's working. He's clearly faster under the water than he is on top of it. In the final, Pankratov uses his underwater skills to their full capacity and the rest of us, swimming across the surface, have no answer. He wins in a world record of 52.27 seconds. Scotty claims the silver medal in 52.53 seconds, a personal best but not what he came for. I finish sixth in 53.30 seconds, another personal best, which gives me hope that my Olympic campaign is not a total flop.

Before the next Olympics, the swimming authorities will restrict Pankratov's torpedo technique by limiting underwater swimming to the first 15m off the dive and the turn, effectively ending his dominance. But it comes too late for Scotty. This is his moment, and he'll never be as fit or fast again. Elite sport can be a cruel business.

On the final day of the swimming programme, the coaches show faith in me when I need it most. My lead-off leg from the 4 x 100m freestyle relay was faster than any of our guys managed in the individual 100m event, and they select me to anchor the Australian 4 x 100m medley team in the final. Our team is Steven Dewick (backstroke), Philip Rogers (breaststroke), Scotty Miller (butterfly) and me (freestyle).

It's an amazing night for the Australian team. After all our struggles during the week, we finally find some momentum. Susie O'Neill wins her first Olympic gold medal in the 200m butterfly and then Kieren and Dan enter the arena for the 1500m showdown. Dan's already won medals in the 200m and 400m freestyle and is the pre-race favourite. By contrast, Kieren has been seriously out of form. He's only just made the 1500m final, and he will swim in lane 8. But when the race begins, Kieren shows no doubt at all. He surges to the front, takes the race by the throat and never lets it go. It's a performance of stunning bravura and defiance under supreme pressure and it lifts our entire team. We're about to head out for the relay so we're the first teammates Kieren sees afterwards, and he grabs us and hugs us in celebration. His euphoria rubs off on us as we prepare to race.

We're still the underdogs here – not even fancied to win a medal – but we're inspired by Kieren's example. The US team is the rightful favourite. The United States has never lost this event at the Olympic Games and it's not about to start now. We know we don't have the firepower to compete with the US swimmers. They win the gold medal in a world record of 3:34.84. Alex anchors the Russian team to the silver medal and I chase down the German anchorman to secure the bronze medal for Australia. I'm starting to feel more comfortable in such an intense environment now and I put together my best race of the week. For the first time, I will stand on the medal podium at the Olympic Games.

It's a salve for my wounds, but it will be a long time before my emotional scars heal from that week.

However, I hide them to join the other swimmers as we celebrate the end of our Olympics.

First, we hit the hospitality area on the top floor of the AT&T Building in the Olympic Park with swimmers from around the world, but they eventually run out of beer so we head on to another bar, Loulou's, which is outside the Olympic precinct. We're sitting there drinking cocktails out of fishbowls when someone tells us that a bomb has gone off in the Olympic Park. We don't pay that much attention at first, and we continue on with our night.

Somewhere I get separated from the others and eventually I try to make my way back to the Olympic Village, but I have no luck trying to hail a taxi. I'm standing next to the road wondering what to do when a cab pulls up beside me with two Australian guys in it who recognise me and offer to drop me at the village. I love the way Aussies help each other out. It's only when I get back to the village that I realise the seriousness of the bombing. We've had a narrow escape because the blast blew out the windows of the AT&T Building where we were partying earlier in the night.

I walk into the Australian team's building to find our management team assembled in the foyer, where they are ticking each swimmer's name off a list as they arrive back. They quiz me about where I've been and who I was with as they try to track down every swimmer who is out on the town. Most of the swimmers don't have working mobile phones because the US system is not compatible with Australian phones, so it's a herculean task to find them and get them all back to the village, to make sure they are safe. The managers are also taking calls from worried swimmers' families. It's a hectic scene and it takes hours to get everyone back to the village, but we're all okay.

The security around the village is ramped up the next day and the atmosphere inside is subdued. We are advised only to go out in groups and to organised events and official venues. More activities and functions are set up for us in controlled spaces where the team managers know we will be safe.

We still have a good time, but there is an undercurrent of tension that wasn't there before the bombing.

All in all, it's been a brutal introduction to the Olympic Games for me. My coaches don't want me to dwell on it too much, so they encourage my return to training before the Games are even over. I'm also conscious that I have one more meet to swim before the end of the season – an exhibition in Toulouse in France. I race Pankratov and most of the Olympic finalists in the 100m butterfly and, surprisingly, I win. This random race is meaningless to them, but it shows me that I can beat the best in the world.

I've planned with my parents to take a family holiday in Poland, but during my break my mind is already back in the pool. I'm an Olympian by name now, but I must perform like one when it counts.

CHAPTER 6

Transformation

By the time I return to the AIS in October, Gennadi has had a lot of time to think about where we go from here. He wants to make changes to my technique and my training, and he has a willing student in me. I'll do anything to avoid feeling the disappointment of Atlanta again. That thought will fuel me through the next four years.

For years, I've been honing my freestyle technique with a high elbow recovery because I want to swim like Alex, just like every other sprinter in the world. He's the benchmark for all of us. But Gennadi is concerned that my freestyle technique is breaking down under pressure. He's noticed that I seem more comfortable when we do a particular training drill that involves both freestyle arms with dolphin kick, and freestyle with a straight-arm recovery. When I use straight arms over the water, I'm regularly pushing 11 seconds for 25m and 24 seconds for 50m. There's something there to work on.

Gennadi thinks this new direction, using a more dynamic freestyle stroke, can also take advantage of my natural athleticism. A lot of swimmers have bodies that are perfectly adapted for the water, but they struggle with land-based sports. Yet I'm comfortable on land too. I'm a reasonable tennis player and I can turn my hand to basketball and other ball sports. Gennadi argues that we should use this strength in my swimming. It's a new path – I'm not just following the herd, and what is ahead is unknown, but that's exciting to me. We keep working on the straight-arm technique and I can feel how much more natural it is to me. It opens me up more across the chest so I can activate those powerful muscles, and I get more range in my arms and shoulders. It gives me better tempo and rhythm, and I find it easier to maintain that to the end of a race.

The other skill we start practising hard is underwater butterfly kicking. Pankratov has changed the game by demonstrating how effective that can be, and not only in butterfly. We plan to bring it into my freestyle events as well. FINA will eventually limit its use to 15m per lap – the sport is not much of a spectacle if most of it happens underwater – but for now we can still make big gains by maximising my efficiency kicking underwater.

Gennadi has also set me another challenge to prevent me feeling anxious on the blocks. He's set a target for me of doing 100 races within 3 per cent of my personal best in the next year. Practising my race plans over and over again means they will become second nature, so automatic to me that I will feel in control no matter what happens.

This isn't going to leave as much time for training, but that does not concern him. In the year before the 1992 Barcelona Olympics, when the Soviet Union was falling apart and resources in the Soviet sports system had become unreliable, he based his squad in Italy to get the stability they needed. But they were short on funds so they became truly professional swimmers, guns for hire at any paying swim meet in Europe, promising fast times to earn their way. That meant they could not do huge training blocks; they had to keep their speed and freshness for the next meet so they could pay their rent.

Through the need to set up a racing programme that could support their training financially, Gennadi discovered that racing could replace training, and that sprinters performed better if they worked continually on their speed rather than burying themselves in high-volume training. Endurance was still important, but it had to be balanced with speed. The intensive racing also gave them the opportunity to perfect their pre-race routines, racing strategies and skills such as starts and turns under the pressure that only comes with racing.

The proof of this new method was the Barcelona Olympic Games. Despite the fallout from the collapse of the Soviet sports system, Gennadi's squad was highly successful as part of the 'Unified Team', as the athletes of the former Soviet Union were called for that Games. At 20, Alex became the Olympic 50m and 100m freestyle champion, defeating the reigning champion Matt Biondi, and Gennadi's squad supplied most of the winning 4 x 200m freestyle relay team.

That experience revolutionised Gennadi's approach. He never went back to the kinds of training methods that many of Australia's coaches were still using through the 1990s. So we've always focused on protecting and developing speed in training, but now I'm going a step further. I'll be racing as much as training. And I must try to execute every part of every race perfectly.

Our first opportunity to test this new approach comes at the 1996 Australian Short Course Championships in Melbourne just before Christmas, and it's an immediate success. I twice break the national 200m freestyle record, which has stood for nine years. I also set a Commonwealth record in the 100m freestyle and I take the world No. 1 ranking in the 100m butterfly, qualifying to swim all three events at the World Short Course Championships in Gothenburg in April 1997. It's time to take this show on the road.

I'm back in international waters in the first week of the New Year, at the World Cup meeting in Hong Kong, and I feel like a man on a mission. I'm completely determined to prove that I can thrive in international competition and my commitment shows. I win a significant 100m freestyle race for the first time. Until now, my 100m freestyle ability has lagged behind the 200m freestyle and the 100m butterfly, but it's coming together as I get older and stronger. I swam it well in the relays in Atlanta, and I want to make it part of my championship programme this year.

The World Cup campaign continues in Glasgow in late January, where I line up the 100m butterfly world record, but miss it by just 0.02 seconds. No matter, there will be other chances as the World Cup series continues in Gelsenkirchen, in Germany. I lower my national 200m freestyle record there, but I don't get my butterfly race right. I'm still not as consistent as I want to be. I head home to Australia for our squad's now-traditional high-altitude training camp at Thredbo. I'm grinding out the laps in the Snowy Mountains when I hear that Pankratov has broken the 100m butterfly world record at the World Cup final in Paris. That just spurs me on, knowing that I'm now at the level where I'm competing with the Olympic champion for the world record.

One of the side benefits of all this racing is that I'm starting to earn good money, but I'm not much good at managing it. While the AIS manages the swimming side of my life, Mum and Dad continue to do my personal admin and handle my finances, and Woody manages my commercial opportunities, leaving me free to focus on swimming fast. Success does complicate an athlete's life, but I have a good team around me.

The next challenge is the national trials in Adelaide, to select the Australian team for the 1997 Pan Pacific Championships, to be held in Fukuoka, Japan, in August. Shaving my head for big competitions has now become a ritual, helping me get into a competitive mindset. It's almost like I reveal a different persona once my head is shaved – one that is tougher, more intense and more confident – and it's that version of me that I need to perform well.

In Adelaide, I extend my national dominance in the 200m freestyle, but an 18-year-old kid called Geoff Huegill upsets me in the 100m butterfly final, bursting through the 53-second barrier (52.95 seconds) that I have been eyeing off. I unveil a 30m submarine start in this race and it works as I set a personal best time of 53.03 seconds, but I still need to perfect it. I'm convinced it will reap dividends once I have more practice.

It's the first national trials since the Olympics and all the kids who have been dreaming of competing at the Sydney Olympics are starting to appear on the radar. The youngest is just 14 and his name is Ian Thorpe. He finishes third in the 400m freestyle behind a 16-year-old Grant Hackett, which means they will both be on the team for Fukuoka. There are a bunch of schoolkids on the team, which only reinforces that I'm not a junior member of the team anymore. It's time for me to step up. Don Talbot thinks so too. In an interview with *The Australian* before we leave for the World Short Course Championships in Gothenburg, Sweden, in April, Don says that this is a stress test for me.

> This is his first chance to really show what he's got since he started swimming very well. In the World Cups, he was unbeatable, but now he's going to run into a stress meet for the first time since the Olympic Games. He's ranked No. 1 and there's no-one been near him this year. It will be interesting to see how he handles that because he's found out how hard it is to defend that position. The question is: Can he manage to get through and win in the face of those pressures? He is much more mature now and he's swimming infinitely better than he was then. He's a great talent across three events and it's critical for him to acquit himself better than he did in Atlanta.

I'll have plenty of opportunity to succeed, or fail, as I have a six-event programme in Sweden, and half of it is on the opening day of the compact schedule. It's less than ideal. My best two events, the 200m freestyle and 100m butterfly, are both on the first day, back to back, then the 4 x 100m medley relay closes out the session. It's a challenge made tougher by the level of competition. Pankratov will be there in the 100m butterfly and Olympic silver medallist Borges in the 200m freestyle. Even if I swim my best, it might not be enough.

I don't make a great start, finishing fourth in the 200m freestyle as Borges takes the title. I claim the bronze medal in the 100m 'fly behind a Swedish newcomer, Lars Frölander, and 'Skippy' Huegill. That's a particularly disappointing result because it's very tight for the medals, only 0.07 seconds between the three of us. Perhaps my previous efforts in the 200m took the edge off me, but I can't help thinking it's a missed opportunity. I put it behind me and refocus for the medley relay, where Skippy (butterfly) and I (freestyle) combine with Adrian Radley (backstroke) and Phil Rogers (breaststroke) to win the gold medal by almost two seconds and break the world record.

In the 100m freestyle, I swim my way onto my first championship podium in that event, finishing with the bronze medal, as we also do in the 4 x 100m freestyle relay. But our team is stronger for the 4 x 200m freestyle relay and I like our chances there. Grant Hackett, Bill Kirby and Dunny are with me, but I have the chance to lead off, and swim a 200m freestyle where I don't have to think about backing up for another race. I give it my all and touch the wall in 1:45.21, a championship record, faster than Gustavo's winning time from the individual final. Hacky is having a great meet and he splits a 1:45, as does Dunny, and it all adds up to a dominant victory and a world record of 7:02.74.

It's a taste of what's to come in that event. Many of the rookies who just missed Olympic selection last year are getting their first chance to impress in international waters, including Hacky, who makes the best of his opportunities, winning his first world title in the 1500m. I'm not alone in thinking it won't be his last.

But I'm still not performing consistently. I have ups and downs, glimpses of brilliance, moments of magic, but still too many dips that bring disappointment. The only time I'm really consistent is when I swim for my country in a relay. Then I have no trouble producing my best performance, but my individual events are another matter. I'm getting better but I still have a way to go. Gennadi's solution is more racing. I've already been to Asia once and Europe twice this year; now we are off to the United States, my fourth continent of the year, then back to Europe.

After a whistle-stop tour through California and Europe in June, we head back to Melbourne for the Australian Short Course Championships in July. By this point I've chalked up more than 90 races this year. I win a tough 100m butterfly–200m freestyle double in 30 minutes and feel that I'm finally finding the reliability I've been seeking since Atlanta. The next event will be the true test as we face off against the world's No. 1 swimming team, the United States, at the Pan Pacific Championships in Fukuoka, Japan.

The event is being hosted in a brand-new regional aquatic centre just outside the city, which entails a long commute four times a day from our city centre hotel, but after the year I've had, I'm not fazed by traffic delays. I'm intent on showing that I can stand up to the pressures of international competition.

I've added the 100m freestyle to my programme, making it one of the biggest programmes of any swimmer at the championships, combining the 100m and 200m freestyle, 100m butterfly and all three relays. It's particularly important that I get off to a good start. In my last two championship meets I've started poorly but ended well, expending a lot of mental energy to overcome the bad start. I need to turn that around and I've done more than 100 world-class races this year with that sole purpose.

I've got the 200m freestyle again on the opening day in Fukuoka and it's time to prove how much I've learned and grown since the Olympics. My main rival in this event is the US champion Josh Davis. He takes the first 100m out hard and turns first at the halfway mark, but I hold my composure and put down the hammer on the third lap and power away from him to win in 1:47.60, faster than Danyon Loader's winning time from the Olympics. Of course, that won't change history, but this is my first major international title, and it does show how much progress I've made in the last year. 'Tonight, I was determined to remain focused,' I tell the Australian media after the race. 'I didn't want to let Gennadi down and I didn't want to let myself down.'

Next on the schedule is the 100m freestyle, which is an even bigger challenge. The Americans have never lost this event at the Pan Pacs. Their sprinters have dominated ours for 29 years. Mike Wenden was the last Australian to get the better of his American counterpart, Mark Spitz, at the 1968 Olympic Games in Mexico City. However, my confidence is up after the 200m and I've qualified fastest for the final, setting a personal best time of 49.52 seconds, which is a Commonwealth record. I'm now officially the fastest 100m man Australia has ever had, and I feel ready to take on the new US champion Neil Walker. However, I'm clearly not ready, because when the gun fires I'm left flat-footed on the blocks. Walker has half a body-length on me by the time I react. A year earlier, that might have been the end of my race right there, but my brain comes up with a solution, calling on my memory of Duncan Armstrong's famous race strategy to win the 200m freestyle at the 1988 Olympics.

I move over to the lane rope next to Walker to 'surf' on his wake down the first lap, and hopefully preserve some energy for the return lap. I hit the turn and explode off the wall, working my underwater kick hard to make up ground. It works and I'm back in the race. I stay strong down the stretch and touch the wall first in another Commonwealth record of 49.46 seconds.

I realise how lucky I am to win despite the almost fatal error at the start. 'At the moment all my swims are learning swims,' I tell the media. 'Even though they are world-class times, there's still a lot of improvement to come.' This performance also gives me the world No. 1 ranking, although I'm not expecting that to last as Alex will be defending his European title in Seville, Spain, the following week. Alex has had a rough time in the last year. He went home to Russia after winning another two gold medals at the Atlanta Olympics, but nearly lost his life when an altercation on a Moscow street with an Azerbaijani watermelon seller turned ugly and he was stabbed in the abdomen. He needed emergency surgery to save his life and his swimming future has been uncertain. The Europeans will be the test of whether he's back to his best.

But I'm not going to make it easy for him to get back to No. 1. I ask to lead off the 4 x 100m freestyle relay the next night in a bid to get the race right from the start, and I do, stopping the clock in 49.15 seconds, my third Australian record in two days. Gennadi starts talking to the media about world records for me. 'His key is the 200m world record, and then the 100m. He has no high speed like some others, but he has toughness and high endurance,' he says.

Everyone's getting excited about my freestyle potential, but my butterfly doesn't go as well. I'm starting to feel fatigued as the meet goes on. Despite Skippy's absence due to illness, I can't get the win in the butterfly, finishing second to Neil Walker. All our relays finish second to the United States, so I end the meet with two gold and four silver medals. I also celebrate the end of my teenage years, as I turn 20 during the meet, but my success in the pool seems far more important.

I want to keep the momentum going, so I don't take much of a break afterwards. In this never-ending year of racing, the Australian championships are just six weeks away, and they are the most important event of the year for us, as they are the trials for the 1998 World Championships, to be held in Perth in January. It's the first time this event has been held in Australia and I have a chance to become a hero at home. Most of our big meets are overseas, so we don't often get to hear Australian crowds cheering for us. No-one wants to miss this one.

After such a massive year of travel, we need to get some training in. But Canberra in September is still cold and not particularly conducive to the work we need to do, so we head up to Cotton Tree on the Sunshine Coast for a three-week training camp. Despite my Polish extraction, I'm really a child of my Indian summers. I gravitate to the sun, and I much prefer swimming outdoors. Wedged between Maroochydore and Alexandra Headland, Cotton Tree is situated where the Maroochy River spills into the Pacific Ocean. The outdoor aquatic centre is on the bank of the river and has everything we need, which is mostly just sunshine, appropriate pool space and some other recreational opportunities. We do three training sessions a day, clocking up 90–100km weeks of training to refill our tanks. But it's not just a hard grind. Some days the afternoon session is surfing or some other activity to break up the work. Part of Gennadi's philosophy is if we feel good, we will swim good. And getting a tan makes me feel good. I feel healthier. The medical profession would disagree, but it's important for my psychology when racing to feel fit and strong and healthy, and a tan helps me do that.

Meanwhile, I'm about to enter the business world. With all the international racing I've done, I'm starting to earn some decent money and Dad identifies a business opportunity for the family. The lease is available at the King Club Leisure Centre in Cheltenham, near our family home at Brighton, which would be an opportunity for us to launch a learn-to-swim programme under my name. We lease the facility under the Klim Swim name. I'm technically a part of the business, but I have very little to do with the day-to-day running. I leave it to Mum and Dad to do all the heavy lifting in terms of managing the facility and expanding the business. We also launch Klim Swim as a learn-to-swim franchise business and we soon have learn-to-swim schools in five centres across Victoria. I may be the face of Klim Swim, but it's Mum and Dad, and Anna, doing all the hard work to make it a success. I turn up for the occasional open day or club meet, but I'm focused primarily on my own swimming.

I arrive at the World Championships trials in Brisbane feeling great. I've now had more than 120 top-class races this year – and we've put in a hard training block, aimed primarily at the 200m freestyle and a possible attempt on Italian Giorgio Lamberti's world record of 1:46.69. I'm less than a second outside it, and closer than anyone has been for years. I win the national title by almost two seconds, but my time is solid rather than spectacular. I'm leaving something in the tank for Perth.

In the 100m freestyle, I become the first Australian to break the 50-second barrier on home soil, but the real fireworks come in the event I have approached as an afterthought, the 100m butterfly. It's being touted as the feature event of the championships for one simple reason: four into two won't go. Australia has most of the best 100m butterflyers in the world right now, but only two can win selection to swim for the world title. It's an old-fashioned shootout between me, Skippy, 200m butterfly specialist Scott Goodman and Adam Pine, who's now training at the University of Nebraska. Theoretically, that should be to my advantage because I'm not relying on this event to earn me a place in the team.

Pressure fills the air as we stand behind the blocks, but I'm feeling pretty relaxed. However, when the gun goes, the starter detects that someone has broken early and fires a second shot to alert us that it is a false start. He then presses a button to drop a rope across the pool at 15m to stop any swimmer who has not heard the second shot. But there is an equipment failure and the rope fails to drop. A second official tries to drop the rope by hand and it jams. Meanwhile, we're still swimming. There's a second rope at the 35m mark as a backup, but our officials are generally not Olympic sprinters, and by the time the designated official runs from 15m to 35m, we've already passed that point. He drops the rope anyway and it finally stops us on the way back.

It's a comedy of errors, but the reality is that we've now swum two-thirds of a race that is to decide the immediate fate of some of the best swimmers in the world. Even at 20, I've experienced a lot in the pool, but nothing like this.

As we try to recover from our efforts – I jump straight into the diving pool to clear out my lactic acid build-up – the officials huddle together and try to decide what to do. Should they delay the race until the end of the session or until tomorrow? In the end, they give us 15 minutes to regroup and be ready to go again.

There's a lot of upset among the guys; even mild-mannered Piney is swearing. He was leading the race when we were stopped. But Gennadi wanders up to us and defuses the situation, telling us: 'This is fantastic – it's like boxing, now you have the second round. You are all warmed up and you can go for a world record.' I think he's joking. Then he gives me some private words to get me refocused: 'You are a bit of a rabbit and a bit of a lion,' he says to me. 'Now you need the lion.' That fires me up and I'm ready for Round 2. I'm no longer thinking about the aborted race or my rivals, only about what I need to do.

When the gun goes, I dive in and move smoothly through my race plan. I can see that I'm in front at the turn and I relax and drive for the wall. I touch and turn to look up at the scoreboard and think there must be another mistake. The clock says 52.15 seconds, which is under the world record, but everyone is quiet – the crowd, the coaches, the media. They are checking to see who finished second and haven't looked hard at the times yet. Then I see my parents going crazy in the grandstand and the surprised announcer finally says I've broken the world record.

Everyone suddenly erupts and I go berserk in the water, jumping on the lane rope and pumping my arms in the air in victory. One of the photographers immortalises the moment, and that image becomes the inspiration for our Klim Swim logo.

The world record is so unexpected, given all the drama around this race. I really have not given a moment's thought to going after Pankratov's time (52.27 seconds) tonight. Yet there it is. I'm now the fastest man in history in the 100m butterfly and the first Australian to hold this record. I'm in the club with guys like Mark Spitz, Pablo Morales and Michael Gross, some of my all-time heroes. I pull myself out of the water and do a little shoulder jiggle in delight while Laurie Lawrence is pushing a TV microphone up to my mouth. It's all so exciting, but I have to remind myself not to get carried away. This hasn't changed any of my ambitions.

'I want to get the 200m freestyle record – this is definitely not a priority,' I tell the media after everyone has calmed down a bit. 'I always wanted to do the 100m butterfly, but I never thought I could do it so quickly. If you break a world record everyone looks at you and measures you, but I want to be a world champion and until I am I won't have accomplished my goal.'

But I have learned something from this race. I know now the mindset I need to perform at my best. When I look back at that race, everything is a blur and I am focused only on the wall. I'm aggressive but relaxed, and I feel totally in control. That's what I've been searching for: that balance between relaxation and arousal that allows my best performance to come out. Now I need to do this again at the highest level – the World Championships.

CHAPTER 7

Bringing Out the Lion

I've got good momentum now. The US-based magazine *Swimming World* names me Male Swimmer of the Year off the back of my world record, but I'm also facing a huge programme of seven events at the world titles in Perth in January – four individual (50m, 100m and 200m freestyle; 100m butterfly) and three relays over seven days. That's at least 11 races. It's a big challenge and I will need every bit of energy I can find.

We go back to Cotton Tree for another camp. I do the biggest mileage of my life, up to 100km a week, to condition my body for what's ahead. There's another challenge that I need to get my head around: the fact that I will be racing Alex in Perth in the 50m and 100m freestyle. The end-of-year rankings for 1997 have us first and second in the world for the 100m freestyle. Alex is No. 1, courtesy of his winning time of 49.02 seconds from the European championships in Seville, and I'm

No. 2, after my lead-off swim in the relay in Fukuoka (49.15 seconds). The swimming community and the media are starting to see us as rivals, and to speculate on what might happen between us in Perth, but we don't want that rivalry to seep into our training squad. Gennadi is careful to design individual training programmes for each of us. We are different athletes who need different training stimuli anyway, but he doesn't want us racing each other in training and we don't want that either. Even with my 140 races this year, I haven't raced Alex over the 100m freestyle at all. We've been on totally different competition schedules.

'Alex and I are very good friends and there's no hard feelings there,' I tell the media. 'We have agreed not to think about each other as rivals until we get on the blocks in Perth.' It's not that difficult for me to avoid getting competitive with him because I regard the 200m freestyle and 100m butterfly as my main events for Perth. I'm delighted that my freestyle sprinting is also developing, but I don't have big expectations around the 100m freestyle. And if we get consumed with each other, there's a danger we could forget that the rest of the world is coming for us. We do another three-week altitude training camp in Thredbo before Christmas to prepare for the onslaught.

In the first week of January, we head to Perth to do our final preparation, but separately. Gennadi and I are with the Australian team and Alex will join the Russian team when they arrive. Alex tones down the talk of any rivalry between us. He says to the media:

> You guys still want to provide a little bit of a battle between us, but I don't want to do that. When it comes to the race, we will see who will win. I have nothing against him, and I hope he has nothing against me. He's maturing and developing and it's good to see a guy from a younger generation who is able to do the same things I did quite a few years ago. I don't feel any pressure that Michael Klim is racing me. We are still good friends, we share the same lane and the same gym, but we did our own preparation – this is where we will see who did it better.

The Australian team goes into camp at the HMAS *Stirling* naval base, south of Perth, where we are in our own world. Don has done this deliberately to get us away from the hype of a home World Championships where we will be the centre of all media attention. Any media trying to get to us would have to get past the base's military security. That is to our advantage when a doping scandal hits the Chinese team on their arrival in Australia. There's been much speculation about the Chinese team since they emerged as a force in the early 1990s – stories about them hiring former East German coaches since the Berlin Wall fell to teach them the same doping methods. Their women swimmers dominated the 1994 World Championships, but at the Asian Games in Japan in 1995 there was surprise drug-testing at their pre-event camp and seven swimmers failed drug tests and were suspended. Since then, the rest of the world has looked upon China with suspicion.

On their way to Perth, the Chinese swimmers arrive at Sydney Airport where they must go through customs, and a flask of human growth hormone is discovered in the luggage of the breaststroke swimmer Yuan Yuan, containing enough for the whole team. She and the team leaders are questioned and the drugs are confiscated, but the team is allowed to board a plane to Perth.

However, while they are on the five-hour flight to Perth, the news of the drug seizure gets out to the media. By the time their flight arrives, every media organisation in the city is waiting for them at the gate at Perth Airport. Cameras and reporters are everywhere. The swimmers are taken unawares as they walk off the plane. They try to escape the attention by weaving through the airport, but the cameras are going backward in front of them, knocking over bystanders and falling down stairs and escalators. It's chaos and there is nowhere to hide as the Chinese then have to wait, surrounded by the media, for their bags to be unloaded before they can board a bus to their hotel. The intense scrutiny continues at their hotel and throughout the championships, especially after four swimmers test positive to a diuretic masking agent in Perth before the championships begin. But we have been shielded from all this mayhem at HMAS *Stirling*. By the time we arrive in Perth and do our final preparation in the competition pool, much of the commotion will have died down. But it has had one benefit for us: it has taken the media focus away from the Australian team for a few days.

HMAS *Stirling* is a fairly sterile environment – the rooms are bare and basic – but I'm used to a dormitory setting. Luckily, I'm rooming with Hacky and we always manage to make it fun, mostly just by laughing at each other. I've started my race taper but I'm not setting the world on fire. I don't feel good in the water and I can't find the pace I need to know that I'm ready to race for world titles. Some doubt is creeping in. Taper is always a nervous time because your body goes into an adaptation as you reduce your workload and freshen up to prepare to race. Technically, you are fresher, but while your body is adjusting to a different routine, it doesn't feel like it. Often you feel worse before you feel better, but the deeper the 'hole' you go into, the higher peak you are likely to reach when you come out of it – at least that's the theory. But it can play havoc with your mind while you are feeling bad in the water. It's hard to trust that it will come good when you need it. I'm definitely in a hole while we're on the base.

But moving into Perth seems to do the trick. I immediately start to feel better in the water. Gennadi and I have developed one particular test we use to measure my final preparation for major championships. I stand up and do a 200m freestyle, no warm-up, no special suit, no competitors, just a time trial, and if I feel good and swim fast, we know I am ready to go.

When the day arrives in Perth, the training pool is crowded with swimmers of every nationality, all trying to get their last preparation in. But that doesn't deter me. I find a tiny bit of room and do my race-pace 200m, and it feels great. I feel light in the water, and I know it's good even before I finish. Gennadi doesn't say a word to me, but I can read his body language. He makes eye contact with me and then he deliberately walks away. I'm ready. Nothing more needs to be said.

The swimming team managers, in their wisdom, have decided to put four young up-and-coming male swimmers together in one apartment at our accommodation. I'm rooming with 15-year-old Ian Thorpe. At 20, I don't feel much more than a kid myself, and I'm at my first World Championships, but I've been teamed with Thorpey to show him the ropes. Grant Hackett and Simon Cowley, both 17, are in the other room. Almost immediately, we get into the mother of all Play Station contests, a competition that will continue right through the championships, when we're not swimming, eating or sleeping.

I definitely start to feel like the adult in the room when they start throwing fruit into the fan to see it being sliced up and spat out around the kitchen. But their enthusiasm and sense of fun are infectious. Thorpey and Hacky seem incredibly laidback considering these are the World Championships. They don't have much experience, but they don't have any baggage either. They don't want to talk about swimming away from the pool and they aren't overthinking it. They prove to be an excellent foil for my natural seriousness at competition time.

I also discover that Thorpey is one of the messiest creatures alive, whereas I'm a neat freak. Yet we become regular roommates on tour, a bit like the Odd Couple. Secretly, I think he likes rooming with me because when he leaves the room, there's stuff everywhere, and when he comes back, I've always reorganised it.

My family has arrived for the championships, but they leave me to my own devices. They know I have a massive workload so they don't expect to see me much except when I'm racing. The best I can do is a quick hello when I get the chance.

My race programme starts with the 200m freestyle, as it did in Atlanta, but this time I'm determined to get it right. I arrive for the heats in the morning and I could not feel more different than I did 18 months earlier. This time I feel totally in control and I know exactly what I need to do. As part of my need for order in my surroundings, I always study the stats around my events. I know what everyone else has done leading in and I know I'm the only one in the field with a sub-1:48 clocking to my name in the past year.

It's a young field, and the Olympic champion Danyon Loader of New Zealand and silver medallist Gustavo Borges of Brazil are not in the form they were in 1996, so there's an opportunity for a new champion to emerge. The other likely contenders are all around my age – Massi Rosolino of Italy and the Dutch kid Pieter van den Hoogenband are both 19 – so in some ways it feels like I'm back in my age group. For once, the Europeans and Americans are in our backyard now, competing out of season and across the world, dealing with jetlag and an unfamiliar culture, and I'm not going to make it easy for them.

In the heats, I swim just fast enough to show them what they will need to do to beat me, clocking the only sub-1:48 time of the session to take lane 4 for the decider. For years, swimming aficionados have been predicting that I will be a world champion. Sometimes that's been a millstone around my neck that has choked me in the past, but when I stand behind the blocks for the final in Perth, I'm excited, not scared. I feel the love from the home crowd and thrust my arms to the sky to acknowledge them when the cheer goes up for me during the pre-race introductions.

When the gun fires, I set a testing pace and lead all the way. I'm under world record pace after 150m. I fade slightly in the closing metres, but it doesn't matter – I'm too far in front by then and I win by a body-length from Massi and Pieter. I'm slightly disappointed with my time, a personal best of 1:47.41, because I had hoped to challenge the world record (1:46.69), but the bottom line is that I've won the world title. I tell the television interviewer afterwards, 'I'm the best in the world – I feel great.' One down, six to go.

Day 2 brings the 4 x 200m freestyle relay and the chance to swim with two of my roomies, Thorpey and Hacky. But first they need to earn their places on the final team – which they do, along with Dan Kowalski, by shepherding our team through the morning heats as the fastest qualifier.

Dan and I were on the relay team in Atlanta that flopped in this event; now we want to make amends. For the two teenagers, it's all gravy. We've put the experienced guys first and last in our relay order and tucked the kids in the middle, where they will be a bit protected as they swim their first World Championships final.

I've become a bit of a specialist lead-off swimmer in the freestyle relays. I like the challenge of leading off and somehow the fact that I'm doing it for a team, and not just for myself, takes me outside my own expectations and relaxes me. I give the team a nice lead in the opening leg, then hand over to Hacky, who is followed by Thorpey.

Swimming for Australia, they both set personal best splits and extend our advantage, delivering Dan a five-second margin when he dives into the water. The race is effectively over: they won't catch us from here, but the world record is in play.

Dan puts in a solid anchor leg to stop the clock in 7:12.48, just half a second outside the world record (7:11.95) set by the Unified Team at the Barcelona Olympics, which was also coached by Gennadi. For the first time in decades, the Australian men have won a world relay title, finally converting the hype into hardware. And this relay team is just getting started. With three members under 21, the potential is there to dominate this event for years to come. After two days of the World Championships, I have two gold medals and I'm surfing a wave that I want to ride forever.

On Day 3, I turn my attention to the 100m freestyle and the looming clash with Alex. Neither of us has wanted to think about this race, but now it's here. To be honest, I don't think I'm ready to beat him, so I don't have big expectations of victory. I just want to perform well. I qualify fastest, so I'll be in lane 4, with Alex to my left and Pieter to my right. Before the final, Alex and I warm up together and keep chatting together all the way to the blocks. We are putting off the moment when we must turn into rivals for as long as possible.

But when we step onto the blocks, the time has come. I'm in a good position at the turn, but Alex puts the hammer down when he accelerates off the wall and takes control of the race to win in a championship record of 48.93 seconds. I take the silver medal in 49.30 seconds, and I'm satisfied with that. It's great to be up there with him, but I still feel like he's the master in this event. We emerge from the water laughing now we know we will share the medal podium.

To the media, I say, 'I will never forget this race. It's special because it's good for me and it's good for Alex and it's good for Gennadi. I don't really care that I came second.'

I'm relieved this race is over. I didn't like being pitted against Alex by the media. I've found the hype around our 'duel' more stressful than anything else leading into the meet. To me, we are brothers in arms. We've been in the trenches together for six weeks of training camp at Cotton Tree and three weeks in Thredbo leading into this event, and Gennadi has managed us perfectly. I've never felt that he gave either of us preference or priority, and we've both swum well enough to beat the world. I'm now three events in and I've got two gold medals and a silver. It's more than I ever dreamed of and I'm still not even halfway through my programme.

Day 4 also features a race between mates: Hacky and Thorpey in the 400m freestyle. Hacky is the Pan Pac champion and he's improving fast, but European champion Emiliano Brembilla has a better time, so he's technically the favourite. We have high hopes for Hacky to win. Everyone knows Thorpey is a huge talent, but 15-year-old boys don't win world titles against men. Hacky attacks the race and he's leading comfortably after 300m, two seconds clear of the field, but then Thorpey starts to eat into the margin. Hacky still leads by more than a body-length at the final turn but he's starting to die and Thorpey is charging. Hacky fights to hold on but the kid can feel the opportunity now and he brings in that extraordinary kick to surge to the finish and win by 0.15 of a second. He's now the youngest male world champion in history, and the way he's won the race is nothing short of sensational.

That race gets the Australian team up and humming, which is great for our 4 x 100m freestyle relay team, who are taking on the almost unbeatable US team at the end of the night. I grab us a half-second lead over the Americans on the opening leg, but Piney and Richard Upton can't hold it and Fydes as our anchorman goes into the water 0.35 seconds behind Gary Hall Jnr. He can't quite overhaul him, but he does cut into the lead. The Americans win in 3:16.69 and we are second in a national record of 3:16.97. But we've come close to the US team for the first time in decades and that gets us thinking about what may be possible at a home Olympics in two years' time.

I've now got two gold and two silver medals from my four events, Thorpey has two gold medals and Hacky has one gold and one silver, with his best event yet to come. The media get to know that we are rooming together and christen our apartment the 'Golden Room'.

I wake up on Day 5 of the championships and I know I'm in trouble. I have no energy at all. After four days and nights of high-class swimming, I feel exhausted. I've raced every day and been on the medal podium every night, which has meant four very late nights, once I've completed my warm-down, massage, media commitments and drug-testing. I've been virtually the last person out of the aquatic centre each night, and mostly eaten dinner on my own when I've arrived back at our accommodation. It has taken a toll. And this wave of lethargy has hit at the very worst time, on the morning of the 100m butterfly – my world record event.

This is where all those races in the last year will show their worth. I've raced well in every circumstance and under every condition, no matter how I am feeling, and I will need to use all that experience and confidence to produce good races today. I drag myself to the pool and begin preparing for my heat. I still feel flat, but I tell myself it doesn't matter. I know I'm in good form and the performance will be there when I need it.

I also have the crowd to help me. After four days, they are cheering my every move and I'm feeding off their energy. Skippy is coming in fresh and raring to go after missing the chance to compete at the Pan Pacs due to illness, and he flies through his heat and sets a championship record of 52.93 seconds to take lane 4 for the final. I qualify a solid fourth, behind France's Frank Esposito and Sweden's Lars Frölander. It's all I need to do. I've secured lane 6 for the final, which is always nice as an Australian swimmer. Both Jon Sieben and Duncan Armstrong won their Olympic gold medals in lane 6, so for us it's a lucky lane. I go home from the pool to rest and get my mind right for the evening.

When I come back, I feel like a different swimmer. Everything feels light and easy and I'm back in the zone. I'm so determined to get this race right and prove that the world record was not a fluke. The crowd is rocking again and the cheer I get when I'm introduced is the biggest of the week so far. The sound surrounds me like a blanket. I feel warm and safe inside it. They know this race is mine, and so do I. When I break through the surface after 20m of underwater kicking, the first five strokes feel smooth and strong, and I go into autopilot, not thinking, just focusing on my technique. Doing my underwater kicks off the wall, I can see I'm in control of the race and I don't let up until I stop the clock in 52.25 seconds, the second-fastest time in history, just a tenth outside my world record.

A wave of relief washes over me and I finally let out the emotion I've been trying to hold in all week. I leap onto the lane rope and raise my arms, my forefingers pointed to the sky. It's my third gold medal and I have five medals in total. I couldn't have imagined it would go this well, and it's not over yet. I still have two events to go.

I don't have high hopes for the 50m freestyle on Day 6. I'm surprised even to be swimming it as I'm not ranked in the top ten in the world. But there was a spare spot, no-one else had qualified in the team and it's always better to have two Australians in an event. This will be my one 'fun' event of the week because I have no expectations.

The 50m is also called the 'splash and dash'. It's a bit of a lottery in some ways because everyone is so close in ability. It's generally the swimmer who makes the fewest mistakes who wins, because there's no time to overcome an error. It's not really my bag so I'm amazed when I qualify equal fastest for the final with Alex, ahead of some of the renowned 50m specialists. There's a lot of pressure on them, but none on me and that's a weapon I can use in the final.

Alex is the favourite, after winning the 100m freestyle and maintaining his perfect record in championship races since 1991. But he's left standing on the blocks in the final, while unfancied American Bill Pilczuk gets a perfect start – almost a flyer – and that gives him a crucial advantage. Alex tries to chase him down but it's too late, the race has been decided in the first instant. Bill claims the world title in 22.29 seconds, from Alex in 22.43, in what is arguably the biggest upset of the championships.

Meanwhile, I'm focused on putting together the best race I can. When I hit the wall, with the white water frothing around me, I look up at the scoreboard and I'm stunned to see that I've won a medal. I've tied with Puerto Rico's Ricardo Busquets for the bronze, in 22.47 seconds, another personal best time. It just goes to show what momentum and confidence can do. There's a funny moment when I walk into the medal room after the race. Alex looks at me puzzled, as if to say, 'What are you doing here?' He's so shocked to lose the race that he hasn't even noticed that I've won a medal. I've now got three golds, two silvers and a bronze – a medal in every event I've contested. It is way, way beyond what I dreamed I could do.

Finally, it's the last day of the championships. Today I have the 4 x 100m medley relay. It's always one of my favourite events and we have a strong team, based on the results of the four individual 100m finals. I've won the butterfly and finished second in the freestyle, but the coaches have decided that the team is stronger if I do the butterfly, because of my winning margin over the rest of the world in that event. Fydes has finished seventh in the freestyle final, but he's a terrific anchorman and we know he won't let the team down. Skippy is unlucky to miss out, given that he also won a medal in the 'fly. That's the back end of the relay sorted.

Victorian Matt Welsh has emerged as Australia's best backstroker over the last few months. He's a late bloomer who started off as a butterflyer before switching to backstroke on the advice of his coach, Ian Pope, 12 months ago. Since then, he's made massive gains, charging up the world rankings. He's still new to the international scene, but he's done well to finish sixth in the 100m backstroke final. For the breaststroke, we have the ever-reliable Phil Rogers, a veteran at this stage who finished fourth in the 100m breaststroke final.

As usual, it's the Americans we will have to beat if we want to win the title. We know they will be out fast, courtesy of their new backstroke star Lenny Krayzelburg, and we will have to hunt them down. Matt does a brilliant job to keep Lenny in check, finishing just a quarter of a second behind to give us a shot and Phil keeps us in contact in the breaststroke. As I dive into the water, the deficit is under three-quarters of a second and this is my opportunity to give us a winning lead.

The US butterflyer Neil Walker, who beat me at Pan Pacs, is out of form and now is my chance to make amends. I surge down the pool and back in 51.80 seconds, the fastest split in history, and our lead is now nearly a second. The United States team has its legendary anchorman, Gary Hall Jnr, but the job is too big – even for him. He challenges Fydes down the first lap and even turns first, but he fades on the return leg.

Fydes only needs to swim a measured race to seal the win and he does, celebrating wildly in the water once he realises we have won. We all jump in to celebrate with him while the Perth crowd launches into orbit. It's the first time we've won the medley relay at a global championship since the Mean Machine triumphed at the 1980 Olympic Games.

This is the final event of the championships and marks a hugely successful meet for the Australian team. Hacky has also won the 1500m on the last night, and that brings our medal tally to seven gold, six silver and seven bronze, our best ever total from the World Championships. It leaves us second on the medal table, behind the United States. Four of Australia's five individual gold medals rest in the 'Golden Room' – as well as a selection of relay gold medals.

I have four gold medals. Thorpey and Hacky have two each. We're all young and it's clear that we will form the nucleus of the Sydney Olympic team in two and a half years. My individual tally of four gold, two silver and a bronze is the best that a male swimmer has ever achieved at the World Championships and earns me the Male Swimmer of the Championships award.

But there's not much time for celebrating. We have another competition coming up, a World Cup meet in Sydney, so I still need to go through my full warm-down routine, as well as drug-testing and a final press conference. By the time I'm done, the stadium is empty – everyone has gone. I see my family quickly and then head back to our accommodation. The busy schedule has served me well because I haven't had time to overthink anything. I just got into a routine and rode the momentum that I had after the first day. The success has been transformative for me, as Alex explains to the media: 'It brings you such confidence. All of a sudden you understand that you can do many things – like winning and winning easily. It becomes a pleasure and you become addicted to it.'

I am unrecognisable from the kid who was so scared and uncertain in Atlanta. Under Gennadi's guidance, I have done everything possible to grow into a different athlete in the last 18 months, one capable of conquering the world – and I have.

Some athletes – Alex, Kieren and Thorpey spring to mind – naturally have a mindset and emotional control that allow them to perform under pressure. Others, like me, have to learn these things. I'm not an iceman, and my confidence is not innate. It rises and falls based on how I'm training, how I'm performing. In my early years, I was very self-conscious – about my body and my less-than-perfect English. I was never sure I had what it took to be great. Others were far more confident about my abilities than I was. But I wanted it so badly that I just kept going, taking every opportunity, overcoming my fears, pushing through the setbacks, and now I've arrived. Don Talbot sums up my performance like this: 'At Atlanta he was a boy in a man's body, now he's a man in a man's body.' But a historic performance like the one I've been able to produce in Perth, in a sport that is so beloved by Australians, brings its own challenges. Before, I was well known within the small tight-knit swimming community but reasonably unknown to the Australian public. I'm now famous, and I don't realise how famous until I leave Perth and go back to the east coast.

CHAPTER 8

Life Gets Complicated

That one week in Perth changes my life – and my family's lives, because it isn't only me who becomes famous. The whole family is now receiving regular media attention. The name Klim is unusual in Australia, and it now has a recognition factor that puts us all in the spotlight. I've been on the television and in the papers every day for a week and the interest in me is enormous. My manager Woody is handling all the media and commercial inquiries, but my diary is filling up with interviews, appearances and engagements.

I know how to handle the pool stuff, but everything else is completely outside my realm of experience. *Sixty Minutes*, one of the highest-rating programmes on television, decides to do a profile on me. Liz Hayes is the interviewer and her TV crew follows me around Sydney as I prepare to compete at the World Cup meet, less than a week after the World Championships.

Alex and I race again in the 100m freestyle, with the same result, but my focus here is on the 100m butterfly because there is a $43,000 car being offered as a prize for the first world record of the meet. No-one breaks a world record on the first day, which means the prize is still up for grabs when I arrive for the 100m butterfly heats on Day 2. The whirlwind of the past two weeks is catching up with me, but I know I'm not the only one eyeing off the car, so I don't think I have the luxury of waiting for the final in the evening and I know I'm capable of breaking Pankratov's mark of 51.78 seconds.

As an added incentive, Liz and the *60 Minutes* crew are waiting poised on the pool deck. My warm-up is awful. I have no rhythm at all, so I cut it short and sit in a chair to rest until I race. I felt much like this on the morning of the 100m butterfly in Perth, so I know I can find the energy when I need it. When the time comes, I push my tired limbs and even more fatigued mind into action, dashing through the four laps in 51.16 seconds to break the world record.

Afterwards, a journalist asks when I will break the 200m freestyle world record, and I realise how high the expectations are now. 'You guys are very hungry – I've just set a world record and you are asking for another one,' I chide them. Yet I do deliver a second world record that day.

I feel better for the 100m butterfly final in the evening, and it shows in the race as I swim a touch quicker again, improving the world record to 51.07 seconds and winning a share of a $10,000 world record bonus. Once again, I'm the centre of media attention and I take the opportunity to shine the spotlight on Gennadi and Alex and Matt Dunn, the people who have helped me reach this point. 'People only see my results, but it wouldn't happen without them,' I say. 'There's more to two world records than one person.'

Woody and I also need to do some quick, and quiet, negotiation with the meeting organisers as the car is a Honda and I have a Mazda sponsorship. We take a cash offer instead.

When I get back to Melbourne, I'm invited to the Australian Open tennis and I attend with Dad and Anna, whose promising tennis career has ended before her time. While training at the Nick Bollettieri Tennis Academy in Florida, she stepped on a ball on the court and fell heavily on her right wrist, breaking it badly. It did not heal well and prevented her from playing again at the highest level. She's a left-hander but had a two-handed backhand. She tried to adjust to a one-handed backhand but after two years of struggle it became obvious that she would not be able to continue as an elite player. It's a devastating outcome for her because she still loves tennis.

We arrive at Melbourne Park just like everyone else, but pretty soon it becomes apparent that I'm not like everyone else anymore. As we walk through the grounds, I start to attract a crowd, then it becomes a well-meaning mob, and we are swamped. We lose each other and the tournament security people have to help me through to Rod Laver Arena. Once we are in our seats, the announcer also draws attention to me, and asks the crowd to welcome me. They applaud, I stand and wave, but then everyone stands and cheers. The moment feels surreal, like I've suddenly morphed into being Andre Agassi. I've spent a lot of time in this arena, but it was mostly as Anna's little brother. To add to the strangeness of it all, the Australian Open organisers ask me to join a talk panel where we are interviewed by the puppet Elmo from *Sesame Street.*

Meanwhile, Woody is working hard to turn the hype into dollars. The next commercial deal is with Nintendo. I knew all that gaming in Perth would come in handy; they sign me up as an ambassador for Nintendo 64 and GameBoy. I've moved out of the AIS residence now, into a flat in the suburb of Bradden with Dunny, where our priorities are pretty clearly displayed in the living room. It features two La-Z-Boy recliners, the biggest TV screen we could find, surround sound and now, courtesy of Nintendo, the latest gaming consoles and games. Dunny's a complete tech-head, so he's delighted with the new additions to our collection.

Then Gillette Australia comes on board as a partner, through its Braun brand. Gillette's Head of Marketing, Ian Scott, decides that they're a natural fit for what is now one of the best-known shaved heads in the country (it's between me and Peter Garrett) and we become close friends. The commercial support is welcome, but the new level my fame has reached only hits me when I'm driving down William St toward Kings Cross in Sydney one day and I see my face on a Braun billboard, right next to the iconic Coca-Cola sign.

Westfield also signs me up, along with Susie O'Neill, and we are booked in for appearances in shopping centres across the country. We even do an event with one of my

St Kilda footy heroes, Robert Harvey. The appearance at Southlands, near my family home in Melbourne, is particularly memorable. Thousands of people are gathered on the ground floor of the atrium, but also on every level going up to the roof, all looking down at me.

I want to show my appreciation to Gennadi, without whom none of this would have happened, and I have found the perfect token of my appreciation. Gary Hall Jnr, who I've gotten to know at international competitions, has given me a beautiful white guitar made by his sponsor Gibson. It's an incredible gift, a collector's item. I don't have the playing skills to do it justice, but Gennadi does. I present him with the guitar and his obvious delight is worth as much to me as any of my gold medals.

My life has changed immensely. The AIS bubble in Canberra protected me for years, allowing me to train and prepare in anonymity and without distraction for each championship. But that bubble has well and truly burst. Now there are distractions almost every day – the media, the public, the sponsors.

I need to get a handle on all this. These demands can't be allowed to interfere with swimming or my performance level will drop, then the interest in me will disappear as suddenly as it has arrived. But at the same time, I'm trying to capitalise on my new status because an athlete's career can be short. An untimely injury can end everything, as my sister found out, and I don't know what the future will bring. So I'm bouncing between Sydney, Melbourne and Canberra, doing appearances and photo shoots between my training commitments. I have to confess that part of me is enjoying the opportunities and social occasions that are now coming my way.

Courtesy of my relationship with the Nine Network, which is using me in its sports promos, I'm invited to the Logies but my flight back to Canberra afterwards is delayed and I am half an hour late for training. Gennadi is not impressed. I'm struggling to find the balance between all these competing demands and I don't have much time to do it, because the competition calendar is remorseless. The Commonwealth Games trials are scheduled to start just three months after Perth finishes.

I arrive at the trials in Melbourne thinking I've done enough training to maintain my position, but what I haven't had is the rest and recovery between training sessions, which was a crucial part of my success in Perth. I'm still emotionally drained from that massive high of the World Championships and all the craziness that has followed. But the expectations of me are higher than ever. And while I've been in the spotlight, younger swimmers like Ian Thorpe and Skippy Huegill have had their heads down working hard.

When I arrive, I don't feel great in the water, but I've bluffed and won before. In the 200m freestyle final, I go out hard, but I don't have the endurance to hold on. Thorpey, still 15, has risen to a new level since Perth and he comes over the top of me, using his now trademark finish to win in 1:47.24, faster than my World Championship time.

I finish second, which means I've qualified to swim the event at the Games in Kuala Lumpur, but it's still a bitter pill, and there's another one to come. Skippy lowers my colours in the 100m butterfly, my world record event. I finally get one back in the 100m freestyle, winning by a body-length, but it doesn't feel like much compensation. The bumpy ride continues in the 50m freestyle final, where I again finish second to Nathan Rickard. I end the week with a win and three seconds.

Looking at the big picture, there's no harm done. I've qualified to swim all four individual events and the three relays in Kuala Lumpur, so it's the same programme I swam in Perth, but I feel humbled all the same. My aura of supremacy has gone and the young wolves are gathering.

There's another challenge looming, this time created by the International Swimming Federation (FINA), which reveals that it is working with the International Olympic Committee to introduce semi-finals for the Sydney Olympic Games. Such a schedule would make my seven-event programme even more difficult to execute. There's an outcry from Australia's leading swimmers and officials, who believe the introduction of semi-finals will hurt the home team's chances. But the other side of the debate is that semi-finals will expand the swimming schedule at the Olympics and therefore make it more commercially attractive, and that argument wins the day.

The FINA technical committee approves the introduction of semi-finals for all events from 50m to 200m in June 1998 and releases a draft schedule that is disastrous for me, and for some of our other leading swimmers. The proposed schedule leaves me with a clash between my best two events, the 200m freestyle and the 100m butterfly, requiring me to contest the 100m butterfly semi-finals four events before the 200m freestyle final.

I don't hide my disappointment at this eventuality. 'Why are they trying to limit excellence?' I say to the media. 'I don't want to eliminate any of my events and I don't agree that money or TV rights should influence sport in this way.' I'm not the only one complaining – the proposed schedule also moves the 1500m freestyle final to the fifth day, before the 4 x 200m freestyle final. There's a chorus of disgruntlement from around the world, which forces FINA and the IOC to consider the details of the schedule again, but the introduction of semi-finals for the Olympics is here to stay and I will have to adjust.

It's a hectic year, but I find time to celebrate my 21st birthday in Melbourne in August. I don't usually go in for the big birthday bash, but what starts as a plan for a small celebration at a yacht club morphs into a party for 200 in a ballroom at Albert Park Lake. The whole thing is completely over the top. The theme is 'A Touch of Gold' and I wear a gold jacket I've borrowed from Channel 9's wardrobe department. Among the guests are my 'Golden Room' mates Thorpey and Hacky.

I happen to know an up-and-coming comedian named Eric Bana, so we convince him to do his stand-up show as part of the entertainment, for mates' rates.

Once the party is over, I again focus on the Commonwealth Games, where the challenge in at least some of my events may be tougher than at the World Championships.

Thorpey's emergence as a contender in the 200m freestyle has turned the race between him and me into box office gold – or at least that's how the media see it. They tip us to challenge the world record. Well, one of us will.

It turns out to be no contest. Thorpey takes off in the third lap and I can't stay with him. He wins in 1:46.70, just one-hundredth outside the world record I've been chasing for the last year. I'm more than a second behind. I can't begrudge him – it's amazing to see what he's doing at the age of 15 – but I'm demoralised by how quickly the tide has turned and I take that negative attitude into the 100m butterfly the next day. The shocks keep coming as I finish third in the final, behind both Skippy and Piney. But there's no time to think about it as we also have the 4 x 200m freestyle that night and with Thorpey's improved speed we think we can get the world record that we just missed in Perth. This is Gennadi's baby and I want to perform well for him.

Given that Thorpey just missed the world record in the individual 200m, he's given the opportunity to lead off and make another attempt. Daniel will follow him, then Matt Dunn, and I will anchor the team. Thorpey's not as fresh as he was at the start of the week, but he still puts in a strong opener of 1:47.48. Daniel is in better form than he was in Perth and improves to 1:47.81, Matt is solid with 1:49.15, but the record is on a knife edge. I need to lift my game if we are to succeed. I finally find some of the energy that I had in Perth and fly through my leg in 1:47.42 and we snatch the world record in 7:11.86.

I know how much that world record means to Gennadi, so I give him my gold medal as a thank you. I don't need it – the race was a much-needed morale booster for me ahead of the 100m freestyle. I've finally found my mojo by that final and I hold off Fydes to win in a Games record of 49.43.

There are highlights away from the pool too. I play backyard cricket in the village with Steve Waugh's men, meet Jonah Lomu coming off a bus and encounter Viv Richards in the dining room.

By the end of the Games, we have won all three relays, which brings my personal medal tally to four gold, one silver and two bronze. It's pretty similar to my count from Perth, but my own feelings about my performance are vastly different. The start of the year was brilliant, but it's ended in an anti-climax. I can't wait to get out of there and reset. The Sydney Olympics are just two years away.

I take six weeks off – the longest break I have had from training for many years. Long breaks are problematic for swimmers because movement through water is so different from movement on land. As a rule, for every week a swimmer takes off, it takes two weeks to get back, so long breaks are generally frowned on by coaches. However, Gennadi recognises that I'm completely fried by this stage and I need to recoup my energy – primarily my mental and emotional reserves – before I can go again. This is the last chance for a decent break before the Olympics, when I need to be at my absolute best.

My parents have organised a trip home to Poland, and Dunny decides to come with us. I'm looking forward to the break until I'm sitting on the plane and I open the travel schedule Dad has put together. That's when I realise it is chock-full of official engagements. I've left all the arrangements to Dad and this now looks more like work than recreation. There's a press conference at Warsaw Airport when we arrive, followed by a dinner with the Polish Olympic Committee three hours later. I'm pretty unhappy about the plan initially because I'm so tired, but it's the first time I've been to Poland since I became 'somebody'. My parents want to show me off to their home country and the Polish sports community wants to recognise me. I've always made a point of talking to the Polish team and coaches when we're at the same competitions and I know I'm the closest thing Poland has had to a swimming world champion in the last decade.

I'm greeted like a returning hero when we step off the plane, so I put on my best face and go through the whirl of functions, meetings, dinners and appearances that have been organised through the Polish Olympic Committee, Polish Swimming Federation and TVP, the national television network. It turns out that I'm doing a victory tour of Poland. President Aleksander Kwaśniewski hosts us at the presidential palace and I do a national TV interview. We visit swimming clubs and schools, meet top Polish athletes from different sports and travel around Poland from Warsaw to Kraków, Zakopane and Gdańsk. Everywhere we go we are given the VIP treatment, and I can see that it means a lot to my parents.

One meeting stands out, when we are ushered into the presence of Lech Wałęsa, the grand old man whose actions have transformed Poland since my family left ten years earlier. He's no longer president, having been defeated in the 1995 election, but he's the most important figure in Poland's history in my lifetime and it's an honour to meet him. He asks about my training and about living in Australia, then he smiles and says I'm like Leonid Brezhnev, the former Soviet leader. I don't get the reference, so I ask why. 'Because you have so many medals on your chest,' he says, roaring with laughter. He's poking fun at the former Soviet leadership who liked to appear in public with a chest full of medals.

I haven't had much down time when I return to the AIS, but I feel refreshed and raring to go. The disappointment of the Commonwealth Games lingers and I'm determined to get back to my peak, but there's a new challenge for me to get my head around.

The new Olympic programme now amounts to a gruelling 15-race schedule over eight days if I am to continue with my seven-event programme from Perth. The competition schedule has undergone a couple of revisions since June, when the semi-finals were introduced, adding four more races to my schedule. At first, my Perth programme looked impossible. Now it looks more reasonable: the 200m freestyle and 100m butterfly have been separated and there's only one really heavy day, when I will have to back up from the 100m freestyle semi-final into the 100m butterfly final and follow up with the 4 x 200m freestyle relay.

Gennadi and I discuss reducing my programme, but I'm willing to take it on. I think racing every day was to my advantage in Perth. Once I was in that rhythm, I developed huge momentum and it was easy to keep going, so I want to replicate that at the Olympic trials and the Games if I can. I tell the media, 'I will have 15 swims, which is a lot more than I have done in the past and it will require a lot of physical and mental strength but, with the right support, I am pretty excited about the challenge. Mark Spitz did it in 1972, so it has been done and maybe we should try to do it as well.'

I make that declaration just weeks before the IOC is to meet and confirm the final schedule for Sydney. Behind the scenes, we're also talking to the Sydney Organising Committee (SOCOG), hoping they will lobby the IOC for a few tweaks to the schedule that will allow me to do all of my preferred events. It's been done in the past. The athletics programme for the Atlanta Games was adjusted slightly to allow Michael Johnson to do the 200m and 400m double at home, so I'm hopeful that the IOC will also see the sense of changing the programme for me. When the IOC makes the decision, the SOCOG president Michael Knight rings me directly from Lausanne to let me know we've won. The Olympic programme now separates all of my main events, with just a small crossover between the 100m butterfly and 50m freestyle, which I can handle. It's the best possible outcome.

'I feel like a chance has been given to me and I don't want to waste that chance,' I tell the media, although I remind everyone that it is my performance at the Olympic trials that will ultimately decide how many events I swim at the Games. I don't want to take it for granted that I will qualify in every event I want to swim. If the Commonwealth Games has taught me anything, it is to not under-estimate the strength of the competition at home, and that is only likely to get tougher as the Olympics approach.

I still have mixed feelings about my year as 1998 winds down. The euphoria of Perth has been overlaid by the disappointment of Kuala Lumpur, so I'm shocked when I'm named the Australian Swimmer of the Year ahead of Thorpey and Hacky, who have both had brilliant years at the World Championships and the Commonwealth Games. It gives me a bit of a lift to know that my performance at the World Championships is still so highly rated. The goal now is to find consistency at that very highest level.

CHAPTER 9

Sprinting Toward Sydney

I guess when you've lived in five different countries growing up, you tend to become adaptable. Some people feel uncomfortable with change, but not me. I embrace new ideas and experiences.

That makes me the perfect pupil for a coach like Gennadi, whose restless and ingenious mind is always searching for new ways to look at swimming, and the world. When I switched to the straight-armed freestyle technique, he described it to one journalist as 'snake with kayak'. I turn my body onto the side (the snake) when I take each stroke, while my arms mimic a kayak paddle. My hands are the blades scything through the water, pulling my body forward.

I was one of the first swimmers to adopt the track start, well before they changed the design of the starting blocks to accommodate it. For us, this is all about problem-solving – finding an area in which I am weak and making it strong. I was not particularly explosive off the blocks when

I used the traditional start with both legs forward, and occasionally I would miss the start altogether. That almost cost me the 100m freestyle win at the Pan Pacs in 1997, so we looked for a better method. I used the track start in Perth, and before long it seemed that half the world's best swimmers had started using it.

We know we need to keep innovating to stay ahead of the pack. The sport keeps progressing and my times from Perth won't win in Sydney, so I have to get better to remain on top. At the very highest level, there are more physically gifted swimmers out there – including Alex and Thorpey – so I need to maximise every strength I have and eliminate as many weaknesses as possible.

My swimsuit sponsor Speedo has been doing some interesting research in racing suits and, as one of its top athletes, I'm working with it on the development. Gennadi has long believed that a tight suit around the core of the body would help a swimmer to maintain a better body position in the water, particularly under fatigue, so he's enthusiastic about this direction. And he's also obsessed with reducing drag, which the suits will aid. The fabric is designed to break through surface resistance. It's like the skin of a shark or a dolphin: it looks smooth, but when you touch it, it feels rough. Speedo's boffins have taken inspiration from Mother Nature. The raised surface carries small air and water particles with us as we move, reducing frictional drag.

The swimsuit manufacturers work years in advance to produce the latest hi-tech suits for each Olympic cycle and

I'm excited to be part of this evolution. It's not ready to be revealed yet, but it's coming soon.

Meanwhile, Speedo has also hired the renowned British art photographers Anderson & Low to shoot an advertising campaign with me, and they book a day at the AIS pool in Canberra. They shoot images of me above, in and below the water over several hours. In a break while they reload the camera, I'm just playing in the water, wearing briefs and goggles. I sink to the bottom and stand on the floor watching them through the portholes in the walls of the pool. I'm holding my breath so there are no bubbles around me, just still water. They notice me and start snapping away. They end up dumping everything else they've shot and focusing on this one image. My feet are planted on the pool floor, my arms hang by my sides with my hands in fists and I stare straight at the camera. Light outlines my body and reflects off my feet, hands, shoulders and head, but the rest of my form is in shadow. That image ends up becoming the poster for the Speedo campaign, and later it is purchased by the National Portrait Gallery, where it still hangs, in Canberra.

My next swimming assignments are the Australian Championships in Brisbane and the World Short Course Championships in Hong Kong. This year's national titles are the trials for the Pan Pacific Championships being held in Sydney in August, which shape as a perfect dress rehearsal for next year's Olympics in the same pool.

The 200m freestyle final is billed as a rematch between Thorpey and me, but that's not how it turns out. Hacky takes out his frustration at being left out of the world record-breaking 4 x 200m freestyle relay team at the Commonwealth Games, and a series of losses to Thorpey over 400m, by showing us both up.

Unbeknownst to us, he's done more 200m pace work since Kuala Lumpur and hit the gym to get a bit stronger, and he mugs us in the final. He charges through the race to stop the clock in 1:46.99, just short of Giorgio Lamberti's world record. Thorpey finishes a close second in 1:47.08 and I swim my fastest race since Perth (1:47.97). But it's still a third-place finish in an event where I am the world champion, and while three can swim the race at the Pan Pacs, only the top two can qualify for the Olympics.

The 200m freestyle is getting away from me and it gets a little bit further away when Hacky decides to have another crack at the world record the next day, leading off the Miami Swimming Club's 4 x 200m freestyle relay. He takes advantage of the clear water in front of him and puts the pedal to the floor from the start, smashing out the race to break the barrier that Thorpey and I have been chasing for the last year. We're watching in the grandstand as he stops the clock at 1:46.67 to become the fastest man in history.

I'm now under pressure in the 200m from the two young guns, but I'm holding my own in the 100m events. I win the 100m freestyle and take back the 100m butterfly title from Skippy. We all head off to the World Short Course Championships in Hong Kong, where Hacky continues on his winning way. Thorpey and I have a great duel for the 200m freestyle title, but he just pips me, and Lars Frölander takes the 100m freestyle–100m butterfly double to leave me with three individual silver medals. My two gold medals come from the 4 x 100m freestyle and medley relays, the latter in a world record. It may not look it from the medal count, but it's an encouraging meet for me. I've set personal bests in both the freestyle events, so I feel as if I'm back on track for the Pan Pacs.

But first – in one of two major 'reveals' for the year – Woody has negotiated a deal with SOCOG, which will result in my face appearing on the cover of nine million copies of the Official Olympic Games Ticket Book. The image selected is of me in the moments after I broke the 100m butterfly world record in Brisbane in 1997. I'm sitting on the lane rope, arms in the air in triumph, mouth open as I roar my delight. For the Australian public, this is the most anticipated moment leading into the Games – when tickets are finally on sale. With the launch of the book, five million tickets to 640 sessions of 28 different sports become available. Every Australian will have the chance to request tickets, although for over-subscribed sessions, all those who have requested tickets will be placed in a lottery to decide who gets them. The hopes of all Australian Games fans rest in the pages of the book and on the allocation process that will follow after the application deadline of 16 July.

The Fairfax newspapers arrange a photoshoot with me in advance so they have a unique photo to use for the day of the ticket launch. When I arrive, they cover me in gold body paint and photograph me for the front page of their newspapers. By the time the ticket book is launched, I'm back in Europe competing on the Mare Nostrum circuit as a warm-up for the Pan Pacs, so I miss most of the hullaballoo. At this stage, it would be a distraction. It's always a fine balance between the demands of being in the public eye and the demands of training. My managers at Elite Sports Properties are very aware of this and work hard to make sure the balance is right.

But the world is a small place these days. Our AIS squad arrives in Barcelona late at night and we're waiting in our hotel foyer for room keys to be handed out when a busload of Australian tourists arrives to check in. One spots me and shouts, 'It's Michael Klim!' Before I know it, I'm surrounded by a group of enthusiastic fans. Gennadi is telling them, 'It's not Michael Klim, it's his brother,' as he and Rohan Taylor, a young coach who has joined us for the tour, shuffle me into the lift.

The same tour group is there when we go to breakfast the next morning and a woman approaches me from behind and wraps her arms around me, saying I'm her favourite swimmer. Later, Rohan asks me what it's like to be so recognisable. Most of the time, I don't mind it. I try to be kind and generous with fans who want to show they appreciate me. The tricky thing is that they know me, but I don't know them. Strangers move into my personal space without a thought, and I have to detach myself gently and create my own space again without offending anyone. Who knew that becoming a world-class swimmer required the skills of a diplomat?

It's an interesting role reversal for Gennadi to be acting as my bodyguard, although he's accustomed to doing that with Alex, who is a huge star in Europe. Much of the time, our swimming squad acts as Gennadi's minders when we are on tour because of his habit of wandering off and losing track when we are away from the pool. By contrast, he's intensely focused at the pool. At the Monaco Grand Prix meeting, I win the 50m butterfly sprint – an elimination sprint series, in which the slowest swimmer in each round is cut until it is a head-to-head competition between the final two. There is good prize money for the winners, and I face off against Pieter van den Hoogenband, now one of the biggest stars in Europe.

I'm excited to win and I bounce up to Gennadi expecting congratulations, but that's not what I get. He's exasperated and he says to me, 'What are you doing? You swim like a sausage.' To be fair, he's right. The whole reason for me to swim this 50m series was for me to practise the first 50m of my ideal 100m race, with a view to bettering my 100m butterfly world record later in the year and preparing for the Sydney Olympics, still more than a year away. We've worked out that my optimum stroke count for the first lap is 16 strokes and that's what I'm supposed to be doing in every 50m race. But in the final, I was caught up in the moment, forgot my race plan and took 18 strokes. In Gennadi's eyes, this is not a cause for celebration. He has a memorable way with words when he's correcting me. Another time he describes me as being 'like a cow on ice' to illustrate that my hands are slipping rather than grabbing the water.

When we get back to Australia, I prepare for my second 'reveal' of the year: the new bodysuit that Gennadi and I have been working on with Speedo for more than a year.

By 1999, the sport is advancing so quickly that I know I'm going to need every legal edge I can find to win in Sydney. I want to use every tool that's available to me, and so does Gennadi. Tim Lees, the Speedo Australia marketing manager, has come to us and asked us to help design a new suit. I'm very excited by the opportunity, knowing it will put me in an advantageous position to make use of this new technology before anyone else.

We embark on a secretive process from late 1998 into 1999, giving feedback on various early versions of the suit. Some have arms, but I don't like the way they feel around my shoulders. It's too restrictive, but from the waist to the ankles the suit feels great.

In one of my first suit tests, I swim a 48.3–48.4 100m freestyle in training, hand-timed by Gennadi. I'm a convert immediately, but the more I test the suit, the slower I am going, which indicates that my body is getting used to the neural stimulation it offers. To get the most advantage from it, we decide it's best not to wear it too often in training, but rather to save it for race day so I get that neural boost when it matters most.

By the time the new suit is ready to be revealed to the world, Speedo has custom-made the latest version for me, creating it to my exact measurements so it fits like a glove. My new suits are neck-to-ankle for freestyle, now the fabric technology has advanced to the point where the fabric slides through the water more easily than bare skin. The downside is that they are so tight that it takes a good ten minutes to squeeze into them.

The Speedo suit has been named the 'aquablade' and has narrow raised stripes on the fabric to channel the water past the body. It goes from neck to ankle with wide armholes to give the shoulders free movement, but Adidas has a Teflon-coated Lycra version that goes from wrist to ankle, covering the whole body.

In my last competition before the Pan Pacs, the Telstra Grand Prix meeting in Brisbane, I come out in my new bodysuit and set my fastest 100m butterfly time since Perth, which lifts me to No. 2 in the world rankings for that year.

The suit, combined with my performance, create a sensation and also a controversy. Don questions its legality, as it has not been officially approved by FINA yet and he says it should only be allowed for the Olympics if all swimmers have access to it. FINA's rules say that a swimsuit should not be a flotation device, which means that unless the suit pops to the surface when it is submerged, it's likely to be approved.

I'm not deterred by the drama. I wear the new suit for all my races in Brisbane and put together a series of fast swims. In the same week, two British swimmers win gold medals at the European Championships in Istanbul, wearing the Adidas suit. By the end of the week, swimmers all over the world are clamouring for bodysuits.

I'm feeling good going into the Pan Pacs in Sydney, which is being touted as a fight for ownership of the Olympic pool between us and the Americans. 'This is our home pool, it's our turf, so we have to defend our fort,' I say at the pre-event press conference.

It's also our first chance to road-test the Olympic programme, with the inclusion of semi-finals, and it's the first time some of us will wear bodysuits at a championship meet. Not everyone is convinced of their merit yet, or has access to a custom-made suit, although Speedo has imported a body scanner to measure the whole Australian team for them during the meet. Thorpey still wears briefs at this meet, some swimmers are in jammers (a waist-to-knee suit) and a few, like me, are in the full-length suit.

Thorpey gets us off to a brilliant start by smashing the 400m freestyle world record. We then give the Americans a taste of what is to come in the 4 x 100m freestyle in the last race of the night. I lead off and set an Australian record of 48.73 seconds, my first time under 49 seconds, which gives us a big lead. Jeff English swims second, with Fydes third. Thorpey, who is trying out my straight-arm action for the first few strokes to help him accelerate more quickly from the start of the 100m, brings us home in 48.55 seconds to seal the win.

It's the first time an American team – albeit one without its biggest gun, Gary Hall Jnr – has ever lost that race in international waters. The Australian team used to suffer from poor starts at major championships, but no longer. We've dominated the first night and we're determined to keep it going.

My individual programme starts on Day 2 with the 200m freestyle heats and semi-finals. With only two Australians able to qualify for the final, and Thorpey and Hacky swimming in the next race, I have no choice but to attack my semi-final. I'm under world-record pace after 150m but I tire slightly in the final 25m to stop the clock at 1:46.82, another big personal best and just a fraction outside Hacky's world record.

I've now set a benchmark, but I don't know if it will even be enough to reach the final, with the second semi-final still to come. Thorpey is brimming with confidence after his first-day heroics and sets his second world record of the meet, clocking 1:46.34. He's so dominant that Hacky doesn't even get a look in, and he swims 1:48.20.

I've achieved my first individual goal: I'm in the final. When the competition is this hot, that's an achievement in itself. Now I've got to figure out how to beat Thorpey in the final. I know I've still got superior speed so I gamble it all on a fast start, but that just sets up the race for him. He's still with me after 100m and from there he powers away to win in another world record (1:46.00), his third in as many days. I take the silver medal in 1:47.40, faster than my winning time in Perth but now light years away from the standard he is setting.

I tell the media, 'He's just having one of those meets. I don't think anyone can stop him at the moment, I hope I can tomorrow [in the 100m freestyle].'

My own performances tell me I'm in career-best form, so I turn my attention to the 100m freestyle where I still like my chances. Thorpey proves to be human after all, as he doesn't beat me or Fydes to snatch a place in the 100m final.

We combine again in the 4 x 200m freestyle relay at the end of the night with that world record squarely in our sights. The numbers don't lie: we know we have a far better team than we had when we established the world record at the Commonwealth Games – we're all in better form than we were then.

This time, Thorpey leads off and I anchor, with Bill Kirby and Hacky in between. Thorpey sets the second-fastest time in history (1:46.28) to give us an unbeatable lead from the start. Bill is the new member of the team and puts in a solid split of 1:48.96. Hacky has been waiting for two years for his chance to be part of this relay and he doesn't waste it, putting in a monster leg of 1:46.30. I bring it home in 1:47.25 for a total of 7:08.79 – more than three seconds inside our previous record.

Satisfyingly, the Americans are more than eight seconds behind and it's hard to see them making up that kind of deficit in the next year. We're now at unbackable odds to win this event at the Olympics.

In the 100m freestyle final, I get my first individual win of the week, beating my old sparring partner Neil Walker in 48.98 seconds. Fydes comes in third to confirm that our sprinters are going better than theirs at this stage of the cycle.

After five days, I have three gold medals and a silver, but there's still quite a significant challenge ahead. My rivalry with Skippy in the 100m butterfly has grown with each meeting in the last year. We're so close in ability that there's a lottery every time we race. He wins some and I win some, but as the world record-holder, I'm desperate to put my stamp on this event.

Skippy leads narrowly to the turn and is still just shading me at the 85m mark, but I've judged my race just right and I outlast him in the final stretch to the wall, clocking 52.49 seconds to win by 0.02 seconds. There's really nothing between us.

The competition is equally tight between the Australian and US teams. We're matching each other gold medal for gold medal on the tally, and there's a realistic chance that we can beat them at a major championship for the first time since the 1956 Olympic Games. We are one up on gold medals on the eighth day (13 to 12), with just one event still to come – the men's 4 x 100m medley relay.

If we win the race, we win the meet. We have a reasonable chance after upsetting the US team at the world titles in Perth. The Americans are superior in the backstroke, where Lenny Krayzelburg has set three world records this week, but we've beaten them in the individual 100m breaststroke (Simon Cowley), butterfly and freestyle (both me). Skippy will do the butterfly. We'll lose nothing with him there, and I will do the freestyle. Matt Welsh will have to put in the swim of his life to keep us in the race after the opening leg and we'll be chasing right through the race, but we won't give up.

By the time I'm on the blocks, the Americans still have a half body-length lead and I know I have no margin for error if I'm to make up that ground on Neil Walker. But I'm a little too eager and I leave the blocks before Skippy has touched. I know I've broken and we'll be disqualified, but I give it my all and make up more than half a second on Walker. We stop the clock in second place, and my split of 47.78 seconds is phenomenal, but it will remain unofficial.

The timing shows I've gone 0.06 seconds too early and we are rubbed out. I've just been a little bit too gung-ho. Australia is still on top of the medal table, with more silver medals (13 to 10) than the US team, but it's a technical knockout now, not the knockout blow we all wanted.

However, it hardly dampens the mood at all. We have a team celebration on the pool deck after the formalities are over and everyone's feeling pretty jovial. Our team is a perfect mix of talented young guys coming through and those of us who have experience. Hacky and I are mucking around, laughing and being cheeky. We know the next time we see the US team will be at the Olympics, and we feel like we're in a great spot to take them on again. This has been a perfect morale-booster. The wave is lifting all of us now as we rush toward the Olympic year.

It's been an extraordinary meet for everyone. By the end of the eight days, 12 world records have been set. Thorpey has four, Krayzel and South African breaststroker Penny Heyns have three each, Jenny Thompson has broken the 100m butterfly mark and our 4 x 200m freestyle relay team has set a new standard. We all know there will be more fireworks when we assemble here again one year from now.

I'm flying high, and it takes almost no effort to keep the momentum going, so I roll right on to the Australian Short Course Championships, being held in my home pool at the AIS in Canberra. I want to make a splash for the locals, and for the AIS, given their great support of me.

We put together an AIS quartet to break the 4 x 200m freestyle relay world record in a time trial on the first day, then I burst through the 51-second barrier in the 100m butterfly, setting a new world record of 50.99 seconds in the semi-final.

The next day, I come down with a chest infection: my immune system is depressed from all the racing and I feel pretty awful. But I wake up feeling better on the last day of the meet and I attack the 50m butterfly world record. I just miss it during the semi-final and final, then appeal to the meet director to let me do a solo time trial, where I finally get the race right and reduce the world record to 23.21 seconds. It's a nice way to end the season as we start the one-year countdown to the Olympics.

There's one very left-field opportunity that comes my way before the end of the year. At a training camp in Hawaii earlier, I'd bought a copy of the Foo Fighters' album *There Is Nothing Left to Lose.* It came with a temporary tattoo of the Foos' FF logo. For fun, I put the tattoo on my left shoulder while I'm at an Australian team training camp and during a media day I'm photographed with it in the pool. The image is spotted by the Foos' record company Sony, and they put it on a special edition of the album produced for the Australian market. As a fan, I'm thrilled. It gives me the kind of street cred that swimming alone could never achieve.

CHAPTER 10

Pressure Test

Everything is bigger in the Olympic year – the stakes, the publicity, the competition, the pressure – and Sydney is the biggest Olympics of them all for those of us in a position to represent Australia. An athlete's career at the highest level is mostly short – 10 years if you are lucky – and no Australian swimmer has been to more than three Olympic Games. Most only go to one. So the chances of getting a home Olympics in your career are infinitesimally small. Those of us who survive the Olympic trials and win selection will have achieved the sporting equivalent of winning the lottery.

I know how rare this chance is. Every Australian swimmer of my generation has hoped and dreamed about this. I must succeed.

It's not only us athletes who are preoccupied with the Sydney Olympics now. Every little event related to Sydney is being blown up to huge proportions in the media.

Thorpey breaks his ankle while going for a run in a bush

reserve and there's much anxiety around how he will recover from that and what effect it will have on his training for the Olympics. He'll be swimming in a cast for the next month. But if you are going to break your ankle, October is the best time of the year to do it. He has a few months before he needs to be back in shape.

We do a three-week altitude training camp in Thredbo in November to get back to peak fitness. I'm lucky in that I have an almost perfect response to altitude training. I get all the fitness benefits that are supposed to accrue from training hard in thinner air.

Mountain climbers were the first to document the fitness benefits from adjusting to high altitudes, but it was the experience of athletes at the first high-altitude Olympic Games – in Mexico City in 1968 – that brought the concept to the wider sports community. At first it was thought that altitude training was only useful for endurance athletes, but over time it has been proven useful for most athletes who compete in aerobic events, although interestingly some athletes don't seem to derive much benefit from it at all. It depends on your individual physiology.

At around 1400m above sea level, Thredbo is at a less extreme altitude than many other training camps around the world – such as Sierra Nevada, Font-Romeu or Colorado Springs, which are all above 1800m – so we get a smaller benefit. It does have the great advantage of being only two and a half hours from Canberra, rather than halfway around the world. That means we can go more regularly at less cost and without having to deal with jetlag.

This camp is timed so we head straight into competition afterwards, first at the US Open in San Antonio, Texas, and then at the annual AIS meet in Canberra just before Christmas. I usually get a good performance spike directly off altitude training. The plan is for me to make a statement in the 100m butterfly in the United States by taking down the world record. But that goes awry when I struggle with jetlag after the trip from Australia. I still swim well – I win the 100m butterfly from Skippy in 52.90 seconds and finish a close second to the Dutch star Pieter van den Hoogenband in the 100m freestyle – but I don't feel as fresh as I need to be if I am to challenge world records.

Back home, I adjust to the time zone quickly and decide to have another crack at the 100m butterfly world record in my home pool. I usually get a second performance spike off altitude training about three or four weeks later, so the timing is right. I've had some rest, through travelling, but I'm not fully prepared for competition. However, I've learned that I don't need everything to line up perfectly in order to swim fast so long as I've done the work.

I do a 100m butterfly time trial on the first day of the AIS meet and lower my world mark from 52.15 seconds to 52.03 seconds, but I catch my left hand on the lane rope just before the finish. That costs me a fraction of a second, so I know I have a better swim in me.

I'm so close to becoming the first man to break 52 seconds in the long course pool, and I want that accolade. The next day I play with my race pacing during the heat and final of the 'fly, but I don't quite get it right. In the final, I misjudge my touch on the wall. Gennadi immediately organises another time trial for the next day. I can see by the gleam in his eyes that he thinks I can smash through that barrier.

On the third day, I prepare myself for one final effort. There's no-one else on the blocks, no crowd, no atmosphere. It's the kind of mental challenge that Gennadi likes to use to prepare me for the big occasions to come. After three previous 'rehearsals', I hit the fourth attempt perfectly: right pace, no errors with my skills, great technique, and there it is. I stop the clock in 51.81 seconds. It's my seventh world record of the year, and this one feels like my masterpiece. I hope it will send a signal to the world that I'm the one to beat for the gold medal in Sydney. I'm confident now that I can perform in any circumstances.

It's arguably my greatest swim, but there is no fanfare or celebration. Gennadi and I walk through the almost deserted AIS grounds afterwards and do a debrief of our recent training block and the weekend races. We treat this like it's just another day.

On the same day in Sydney, Thorpey makes his return to competition after his ankle mishap, proving he's lost nothing. He may even have gained something. While his tremendous kick has been out of action, he's focused on improving his upper-body strength, and it shows in a more-balanced freestyle stroke. He stands up with the kids at the low-key Metropolitan Championships and smashes out the fastest 400m freestyle that's ever been recorded outside a major championships, silencing his own and everyone else's doubts about the impact of the injury. He's back, possibly better than ever. That has implications for me as I try to figure out which events to focus on for the Olympics.

As the calendar flips over to 2000, I'm in Sydney with the AIS team and our family and friends. Dunny's twin brothers have organised a party at the Australian Maritime Museum on the harbour where we can see the fireworks. There's a countdown clock and they give me the honour of counting down the final seconds until 2000. It's a great night, and one of the last times we will get a chance to let our hair down before the Games. Everyone we meet wants to talk to us about the Olympics now. The hype has gone to another level.

At the World Cup meet in Sydney in January, Thorpey brings down the world short course record in the 200m freestyle, and that's more food for thought for Gennadi and me. I'm still one of the best in the world in the 200m, but I'm no longer the best, so should I continue doing the event when it comes first in the Olympic programme and could take the edge off me before I get to the events in which I have a better chance of a gold medal? On the other hand, I've always swum better when I have a big programme because it gives me less opportunity to over-analyse each performance. I find it easier to overcome a disappointment when I have another event to focus on the next day, and if I swim well, I get on a roll. Each approach has advantages so we go back and forth on the issue. However, there's no question about my form: I win eight straight gold medals in 50m and 100m events across the two World Cup meets in Sydney and Hobart.

With the Olympic trials and the Games so important this year, most of Australia's best swimmers opt out of the World Short Course Championships in March in Athens, including me. But I wonder whether it is the right decision after the Europeans and Americans blitz the world records there. Sweden's Lars Frölander breaks my 50m and 100m butterfly marks and the US team breaks Australia's 4 x 200m freestyle and medley relay records. That's four world records I've lost in a few days. It's a warning shot that I need to heed. The world is coming for us in Sydney.

The swimsuit furore has continued to bubble away since the new bodysuits were unveiled in mid-1999, but it really blows up in March when the Australian Olympic Committee president John Coates gets involved. FINA has approved their use, but Coates is not convinced they are legal. He calls for a second opinion from the Court of Arbitration for Sport.

Even the Queen is interested in the issue. Louise Sauvage and I are invited to a State Dinner for Queen Elizabeth II at Government House in Canberra during her Australian tour in March 2000. When I'm presented to her, she asks me about the new suits and wants to know how difficult they are to get on. I'm more worried about watching my manners at the dinner table.

I have one of the first of Speedo's revolutionary new Olympic suits. It's called the Fastskin – a full bodysuit made of knitted fabric with a surface print designed to mimic sharkskin in its ability to cut through the water. It hasn't even been launched officially yet, but I've been planning to wear it in at the NSW Institute of Sport meet at the end of March.

It's meant to be a low-key meet, but suddenly there's huge noise around the suit and Speedo advises me to hold off, given the circumstances. There are two issues: the first is those who believe the suit is illegal; the second is that the suit is not generally available yet and if it provides the kind of advantage that Speedo says it does, that could create unfair competition if not all swimmers have access to it. The AOC's main concern is that suit access could affect qualification at the Olympic trials in May, and lead to legal action from swimmers who have been disadvantaged, throwing team selection for the Sydney Games into chaos.

As the poster-boy for Speedo's new suit, and the swimmer most involved in its development, I'm suddenly at the centre of this storm. I tell the media, 'I'm a bit surprised by the uproar because it didn't happen when Adidas launched its suit six months ago. If you compare the suit with my old one, it's an advancement but it's not that different. I can swim well with or without it, so that doesn't concern me.'

Eventually, Speedo does permit me to swim in the suit at the NSWIS meet and I immediately break the Commonwealth 100m freestyle record, clocking 48.72 seconds. A day earlier, Hacky, who is also a Speedo swimmer, has worn his new suit at his home club meet at Miami on the Gold Coast, beating Kieren in the 400m.

The advent of these suits splits the Australian team down generational lines. Thorpey, Hacky and I are in favour. Kieren, Fydes and Scotty Miller are against. Kieren says the arrival of the new suits is 'almost the beginning of a new sport' and they should be banned. I respond, 'I think sport has to evolve and it's the young people, like me and Ian and Grant, who want to take the sport forward. It's the older guys, like Chris Fydler and Kieren Perkins, who are the ones taking a completely different stand on it.'

I've been involved in the development of the suit all along and I understand the logic behind it. For me, it's a new resource that we can use to help us swim faster, and I'm all for it.

The Olympic trials are always our most nerve-wracking national meet because there's so much more on the line than in other years. Dreams are made and dashed. There's elation for those who make the team and devastation for those who don't, because the chance is lost for at least another four years, and perhaps forever. The stakes don't get higher for swimmers than this. Add in the fact that this time the prize is a home Olympics, and then the ongoing uncertainty about the availability of the new suits that clearly offer an advantage, and the stress for swimmers hoping to make the Olympic teams is dialled up to eleven in April 2000.

Speedo moves heaven and earth to get enough suits distributed before the Olympic trials to quell the suit anxiety, but that's only part of the equation.

I don't have to worry about the suit – mine is custom-made and I'm already comfortable wearing it and convinced that it will aid my performance – but I'm going to need every edge I can find to succeed because of the standard of competition in all of my events. In the 200m freestyle, I am going to have to beat either Ian Thorpe or Grant Hackett to qualify. In the 100m freestyle, Thorpey and Fydes stand in my way. In the 100m butterfly, I have Skippy and Scotty to beat. And I have one of the biggest programmes of any swimmer at the trials, with nine races in six days. At least I don't have to do relays this week, but if I'm off my game at any stage, there will be a world-class swimmer in the next lane who will make me pay.

And a lot of people will be there to see it. The new Olympic grandstand, which seats 8500 people, has opened at the Sydney International Aquatic Centre in time for the trials. It's to my advantage that I've swum in front of big crowds at both the World Championships in Perth and the Pan Pacs in Sydney, so I know how to use the crowd's energy to lift me if I need it. They helped me in the 100m butterfly in Perth when I was feeling fatigued and I will turn to them again if my workload starts to bite.

The AIS squad stays in a hotel at Rosehill when we compete in Sydney, and commutes to the pool in minibuses, so the surroundings and routine are familiar when we arrive for the 2000 Olympic trials. But everything else feels different for me from the 1996 Olympic trials. My state of mind is totally different. I have much more confidence in my ability and my place in the sport than I did four years earlier. That's not to say I don't feel pressure. There is pressure everywhere at the Olympic trials and I can see it on the faces of every swimmer I meet. This is a once-in-a-lifetime opportunity to swim at a home Olympics. And such is the standard required to make the Australian team now, that anyone who wins selection will be in a position to win a medal at the Games. This is everything to us, and the media know it. Channel 9 have been running TV ads for weeks promoting its live coverage. The promo features me, Thorpey, Susie, Hacky and a few others. The voiceover says it will be 'Aussie vs Aussie', 'Sudden Death', 'No Second Chances'. Over 100 media have registered to report on those who survive the gauntlet and those who don't.

It's such a peculiar situation for us. Most of the leading swimmers are good friends, many of us are training partners, and we've travelled around the world to competitions together. But suddenly we need to put friendship aside and compete with no mercy. Then once we're selected, we have to come together as a team again to represent the Green and Gold. It's an emotional rollercoaster unique to swimming.

On the first night, 10,000 fans turn up, many of whom have not been able to secure tickets for the Games themselves. Thorpey puts on an Olympic-standard show, taking down his own world record in the 400m freestyle. He's even better than before he broke his ankle, so that's the juggernaut I will face in the 200m freestyle over the next two days.

I win my semi-final to qualify third fastest for the final, behind Thorpey, who sets another world record in 1:45.69, and Hacky. If I want to swim my world title event at the Olympics, I'm going to have to get past at least one of my best friends in the final.

As the moment of truth arrives, the hype keeps growing. It's all a bit nuts, to be honest. On the night of the 200m final, seven guys in the crowd turn up with shaved heads and 'Go Klim' spelled out across their chests in my honour. This has been touted as the best field ever assembled for a domestic swimming race. Dan, Kieren, Bill Kirby and Todd Pearson are also in the field. There's a world-class swimmer in every lane. In the minute before we walk out from the marshalling room, we gather together, clasp hands and wish each other luck. We are all about to face the same test.

Standing behind the blocks, Thorpey and I are a study in contrasts. I'm a jack-in-the-box, bouncing up and down, swinging my arms as we are introduced, waving to the crowd when they cheer for me. Thorpey is sitting on his chair, as immobile as a statue until the announcer calls his name, when he lifts to vertical and raises one arm in the air to acknowledge his reception. When the gun goes, I use my superior early speed to take the lead at 50m, but Thorpey looms up beside me at 75m. We hit the 100m and 150m together. I have a great underwater off the final turn and we're still together at 180m. It's an arm-wrestle but then I start to fatigue and Thorpey's massive kick gives him the edge. He breaks another world record (1:45.51), his third in as many days. I hold on well to secure the second place in the Olympic team in 1:46.89. It's not my best time but I feel satisfied. I put it all on the line because I was trying to win. It didn't work out that way, but I gave it my all.

Hacky, Bill Kirby, Daniel and Todd Pearson secure relay places. The first job is done. I've secured my place on the Olympic team, so whatever happens for the rest of the week, I can breathe easier. But I also know I'm going to have to fend off Thorpey at the top of his game in the 100m freestyle in two days. Fydes, now a practising lawyer at 27 and making his last play for Olympic selection, also knows this is going to be a life-and-death struggle for the top two places. He shows he's in the form of his life by setting a personal best time to lead us all into the final. He's going to fight for his place.

On the day of the final, I feel lethargic – all the emotion at the trials is sapping my strength – but I refuse to panic. Instead, I think about Kieren's 1500m swim in Atlanta and the way he willed himself to victory there. I'm going to have to do the same thing to win tonight.

I need to trust that all the training and racing I have done in the last four years will serve me now. When the gun goes, I commit to my race plan, dashing through the first 50m under world-record pace. Fydes comes at me after the turn, but I have something left and I surge toward the wall, bringing in my dolphin kick to help me keep my stroke long in the last few metres. It works. I stop the clock in an Australian record of 48.56 seconds.

I'm so pumped that I bring out Mats Wilander's famous 'Vicht' salute in celebration. I haven't watched all that tennis for nothing. Afterwards, I tell the poolside interviewer, 'Tonight, I just talked myself into swimming faster. In the heat and the semi-final I was very lazy. Basically, I told myself there was no other way.' Fydes breaks 49 seconds for the first time, clocking 48.85 seconds to snatch second place. Thorpey takes a relay place, along with Ash Callus, Adam Pine and Todd Pearson.

I now have four swims locked in for the Olympics, but the challenge is getting harder as I turn my attention to the 100m butterfly. Skippy is in career-best form, as he demonstrates by breaking the world record in the 50m butterfly as a warm-up for his main event. Scotty is also back in top form, for the first time in four years, and Adam Pine, the World Universities Champion, cannot be discounted. We are all ranked in the world's top ten, but only two of us can win places in the team. It may take a world record to win. In the final, Skippy's freshness proves decisive. I lead early, but I'm running out of gas after eight previous races, and he finishes stronger to take the win in 52.19, just 0.01 seconds ahead of me. We are so closely matched that every race between us seems to be decided by millimetres. Adam finishes third, with Scotty fourth. The silver medallist from the 1996 Games won't make the 2000 Olympic team.

However, I've survived the pressure test that is the Olympic trials by qualifying for all three of the individual events where I have a real shot at a medal, and the three relays. I can sit back and relax on the final night of the trials as Hacky and Kieren go at it in the 1500m. Hacky wins, so chalk another one up for the new guard. The Olympic team is announced live on television the same night, after a short delay to confirm the selections, and much of the crowd waits in the stands for the announcement, including our family and friends. Australia's Olympic swimming legends form a guard of honour as our names are announced as part of the ceremony. As I walk by, I see Dawn Fraser, John Konrads and Shane Gould, and my manager Woody, among them.

It brings home the significance of the occasion, of the torch being passed on from generation to generation of the Australian swimming team. It feels incredibly special, but the overwhelming emotion for all of us is relief. We've been doing our best to smash each other in the pool for a week, and some of the best swimmers in the country have fallen by the wayside, including Sam Riley and my great mate Simon Cowley. Only a lucky few have kept our dreams alive. We're competing at the Sydney Olympics.

The day after the Australian team is named, I make an announcement. I'm going to withdraw from the 200m freestyle for the Olympics. This day has been looming since FINA announced that semi-finals would be introduced at the Sydney Olympics. Gennadi, Don and I have been discussing it on and off for months, but the deciding factor is the way I died at the end of the 100m butterfly at the trials. I'm convinced now that if I do the 200m freestyle before the 100m freestyle and the 100m butterfly, it will hurt my chances in the events where I have a better chance of winning. I may be the world 200m champion, but I don't own that event anymore. Now it belongs to Thorpey. Don, Gennadi and I sat down after the 'fly final and made the decision that night, then I told Hacky, who is in line to get the spot.

'I want to lead with my strong cards,' I tell the media. 'Being the world champion in the 200m, and knowing I am capable of winning a medal, made it hard to give it up but we have a lot of depth in that event and I think I am making the right decision.'

Don agrees, saying, 'In a smaller meet you can do everything, but the Olympics is different.'

That leaves me with two individual events – the 100m freestyle and 100m butterfly – and three relays for the Olympics, which is still five events and at least nine races over eight days. I turn my sights to Sydney.

There isn't much in the way of domestic competition available through the winter in Australia, so for the first time in years I'm in Canberra in the winter, arriving at training when it's dark and frosty, and leaving in the dark at the end of the day. One of the few competitions I find is the Lake Ginninderra club meet that Lynn Fowlie runs in late June. It's very low-key and I have friends in town, so I don't worry when I'm out late at dinner the night before.

But that results in me forgetting to set an alarm for the next morning and I'm woken by Jim Fowlie, reminding me that I'm supposed to be racing. I'm so late to the pool that I don't have any time for a warm-up before the 50m butterfly. I dive in the pool at one end and swim 20m to the start of the short course pool. That will have to do. When the race starts, I'm on automatic pilot. I haven't had time to think about it at all. To my surprise, I dash through two laps in 23.11 seconds, bettering the world record that Frölander set in Athens in March.

It means nothing in the grand scheme of the Olympic preparation, but it does show that I'm now so well drilled in my technique and my skills that I can virtually swim fast in my sleep. My prize for setting the world record is a bag of Chupa Chups.

On the same weekend, Alex competes at the Russian championships and Olympic trials in Moscow, where he reasserts his authority in the sprint freestyle – breaking the 50m freestyle world record and going close in the 100m freestyle. Gennadi hasn't seen either of the world records. When I catch up with him later in the day, he jokes that neither of us needs a coach.

There's a Telstra Grand Prix meeting in Canberra the following week to give us some more race practice, a second tune-up meet in Brisbane in July and a final one in Melbourne in August, but now we're playing poker, keeping our cards close to our chests until the big reveal in September.

In early August, the AIS and NSW Institute of Sport squads, including Thorpey and me, head to a high-altitude training camp at Colorado Springs in the United States for three weeks. That has the benefit of removing us from the Olympic fever growing in Australia.

We train at the US Olympic training centre, with all the history and glory of the US Olympic team displayed on the walls. It leaves us in no doubt about the challenge that lies ahead. Gennadi may have done this on purpose to keep our heads in the game.

The camp also coincides with the US Olympic trials in Indianapolis. The US stars start putting down markers, swimming super-fast because they have no choice if they want to qualify for the Olympics. In many events, the standard is even higher than it was for our trials. Neil Walker wins the 100m freestyle from Gary Hall Jnr and their top three guys go under 49 seconds. On paper, their top four are faster than our top four. A kid called Michael Phelps makes the Olympic team in the 200m butterfly, aged just 15. The times in my individual events are competitive but not daunting. It's good motivation for us to train as well as we can.

I'm really enjoying the camp. Alex, Dunny, Sarah Ryan and I work in a tight little group with Gennadi. We have a very clear idea of what we want to achieve. Each session has a distinct purpose, whether it is working on top-end speed, front-end speed or back-end speed for the 100m.

Given the intensity of the camp, we also need a pressure release when we can get it. Dunny discovers that a death metal band called Danzig is playing near our hotel. We've been in the bubble too long so we decide to break out and go to the concert. It becomes apparent that we are out of our element when we see the hardcore fans of the band, but we survive unscathed. It's a relief not to think about swimming for one night.

CHAPTER 11

Into the Furnace

Before we know it, the moment we've been dreaming of for seven years is almost here. The Australian team goes into its final pre-Games training camp in Melbourne at the end of August. Don has deliberately taken us interstate to avoid exposing us to the ever-growing excitement in Sydney until the last moment, and it's a good move.

Media access is tightly controlled as we go about our business, shuttling back and forward between the Sebel Hotel on St Kilda Road and the new Melbourne Sports and Aquatic Centre at Albert Park for training.

I immediately feel at home in my old stomping ground. It all feels fairly relaxed, more like we are preparing for the national titles than the Olympic Games. Training is getting lighter and more focused on skills and technique than volume as we taper down for competition. That means we have more time away from the pool, and more energy, which can be a dangerous combination with young athletes.

We amuse ourselves with gaming, movies and music, as well as team-bonding activities. Breaststroker Ryan Mitchell produces a killer version of the Green Day song 'Good Riddance (Time of Your Life)' that he plays on acoustic guitar, reminding us that we are not just swimmers.

There's a more formal side as well, with briefings and meetings so we know exactly what we will face when we arrive in Sydney. We also do specific sessions where we practise relay changeovers. As the one athlete who is on all three men's relay teams, I'm getting plenty of practice. Thorpey's coach Doug Frost has responsibility for the 4 x 100m freestyle relay team, while Gennadi has responsibility for the 4 x 200m team. There was a bit of angst over that initially, as both coaches wanted the 4 x 2 – it's clearly our best gold medal chance.

But there's a fair bit of crossover between the freestyle relays, with Thorpey and Todd Pearson also involved in both, and we bond together easily. Bill and Todd and Adam are at the AIS. Hacky and Thorpey have been my roommates in international competition. Dan and Fydes have been constants since I first made the Australian team.

Fydes and I know it's more than likely that I will lead off the 4 x 100m freestyle and he will follow – so we do plenty of practice with that changeover. People think it's the responsibility of the swimmer who is diving in to make sure the change goes smoothly, but it's actually the swimmer who's in the water who's responsible for making it as easy as possible for the next swimmer to predict when they should jump. It's super important to be strong and consistent into the wall, and to finish on a full stroke so the next swimmer can judge when you will finish, because they aren't going to see the touch – not if they are doing it right. By the time I touch the wall, Fydes needs to be out over the water with just his feet on the blocks. We drill that changeover so well we could do it blindfolded.

Our island of calm is only disturbed a couple of times. There's a designated media day when suddenly we are surrounded by cameras at training, and there are interviews and a press conference. As luck would have it, I'm struggling with my start on that day. I know my dive and the first 15m of my race are crucial, not only for my individual events but to get the 4 x 100m freestyle relay off to the best start. We work on my take-off angle from the blocks, but I just can't get it right. This is unusual for me. I'm very coachable, I can usually adjust my body at will and I'm diligent about getting things right. I tick all the boxes with training, I do the hard work and I keep to the structure and routine. But sometimes I overthink things.

Gennadi decides that this is a mental rather than a physical issue and he must get me out of this funk. His solution is to give me a very public serve on the pool deck, right in front of the cameras. He either doesn't care that they are there or he thinks a public dressing-down will have more power. He wants me out of my head and relying on my intuition. He's right and it helps me to change my mindset.

But we don't turn out to be the headline act of the media day. At the press conference later, one of the reporters asks Kieren what he thinks about Gary Hall's prediction that the US team will smash Australia 'like guitars'.

Kieren is a mind game master and he never takes a backward step so he launches in: 'I don't take a lot of notice of drug cheats, so you know, I don't worry about him.' A collective gasp goes through the media. They know a story when they see it. 'He got suspended, didn't he? It's fact then, there you go,' Kieren says.

Gary had been suspended for three months after testing positive for marijuana, but he was not suspected of taking performance-enhancing drugs. Kieren has just poured petrol onto the fire of what was already shaping up as an explosive showdown. I keep my mouth shut and stay out of the crossfire. I respect both swimmers enormously and prefer not to involve myself in the trash talking.

Coincidentally, the US team arrives in Sydney the same day. Gary is kept away from the media and US head coach Mark Schubert plays down the whole thing. 'I was disappointed in Gary's comment but one person's comment doesn't reflect what the whole team thinks,' Schubert says to the waiting media. 'I prefer they don't trash talk, but I think that's just the showman in Gary. Like all of us, he has a great deal of respect for the Australians.'

But the exchange has lit a fuse. Public anticipation of our relay clash is now approaching fever pitch ten days before the Games Opening Ceremony. We spend the rest of the week in our Melbourne camp before we finally head into the Olympic Village at Homebush Bay in Sydney.

Arriving at the village is an exciting moment. Every Olympic Village is different. In Atlanta, we were in inner-city university dorms, but the Sydney athletes' village is a new housing estate, supplemented by temporary demountable accommodation, so it's low-rise and there's plenty of space. It's a beautiful day when we arrive, and everything is still and fresh as we are guided through the village. The Australian team accommodation is based around a quadrangle, where we can hang out with the other Aussie athletes. Thorpey and I are rooming together and Hacky is in the same flat, so it's the 'Golden Room' revisited. Our bedrooms are small and the beds, covered in bright blue covers, seem tiny. But Thorpey and I settle in easily. We're used to being roommates, so we fall into our normal routine. We spend most of our time in the common area of the flat, with Hacky and Dunny and breaststroker Regan Harrison, which reminds me of our Perth adventure. I realise how much more relaxed I feel than I did in Atlanta, where everything seemed so strange and I was uncomfortable.

When we head to the competition pool for training, it again feels very familiar. I have friends in the other teams and it's good to catch up with everyone as they arrive. I'm quite close to the Dutch team; they have a very similar culture to ours, so I visit Pieter and Inge de Bruijn in the village.

Laurie Lawrence and Peter Brock, two of the Australian Olympic team ambassadors, lead team-building activities. John Williamson gives us a private concert. Everything is as Aussie as it gets, and we all feel patriotic. Every volunteer knows who we are and they smile at us whenever we see them. They have orders not to ask for autographs, but some can't help themselves.

On the day before the Opening Ceremony, the entire team is gathered together in our quadrangle to hear the flag bearer announcement: basketball player Andrew Gaze. But the swimming team will not march in the Opening Ceremony as most of us will be competing on the first two days of the Games. We can't afford to go into competition with tired legs, so we put on our Opening Ceremony uniforms and gather with the other athletes who are not marching, sitting in beanbags on the grass to watch the ceremony on the big screen in our village square. It's a light-hearted evening. There are big cheers when we spot our teammates marching in. We're all proud and excited about what's to come.

I'm feeling good. Earlier in the day, I had my last swim before the competition. I put on my competition suit and did a 50m freestyle test, pushing off from the wall and sprinting. Gennadi clocked me at 23.7 seconds, which is only a second outside my competition personal best. 'You're ready,' he says, and that's all I need to hear. I now have 24 hours off before the 4 x 100m freestyle final in the evening. I've been given the option not to swim the heat and I take it. I don't need a morning swim for confidence. I know everything is right where it needs to be. I ask to swim first in the final. I know I can give us a lead and make the Americans chase us.

In the morning, our heat team of Fydes (leading off to put us in a good position), followed by Todd, Adam and Ash, safely steers us through to the final. As our No. 2 100m freestyler, Fydes' place in the final team is secure. He will join Thorpey and me. Todd, Adam and Ash have to fight for the final position, and Ash wins it narrowly, just 0.01 seconds faster than Piney.

Meanwhile, Thorpey has swum and won his 400m freestyle heat, qualifying fastest for the final. It's his first ever swim at the Olympics, but he's handling the whole thing like a veteran. He comes back to the village after warming down, has some lunch and then settles down for a nap. I'm envious of his ability to drop off no matter what the circumstances are.

We have our regular team meeting mid-afternoon, which all team members must attend. It's in a demountable meeting room at the village. Don announces our final line-up for the relay during the meeting. Soon everyone will know, as the team has to be submitted to the officials one hour before the session begins.

From there the first finals session plays out exactly as we hoped. I feel the most clear-headed I've ever felt during the relay final. I find that perfect combination of relaxation and arousal that allows athletes to perform at their very best. That's not easy for me – it doesn't come naturally. I've worked as hard on finding that state in the last four years as I have on honing my muscles and my skills, but on that one magic night, all the work pays off.

One technique Gennadi has taught us to calm ourselves just before a race is nasal breathing. For about 30 seconds we take shallow breaths through our noses. It builds up the carbon dioxide in our systems so when we start taking deep breaths, the oxygen is more easily absorbed. It also helps us get into the right mental state. Breathing through your mouth stimulates a stress response, while breathing through your nose promotes relaxation. Alex is better at it than me – I get too fidgety just before I race. But today it doesn't matter. I am ready to go.

Gennadi has cautioned me to take one less underwater dolphin kick at the start, just to make sure I don't break the 15m limit underwater. I usually do ten, but with the adrenaline surge I get from this situation, ten kicks might get me disqualified, so I pull it back to nine. I break through the surface and catch my first stroke just right. I surge through the lap, breathing only twice, at the 25m mark and just before I start my turn.

I flip over, maybe a bit slow to get my feet on the wall, but then I go another nine kicks underwater, holding my breath for seven seconds before I break out at 15m. By then I can't see anyone else around me, not even Anthony Ervin, so I know I'm swimming fast. On the second lap I breathe every four strokes, just to make sure I have enough oxygen flowing through my body as I start to fatigue.

With 15m to go, I change from freestyle kick into dolphin kick. It's something I tried at the Olympic trials and, with the aid of the new suit, I think it helps me maintain my momentum to the finish as my legs begin to tire. The tightness of my suit supports me in holding a good body position in the water, not letting my hips sink so I can maintain a good tempo with my arms. I feel like I'm surfing now, and I don't need to draw on my reserves of energy. When I hit the wall, it feels like the perfect race and the clock confirms that it is the fastest 100m freestyle that I, or anyone else, has ever done. The rest is history as my teammates force the Americans to chase us down, and Thorpey's race with Gary Hall becomes a duel for the ages.

By the end of the session, the Australian team has two gold medals, as has Thorpey, and we've made a statement before the eyes of the world. It's late by the time we leave the pool. The more you win, the later it gets, what with drug-testing and media commitments. The four of us don't get back to the village until after midnight.

By that time, some of our excitement is dying down and we're starving so we head straight to the dining hall, expecting it to be empty. But when we walk in, the place is packed – a couple of thousand people are here. As the other athletes spot us, they start clapping and suddenly the athletes of the world are giving us a standing ovation. For the first time that night, I feel tears pricking my eyes. It's so special to be acknowledged by our fellow Olympians. This may be the most memorable moment of the greatest night of my life. But the happiest man in Sydney that night is Ash Callus. His Olympics is over – one event, one gold medal, job done. For the rest of the Games, he parties like it's 1999.

Thorpey and I head to bed as soon as possible because we still have a lot of swimming to do. He has the 200m freestyle heats the next morning and he's asleep as soon as his head hits the pillow. I'm not. I'm still too hyped. I've just won my first Olympic gold medal, achieved the dream of a lifetime. Who can sleep at a moment like this? Thorpey, that's who. At least I don't have to worry about waking him while I lie there with a million thoughts dashing through my head.

Luckily I'm not racing the next day because I'm still amped from the night before and I haven't slept well. Everywhere I go, people are congratulating me. I go to do a shakeout swim and I can feel the eyeballs on us around the pool.

It's a rule in the Australian team that if you are not racing in the evening, you must come and watch your teammates for the finals session, so I go along as a spectator on the second night. Our team is placed next to the US team in the athlete grandstand and, as I take my seat, I notice something I've never seen before. The Americans look deflated. They've lost the air of invincibility they usually have. I'm amazed at the effect one race has had on their whole team. There's been a complete momentum shift because our team is up and buzzing. We have had the most amazing night, and the coaches are still peeling most of us off the rafters the next day. Don's actually worried that we're too high, that what will follow is a crash.

Thorpey is back in the water for the 200m freestyle semi-finals. But first Pieter hits the water in his semi-final and lays down a marker – breaking Thorpey's world record with a time of 1:45.35. Thorpey responds in the next race, and his time is almost identical, just 0.02 seconds slower, so the stage is set for an extraordinary final. I know it was the right decision for me to skip this event, even more so now that Pieter is swimming so well, but I can't help feeling a tinge of regret that I won't be in it. Hacky will be, after qualifying in seventh place, so I'm glad for him, but his stroke doesn't look great. He looks like he's spinning his wheels rather than holding the water as he does when he's at his best.

Even with Pieter swimming so well, we still think this is gold in the bag for Thorpey. No-one has beaten him over 200m in a championship race since the 1998 world titles. No matter what the challenge, he's shown that he can rise to the occasion and there's a trail of broken world records behind him to prove it. So we're still optimistic as we watch him step onto the blocks for the final. As his roommate, I've noticed nothing wrong in the lead-up, but he swims the most uncharacteristic race of his career. When he hasn't made a move by the final turn and Pieter is still with him, I get a bad feeling. 'This might be tricky,' I think to myself. I can see him reaching for his extra gear in the final lap, but it is not there. Pieter equals his new world record to take the gold, Thorpey swims half a second slower for silver and Hacky finishes last, which endangers his place in our 4 x 200m freestyle relay team.

I'm not worried about the relay's prospects. We still have so much depth in that event that this result doesn't really make a difference, but Thorpey has become our team talisman. When he lifts, we all lift. When he looks vulnerable, we all feel vulnerable. Now we're the team that looks deflated.

I head back to the village, eat some dinner and wait for Thorpey in our apartment. I'm feeling a bit nervous because I don't know how he's going to react to this. It's the only time I've ever seen him swim another man's race rather than his own. I don't expect that he will want to rehash the race. He never wants to do that, whether it's good or bad. We don't talk swimming in our room. It's our sanctuary from all that. But if he's unhappy, I can tell, because he gets stroppy. Eventually he walks in and gives me a lopsided grin to break the ice. Then he says, 'Well, I fucked that up', and we both burst out laughing. I have nothing more profound to add and we leave it there. He's passed out within a matter of minutes.

He gets a sleep-in on Day 4, but I have one of my busiest days of the Games. The 100m freestyle heats are this morning and the semi-finals are this evening, before the final of the 4 x 200m freestyle. After two days cooling my heels, I'm keen to get back into the groove of racing. It's been a long time since I had days off in the middle of a championship, and I much prefer to stay busy during the meet. Sitting around leaves me too much thinking time, so it's good to get back into the swing of things.

The first three days have been extraordinary but emotionally exhausting. I swim a solid 100m freestyle heat in the morning, qualifying second fastest behind Pieter. But at the back of my mind, I can hear a tiny warning bell. The swim is almost a second slower than my new world record so it should feel easy, but instead it feels laboured. The spark I felt on the first day is missing and I'm going to need to find it before the final. I'm not the only one starting to worry.

In the 4 x 200m freestyle heats, Hacky, Bill, Todd and Dan have been selected to qualify us for the final, which they do. But Hacky is even slower than he was last night, while Bill and Todd are clearly the guys in the best form of that group. They win the places in the final team. It's devastating for Hacky. A year earlier, he broke the world

My first coach in Australia, Gene Jackson. I owe so much to him for his guidance in my early teens.

At my first ever competition at Nunawading after arriving in Australia when I was 11.

Matthew Dunn, Alexander Popov and me at one of many camps in Thredbo in the leadup to the 1998 World Championships.

With Alexander Popov and my coach Gennadi Touretski in Perth for the 1998 World Championships.

With Simon Cowley, my dear friend and roommate at the Australian Institute of Sport from 2000–2001.

I was honoured to be invited to meet Lech Wałęsa, the leader of Solidarity who changed the course of the Cold War and catalysed the fall of the Berlin Wall.

With my sister Anna and parents Ewa and Wojtek at our home in Bentleigh in 1998.

Grant Hackett, Ian Thorpe and me at the closing ceremony of the 2000 Sydney Olympics. Source: Hamish Blair / Staff, Getty Images AsiaPac

Above: Gennadi, my coach of eight years, with the Gibson guitar gifted to me by Gary Hall. 1998.

Right: Prepping for the Athens 2004 Olympics with Matthew Welsh, Ian Pope and Brett Hawke.

Launching Milk Skincare with Mitch Catlin for Myer. August 2008.

Rohan Taylor and Jeremy Oliver analysing my stroke during my comeback in 2012.

Above: Underwater with my gang Michelle, Stella, Rocco and Frankie. It's better down here.

Right: Coaching the next wave of talent at Klim Swim Bali.

Me with my first swimming teacher, Mrs Bathena, 30 years apart (2016 and 1986).

Surfing with Stella. Bonding and fun times!

With my parents, Ewa and Wojtek, at a World Series Swim event in Noosa.

With my amazing sister Anna during one of many trips to Australia to receive my treatment in 2023.

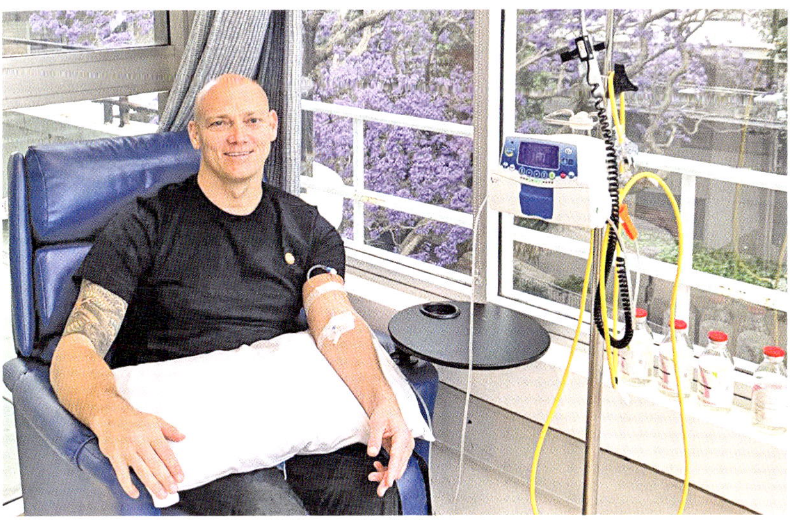

Receiving my weekly IVIG treatment at Royal Prince Alfred Hospital in Sydney 2023.

Celebrating Rocco's 16th birthday with Stella, Frankie and my partner Michelle.

Soon after meeting my partner Michelle Owen.

With the man himself, Gary Hall, during my latest trip to LA in 2023, just before my induction into the Hall of Fame.

record for the 200m freestyle and now he can't make the top four in the country. I feel for him, but I'm also happy for Bill and Todd. They may not be the highest-profile swimmers in the country, but I train beside them every day at the AIS and I know how hard they have worked to earn this moment.

I come back for the 100m freestyle semi-finals in the evening, where Pieter does something no-one has been expecting, even after his 200m freestyle heroics. He smashes through the 48-second barrier, setting a new world record of 47.84 seconds, a third of a second faster than my three-day-old standard. I qualify second, but almost a second slower (48.80), just ahead of Alex (48.84 seconds). Pieter has upended the form book and now we'll all be chasing him. But I don't have time to think about it because I need to warm down and prepare to win another gold medal for Australia.

We've decided to blitz the other relay teams by stacking our team fastest to slowest in the order. It worked for us in the 4 x 100m and we're even stronger in this event. That means Thorpey will lead off, followed by me, then Todd, with Bill as the anchor. Swimming second is an unusual position for me – I'm usually first or last – but I'm fine with second. This is our race to lose. By putting out our biggest guns first, we can shut the gate on everyone else. We won't even give them a sniff. All we need to do is swim to form.

It's a much more relaxing lead-in to this race than we had on the first night. This time I'm the one doubling up, and I'm a bit late to marshalling – but not too late. I'm slightly concerned that Bill and Todd might find the crowd response overwhelming, as they haven't been out there for a finals session before, so I try to prep them, telling them what it's like, but Todd looks at me like I'm mad. They've waited for this all their lives, why wouldn't they be prepared? I take the hint and shut up.

We get another great reception from the crowd as we walk out. Susie O'Neill has fired them up earlier by winning the 200m freestyle and now they are baying for more gold. Thorpey leads off in a 1:46.03 – three or four seconds faster than any other opening swimmer – and right away we have a five-metre advantage. I dive in under no pressure at all and produce a 1:46.40 that makes us unbeatable right there.

US captain Josh Davis has already conceded the race – he starts shaking our hands at that point. But our least experienced swimmers, Todd and Bill, still need to perform if we are to break the world record, and they both rise to the occasion, setting personal best times to seal the victory. We've held the world record for two years, we've taken it down three seconds in that time and the objective is to put it out of reach. Bill stops the clock at 7:07.05, taking nearly two seconds off our previous mark.

Thorpey and Todd and I go into a group hug, and someone suggests we jump in the pool to celebrate with Bill. The next thing we're back in the water waving to the crowd. The rules of swimming say that other swimmers cannot enter the pool before the last swimmer in the race has finished. I'm not sure whether we broke that one, but luckily none of the officials is paying attention right now.

Thorpey now has his third gold medal, equalling Shane Gould's record Australian tally for one Games. His Olympic journey is almost over, but mine is just beginning. I have two gold medals and two world records, but I still have my main individual events and the medley relay to come.

I need to get a good sleep before the 100m freestyle final, but when I eventually get to bed my mind won't release me. Thoughts are ricocheting around my head – what we've already done, what I still have to come, what might happen. I get a sleep-in the next morning but I still don't feel refreshed. I have an internal battle to fight. I have to find something inside to allow me to perform at my best in the biggest race of my life. I know it's there somewhere – my form can't have vanished in three days – but now I just feel flat. All my training and experience, and my coach, tell me to trust my preparation and not to overthink this, but that's always been the biggest challenge for me.

In the final, Pieter is with the early speedsters at the turn and no-one can stay with him on the trip home, but his time is surprisingly slow. He wins in 48.30, slower than I swam on the first night, but he's a clear winner. Alex, Gary and I are all together as we surge for the wall. It's a battle of wills now. Alex uses his long arms to reach out and grab the silver medal and Gary takes the bronze, by 0.01 of a second from me in fourth. It's a kick in the guts. I'm so close to the medals. There's only 0.05 seconds between Alex, as the silver medallist, and me.

I wasn't confident of winning the gold medal, but I thought I would come away with something. I've thrown everything at the greatest sprinters of my era but it hasn't been enough. I'm going home empty-handed tonight. Alex is also deflated. As the defending champion, he was going to be disappointed with anything less than gold. Gary seems the most pleased of us, with the bronze.

However, there's no time for me to wallow in disappointment, and that's the beauty of my programme. There are going to be ups and downs through eight days of swimming, and for good or bad I just have to keep picking myself up and going again because there's going to be another day, another chance to shine. I refocus on the 100m butterfly the next day. The freestyle didn't work out for me, but I've broken the world 100m butterfly record three times since 1997 and no-one else has broken 52 seconds. Surely this is my moment.

But it doesn't feel like it in the preliminaries. I qualify fastest just ahead of Skippy, but he reverses things in the semi-finals, setting the second-fastest time in history and becoming the second man under 52 seconds (51.96 seconds). He's clearly sharp and I'm still feeling sluggish, although better than I had felt in the morning.

I've qualified second fastest for the final, but I'm struggling. I feel emotionally exhausted and I've got to find something fast if I'm going to win that gold medal. Gennadi pulls out all the tricks in his coaching box to get me up for the medal race, trying to convince me that I'm still on track.

On the night of the final, I take the bus to the pool alone and I'm trying to psych myself into feeling great. I tell myself, 'This is my time, this is my opportunity', but deep down I'm not sure I believe it. I do my warm-up, still not feeling great, and behind the blocks I begin repeating two words to myself: 'No pain, no pain'.

For the first 75m, I do feel no pain. I lead through 50m and I'm feeling the best I have for a long time. I know I'm still in front as we enter the last quarter of the race. But then I start to feel the early pace in my arms. Then there is pain. Suddenly, I'm wading through sand and I can barely get my arms out of the water. Skippy is coming at me, and so is Lars Frölander. I make a split-second decision to flow through the last part of the race, rather than muscling it, hoping that relaxation will help me get to the wall without losing speed. With five metres to go, we are all locked together. We lunge for the wall and Lars wins: the momentum is with him. I hold on for second and Skippy is third.

I'm a bit stunned. If it wasn't going to be me, I thought it would be Skippy, either way I thought this would be a gold medal for Australia, but Lars has come through late to snatch it from us. I'm still trying to process what's happened as we are walking back for the medal ceremony, when Jan Talbot stops me: 'Have you watched the race?' she exclaims. 'With 10 metres to go, you had it.' I know she doesn't mean to do it, but she opens up my wounds.

I'm bleeding inside as we stand on the medal dais. My last chance for an individual gold medal is gone. But I put on a brave face to get through the ceremony and the lap of honour. As we leave the pool deck, I rub Lars's head, and say to him jokingly, 'You spoiled a big party for us.' He's a good guy, I like him, and on some level I am happy for him. But the disappointment twists inside me like barbed wire. Sometimes you just want something too much and you get in your own way. I've spent four years learning how to control my emotional and nervous energy – but at the critical moment, I couldn't do it. Now I have to live with the bitter knowledge that my best time would have been good enough to win. Skippy and I will always think about this race and wonder 'What if?'

My saviour, as always, is that I have another event to focus on. There's only one day of the competition left and for me that means the medley relay. We've won both the men's relays so far, but this is a bigger challenge for us. After our upset victory on the opening day, the American team has rallied – as only it can – led by Lenny Krayzelburg, who has taken both backstroke events, and Brooke Bennett, who has dominated the women's distance freestyle. Their veterans Tom Dolan and Tom Malchow have also stood up under the heat, Misty Hyman's shock win over Susie in the 200m butterfly was arguably the biggest upset of the week, and they've won both women's freestyle relays. And in last night's 50m freestyle final, Gary Hall and Anthony Ervin tied for the gold medal.

We got under their guard on Day 1, but they are a different proposition now, with 13 gold medals in the bag and their status as the greatest swimming nation reconfirmed. As Gary said after winning the 50m freestyle, 'I see this as just a great triumph for the USA in swimming. It just shows we're still the best.'

But we still have some shots to fire, with the 1500m freestyle final also on the last day. It's Hacky's last chance to win a gold medal at home after what has been a miserable week for him, and he has to beat one of the all-time greats in Kieren to do it. Either way, this is a gold medal for Australia. The whole country has been looking forward to this one, wondering whether Kieren can summon another heroic effort, as he did in Atlanta four years ago. But this time, it's a step too far for the king. Hacky takes control of the race from the start and just refuses to allow this one to get away from him. His relief at the end is enormous, and I'm delighted for him – even though I'm out the back warming up for the relay, which is the final event on the programme.

We can only do so much in the medley relay as we are unlikely to have the advantage of leading early and able to force the US team into error. They will lead off with Lenny, who has the edge on our silver medal-winning backstroker Matt Welsh, and their breaststroker Ed Moses is also faster than our man, Regan Harrison. We are stronger on the back end, with Skippy doing the 'fly and me in the freestyle, but it's probably going to be too little too late. And so it proves. The US team has a two-second lead at the halfway mark and even heroic performances from Skippy and me wouldn't overcome that margin. The Americans set a new world record to close the meeting, while we secure the silver medal. Gary gets the last word: 'When you're faced with tough opponents, it forces you to work for it. We were able to use the threat of being dethroned as the best swimming nation to step up and reach another level.'

Australia finishes second on the medal tally with five gold, nine silver and four bronze. It's our best performance since the 1956 Olympics in Melbourne. Each time we get on the podium, we are given a Boxing Kangaroo and by the end of the week Thorpey and I have four each, so we've started a kangaroo creche, with eight stuffed kangaroos lined up along the wall.

But a few of us can't help but think about what might have been. My personal tally is two gold and two silver, and I think the 10-year-old me who first got excited by the Olympic Games in 1988 would have taken that in a heartbeat, but my own expectations were greater still. I'm having a hard time reconciling my hopes with this outcome.

There have been amazing moments this week, but tough ones too. My overarching emotion is bittersweet. The 100m butterfly result, in particular, will haunt me for years to come. At one point I had six of the fastest ten times in history. I'd been consistently faster than anyone else. Did I make the right decision late in the race? Would it have changed anything if I'd pushed rather than relaxed? I'll never know. For my own protection, I bury those questions deep inside me.

The swimming programme is over after eight days, but the Games goes on. Part of the beauty of being a swimmer at the Olympics is that we have the second week to watch other sports and cheer on our Australian teammates. There are so many corporate invitations that the second week passes in a blur. I only have snapshots. We finally visit The Last Lap, the club that has been set up for the Australian athletes, family and supporters at Darling Harbour, where the reception is crazy. We step off the bus and there are thousands of people cheering for us. It's our first time outside the Olympic bubble and we're totally unprepared for this frenzy. The organisers hustle us in through the back door and it's like we're making an appearance at a nightclub. Athletes are wearing their medals on the dancefloor and they rush us for photos.

The next night is Cathy Freeman's 400m final and Fydes and I are invited to the Murdoch suite at the stadium. When the race is about to start, we walk down and find seats in the grandstand. There's one seat left beside me and just as the race begins, someone slips into it: it's Kylie Minogue.

Because the Dutch swimmers have done so well, Heineken House has become the hottest ticket in town. I go one night with Pieter and Thorpey, and the energy there is off the scale. I go to Michael Johnson's birthday party at Planet Hollywood. One night at the Sebel nightclub in Kings Cross, I walk outside to talk to my mum on the phone and bump into Elle Macpherson. Inside, I get talking to a large American who is smoking cigars. He says he's in tech. I ask him the name of his company. 'Yahoo,' he says. I'm on the dancefloor at the Establishment nightclub when a stranger comes up to me and says someone wants to say hello to me. I wander over and it's Sting, wanting to chat about sport.

Janusz Hooker, a rower who competed at the Atlanta Olympics, invites us to a toga party at the Australian Museum and sends a car for us. We have a big night. We're on the way home early the next morning when we stop at a petrol station to get a Powerade, and we're already on the front page of the newspaper. We're not even home yet.

It's not my proudest moment. I'm normally so measured in the way I live my life – we all are – but things are getting a bit loose.

One night I have an appearance to do at an Ansett function with Carl Lewis, Ed Moses and Mike Powell. The three Americans take a shot of whiskey before we go on stage and call me over to join them. I'm with some of my personal heroes now. I've always been a track fan and I'm excited to be in a room with three of the best of all time. After the reception ends, Mike suggests we all go out. He wants to find a hip-hop club, and it turns out that the Cave nightclub at Star City is having a hip-hop night, so we go there.

I'm definitely out of my element, and I'm certainly the only guy in the room with no rhythm, but I'm having a good time with the guys until I go to the bathroom. I'm standing at the urinal when two big guys grab me from behind and bundle me into a cubicle. Then they start trying to shove drugs down my throat. I've no idea who they are or what they are trying to give me and I'm struggling to fight them off, when someone yanks the door open and the security guys pull me out. Someone must have seen what was happening and alerted them.

The party is over for me. We've been in the Olympic bubble for so long that it felt as if we were protected no matter where we went. This is a sobering reminder of reality.

By the end of the second week of the Games, we've partied so hard that I'm starting to feel an unhealthy level of fatigue. There's only one event to go, the Closing Ceremony, and having missed the Opening Ceremony, none of us wants to miss this. It's been planned as more party than ceremony. The Games have gone exceptionally well – not just for the Australian team, but for the organising committee as well – so everyone is in a buoyant mood.

I walk into the stadium with Hacky and Hawkey and the exuberance is infectious. Thorpey's up the front, carrying the flag, but once his duties are done he joins us to watch the show, which is unabashed Australiana, from lawnmowers and Hills hoists to surf lifesavers and prawns on bicycles. There's Kylie again, first standing atop a giant thong, then in full showgirl regalia under a pink and silver headdress singing 'Dancing Queen'. Greg Norman hits golf balls from a shark-shaped float, Jimmy Barnes belts out 'Working Class Man' on top of a pineapple ring, Midnight Oil performs 'Beds are Burning' in 'Sorry' shirts, Christine Anu sings 'My Island Home' and Yothu Yindi plays 'Treaty'. Paul Hogan, the Bananas in Pyjamas, Men at Work and Slim Dusty are there too. It's the greatest hits of my Australian childhood, and then some. At some point, one of the Aussie athletes produces an AFL football and we do a little bit of kick-to-kick to contribute to the Australian-ness of the occasion. We all end the Games on a high. When we leave the Olympic Village, we sign our names on the door of our apartment. I don't know what happens to that door, but someone out there may have a unique Sydney Olympics souvenir.

Two days later, there's a ticker-tape parade through the streets of Sydney for the Australian team, the first of several around the country. Hundreds of thousands of Sydneysiders turn out to greet us. It's yet another extraordinary moment. I also do the parades in Melbourne and Canberra to acknowledge my home city and the people who have supported me all the way. But eventually the merry-go-round stops and we have to get off and come back down to earth, although I'm not sure that real life will ever live up to what we've experienced in the last few weeks.

CHAPTER 12

After the Party

When you have spent most of your life climbing a mountain and it's all you can see in front of you, what happens after you reach the peak? You take in the view, allow yourself to feel some satisfaction and relief, snap a few photos, and then what? The only way is down. But once you have that view from the top, you also realise that there are other mountains to climb.

I replenish my reserves of mental and emotional energy, which takes a while, and focus on the next mountain. It's actually easier to do this than it was after the World Championships in Perth when everyone wanted a piece of me. I've done well in Sydney but Thorpey is the golden boy now, so most of the media and public attention is focused on him. That makes it easier for the rest of us.

When I get back into training, I feel ready for it but my body isn't. During my break, I've developed a bulging disc in my lower back that starts to cause me pain and restrict my movement when I try to train through it. I have a lot of treatment on it through November and hope it will be alright for my next competition, the Melbourne World Cup meet in December.

It's my first time competing at home since the Olympics so I want to do well, but my back isn't cooperating. I'm now getting nerve spasms, but I'm determined to swim through it. I wheel out a new multicoloured bodysuit to make a splash on the opening night and win the 100m freestyle, but that has consequences. My back is so sore and locked up the next morning that our medical staff put me in traction to relieve the pressure on my spine.

Still, I want to compete today. It's Anna's birthday and I want to have a crack at the world record in the 50m butterfly for her. I win the race, but I fall a little bit short of the time. Even so, it's a pretty good swim considering my condition. I back up to swim the 50m freestyle on Day 3, but Jason Lezak beats me on the final touch and I think better of doing the 100m butterfly given the state of my back. I'm going to need a lot more treatment, and luckily I have time now to do that.

By January 2001, my back is behaving itself and I'm feeling pretty good in the water. I'm looking forward to our next trip to Europe, not so much because of the three World Cup meetings I will contest in Berlin, Stockholm and Paris, but because I've been nominated for a World Sports Award and there is a gala function at the Royal Albert Hall in London to announce the winners.

I've been nominated in the water sports (men) category, alongside the rower Steve Redgrave, Pieter, Thorpey and Lenny. I know I won't win – they all had better Olympic Games than me – but it will be fun to see everyone who was in Sydney, and from other sports that we don't interact with normally. The special guest is Muhammad Ali and I'm pretty keen to meet him. Woody comes with me and we do get to meet Ali, who is celebrating his birthday, and Lennox Lewis, and have a memorable night with the great and good of the sports world. Pieter takes out the award in our category.

Afterwards, we link up with Pieter and his coach, Jacco Verhaeren, and go on to a nightclub in Mayfair and hit the dancefloor until 3 am. It ends up being a massive night. Pieter is not competing at the World Cup in Berlin that week so he gets a sleep-in the next day, while I have to drag myself to the airport with a hangover to fly to Germany. It's nice to be back racing in Berlin – Germany still feels a bit like home. I keep busy, doing the 50m and 100m freestyle and butterfly at all three meets, back to back, and finish undefeated over 100m, winning seven of my 12 finals over nine days. It's been perfect to get me back into the swing of international competition and I feel as if I'm in good form approaching the national trials in Hobart, which is why I'm unprepared for what happens there.

When I arrive and see Thorpey in the training pool, I realise he's gone to another level again. He's decided to take on the 800m freestyle, because it's been added to the programme for the World Championships in Fukuoka mid-year, so he will be swimming everything from 100m to 800m freestyle. I watch him do a 3km time trial before the meet starts and he's casually holding 1:01, 1:02 for each 100m. It's crazy stuff. If his speed is going as well as his speed endurance, I might be in a bit of trouble in the 100m freestyle final. So I'm prepared for the challenge to my national title to come from him now that Fydes has retired. But I need to park that thought for now because the 100m butterfly is first on my schedule. Skippy and I have another close encounter but he wins this one, bringing his national title tally to three. We've been enacting this annual ritual for five years now and the score is three–two to him. But second is enough to earn my place in the event at the world titles, and that's what really counts this week.

The next night I have the 100m freestyle final and the showdown with Thorpey. He's already set world records in the 800m freestyle, downing Hacky, and the 200m freestyle this week and his momentum looks irresistible, provided he's not too fatigued from what has already been a big programme of racing. However, we're not the only swimmers eyeing off the two 100m freestyle spots for Fukuoka. Our relay teammate Ash Callus has grown in confidence and ambition since that magic first night of the Sydney Games. At 21, he's no longer willing to be a bit player on the international stage – he wants a starring role.

Maybe I should have heard warning bells, but I go in confident that I will seal my spot. However, Thorpey swims over me to win in 49.05 seconds and Ash beats me on the touch (49.46 seconds to 49.53 seconds). He's rightly exultant, but it's a big comedown for me. Six months earlier, I was the world record-holder; now I won't even be swimming the event at the World Championships. I'm bitterly disappointed but as usual I need to refocus, as I still have the 50m butterfly to come. By the end of the week, I've qualified to swim the 50m and 100m butterfly and I'm on the roster for the three relays. There's always a silver lining, and this programme will give me a chance to concentrate on butterfly, but the hits keep on coming.

Only a week later, there is another incident with Gennadi, but this one will change both our lives. His home in Canberra is broken into and a safe is stolen, containing the Olympic gold medal Alex gave him after Atlanta and the Commonwealth Games gold medal I gave him after Kuala Lumpur. But it is another item that is in the safe that gets him into trouble. The safe ends up being recovered by police from a local lake and when they open it, there is also a pack of ten steroid pills inside.

Gennadi is initially charged by the police, but the case is eventually dropped for lack of evidence. However, he is suspended from the AIS while an investigation occurs and the drug-testers are brought in to check that we are all clean. I don't for a moment think Gennadi has been giving steroids to athletes, and I do what I can to support him, but the discovery in the safe has made news far and wide and his reputation has been damaged. He has also been having health issues for much of the year – he will have heart bypass surgery in September – so I'm already training part of the time with Jim. I move permanently into his squad to do my preparation for Fukuoka.

Jim likes to do a lot of cross-training as part of his programme, to activate our endocrine system which tends to be suppressed by swimming. I like playing other sports so that's good for me. It breaks up the routine and as the world championships approach, I feel like I'm back to full fitness for the first time since the Olympics.

We've been playing a lot of basketball, for the cross-training effect, and it gets very competitive, but as the major meet approaches, Jim starts to discourage us, worried that one of us will be injured. With 21 days to go, he says no more, but Piney, Antony Matkovich and I are keen to play, so I convince Jim to allow us, promising that we will just go and shoot for 20 minutes, no running, no jumping. Of course, we get carried away and soon we are in a full-on contest trying to dunk the ball.

It's my turn and I run and leap, putting in extra effort to get above the hoop. The ball hits the ring and the impact twists my body. As I fall, my leg gets caught underneath me and my whole body weight comes down on my left ankle. I hear a little 'pop' and I'm in instant agony. I can see by the looks on the other guys' faces that it's bad. The ankle has already ballooned to double its size. Antony and Piney carry me into the physio's room and then go to tell Jim, and he comes rushing in. Our physio Peter Blanch gives me the bad news. I've ruptured both the anterior ligaments in the ankle. It's not an injury that will heal in three weeks; in fact, once the specialists look at it, they recommend immediate surgery that would rule me out of the World Championships altogether.

Instead, we decide to try an intensive rehab programme that may get me in good enough shape to compete and contribute to the Australian team. The rehab is now my training, and it is even more intensive. I spend hours in a barometric chamber, icing the ankle, walking in the pool with weights. We do everything we can think of to bring down the swelling, but as the day approaches for the Australian team to leave for the pre-event camp, the ankle is still sore and swollen.

Jim and I think the best course of action is for me to stay in Canberra, where I have full medical support, for a few extra days, skipping the camp in Kuala Lumpur and flying directly into Fukuoka. The heat and humidity of the tropics will make the job of rehabbing my ankle harder and I need every minute to get it in shape so I can compete.

But Don refuses. Under his leadership, the team culture is built on every athlete being treated the same, whether it's a rookie or Ian Thorpe. We can't convince him that it will be better for me and the team if I stay in Canberra for those days. As we feared, my ankle does not react well to the tropical conditions, and it is still sore and swollen when we arrive in Japan to compete. But now I'm just going to have to make the best of it.

It doesn't affect me much when I'm swimming, but I can't push off the blocks or the walls, so my starts and turns are substantially compromised. It's far from ideal. It is hard to win a world title even when everything is perfect physically, but it's exponentially harder when you are going in with an injury.

Even if I can't perform at my best in my individual events, I want to contribute to the relays, where we have potentially winning teams. There have been substantial changes to the schedule to accommodate the inclusion of the 50m form strokes, but the first night is still a good one for the Australian team with the men's 400m freestyle and 4 x 100m freestyle relay finals, so we have the opportunity to get the team off to a strong start.

Thorpey does his thing in the 400m final, taking another fraction off his own world record (3:40.17) and then joins us for the relay. Our team is me leading off, Ash swimming second, Todd coming in for Fydes and Thorpey to anchor. Why change a winning formula? Again, the Americans have never lost this event at the World Championships, but this time they have no illusions about the potency of our team. I lead off in 49.12 seconds, my fastest time since the Olympics – and not bad, considering. I've been helped by the cortisone injection I had in the ankle joint beforehand, which has numbed the pain. I give us the lead and we never relinquish it. Ash does his best-ever split (48.31 seconds) to extend the margin and Todd consolidates (48.80 seconds) before Thorpey brings it home (47.87 seconds), for a combined time of 3:14.10, a shade outside the world record we set in Sydney. This time there isn't any suspense: we're clear winners, even when Pieter puts in a barnstorming anchor of 47.02 seconds to drag the Dutch team into second place. The US team is later disqualified for using an unregistered swimmer.

The gamble of swimming with my injured ankle has already paid off and I now have a couple of days to prepare for my main individual event, the 100m butterfly. I get another shot of cortisone before the heats and manage a good swim to win my semi-final in 52.50 seconds, qualifying second fastest for the final behind Lars. At that point, my hopes are high that I can contend for a medal in the final the next day. But they are dashed when I wake up the next morning.

The cortisone has worn off. I can hardly walk and it's not safe for me to have another injection today. I limp to the blocks to defend my title in the final, but there's little I can do as Lars wins in 52.10 seconds, with Skippy getting the bronze. I struggle into seventh place. I don't have any big expectations for my other individual event, the 50m butterfly – that's never really been my bag – but I do for the 4 x 200m freestyle relay. All the data are telling us that our team is stronger this year than it was in Sydney, even with me on one leg, so we are targeting our world record.

My roommate Hacky is swimming brilliantly this year and he's delighted that he's fought his way back into the relay team. He will lead off in the final, followed by me, Bill and Thorpey. He's less delighted when he takes a look at me after lunch on the day of the final. We're in our room and I'm covered in sweat, like I have a fever, looking more like a candidate for a hospital bed than a gold medal. It's some kind of weird reaction to the pain and the cortisone injections. He's worried about me even making it to the pool. He gets me a wet towel from the bathroom to mop my brow. I still don't feel great when it comes time to leave for the pool, but I'm determined to swim.

Hacky gives us a great start, setting his personal best time of 1:46.11. I dive in over a body length ahead of the Italian team. I'm desperate not to let the other guys down so I dig in and extend the lead, clocking a 1:46, which Hacky later declares to be a miracle based on what he'd seen a few hours earlier. We keep building with each leg. By the time Thorpey stops the clock with a world record of 7:04.66, we are more than 10 metres ahead of the second-placed Italians.

Virtually the whole Australian team is firing. That's Thorpey's fifth gold medal, and fourth world record, of the week and he still has the 4 x 100m medley relay to go. Matt Welsh wins the 100m backstroke and Skippy wins the 50m butterfly. Giaan Rooney takes out the women's 200m freestyle and Petria Thomas claims the 100m/200m butterfly double. The one hiccup has been in the women's 4 x 200m freestyle relay. The team was disqualified after Petria jumped in the water, at the suggestion of a FINA photographer, to celebrate with her teammates before the final team had finished.

Don is apoplectic at the ruling and storms down onto the pool deck, shouting and waving his arms about, followed by the Australian media. But that moment aside, the team is travelling brilliantly and by the last night there's little doubt that we are going to win the meet, beat the Americans on gold medals and achieve the goal that Don set when he came back as Australian head coach 12 years earlier.

Hacky saves his best for last, taking down the world 1500m freestyle record to finish his week. Winning the medley relay would complete our dominance of the men's programme. For the first time in six years, I'm not swimming that event, not even in the heats. Skippy does the butterfly leg and Thorpey the freestyle. I have mixed feelings watching them win the last gold medal of the championships without me.

It brings our gold medal tally to 12, well ahead of the young American team on seven. Without the old heads who got them back on track in Sydney, they haven't been able to rally the same way. But there is huge talent in this young American team. A 16-year-old Michael Phelps has won his first world title in the 200m butterfly, Anthony Ervin has won the 50m and 100m freestyle double, Aaron Peirsol has won the 200m backstroke and Natalie Coughlin has taken the 100m backstroke. We've seized our chance to lower their colours, but it will be tougher to do that at the Olympics in Athens in three years.

There are two more competitions to come before the end of the season and I've been advised that I can't do any more damage to the ankle by racing, so I swim through the pain at the Australian Short Course Championships and fulfil my final Australian team engagement for the year at the Goodwill Games in Brisbane. My ankle holds up well enough there for me to win the 100m and 200m butterfly in what is virtually an exhibition meet. I'm already booked in for surgery to fix my ankle with orthopaedic surgeon Martin Sullivan in Sydney. According to him,

I've completely torn one ligament, partially torn the other, damaged the cartilage and there are bone fragments floating around in there. That's exactly what it feels like and only surgery can fix it, so I prepare to go under the knife.

CHAPTER 13

Down but Not Out

When I leave the hospital on crutches, I'm papped by a photographer eager to capture my misery. My immediate future is uncertain. Gennadi has undergone triple bypass surgery and is also recovering so he's in no position to support me right now. I don't really want to go back to Canberra, so instead I do my rehab on the Gold Coast.

Giaan Rooney and I have started seeing each other quietly. It's still new and we both have high profiles now, so we don't want to go public until we're confident things will work out. We know there will be a media storm once our relationship becomes news.

When my ankle is strong enough, I start swimming with the Miami squad under Denis Cotterell, who coaches Gi, Hacky and Daniel, three of my closest teammates. It's a comfortable environment for me, the change of scene is refreshing and I can't fault the climate. Despite my Polish roots, it's hot weather that makes me feel alive. I rent an apartment on the beach and adapt easily to a new lifestyle surrounded by friends. As I'm trying to regain fitness, Denis's more endurance-based programme is ideal for me at this stage.

I stay in contact with Gennadi. It helps that he and Denis are also good friends and unlikely roommates on national teams. They have bonded over their shared musical taste, and often jam together on guitar and harmonica on tours. Gi and I are still going well together and eventually the local newspaper blows our cover, but being on the Gold Coast means we're not bothered much by the metropolitan-based media. By December, I'm still on the Coast, and I decide to stay through to the Commonwealth Games trials in March 2002.

Now I'm fit again, I'm keen to make some strength gains and I embark on an ambitious gym programme, but without the supervision I'm used to at the AIS. I put new exercises into my programme, including dead lifts, but that aggravates the bulging disc in my back that grounded me a year earlier. This time, I can barely move. The disc is now prolapsed and impinging on a nerve, which gives me pain and weakness down my right leg. I try everything to get some relief – physiotherapy, massage, acupuncture and other alternative therapies – but nothing works.

Eventually, I have a nerve-block injection in my spine in Brisbane, then go to Melbourne for an MRI scan and an appointment with spinal specialist Gary Speck. It's not good news. He recommends spinal surgery immediately, which will rule me out of the Commonwealth Games in

Manchester, the Pan Pacs and the World Short Course Championships. I hate to miss any opportunity to represent my country, but I've now lost more than a month of training, and in reality I'm no longer fit enough to swim for a place in the team at the Commonwealth Games trials in six weeks.

The Olympics in Athens are a little more than two years away, so I don't want a chronic back problem hanging over my preparation. With a heavy heart, I agree to the surgery. Given the media interest in my situation, Woody calls a press conference in Melbourne, where my condition is obvious to all because I can't sit down. I announce my decision while kneeling at a table in front of the cameras.

Despite two major surgeries in six months, I throw myself into rehab afterwards. I spend a month in Melbourne working with the post-op team, and make good enough progress that Gary gives me the green light to return to the Gold Coast and get back in the water. He'd predicted this part would take two months, but I've healed quickly. A week later, I'm juggling three training programmes. I'm back swimming up to 7km a day with Denis in Miami, doing my rehab with my physio and taking on a strength and conditioning programme with my trainer, Gavin Hopper. I'm eager to get back to where I was before the accident.

Gi and I are still going strong but one of my most formative relationships is ending. Gennadi has experienced another incident on an international flight and the Australian Institute of Sport chooses not to renew his contract. He secures a new post in Switzerland, and Alex goes with him. It's the end of an era. Life felt so simple at the AIS and there was such purity of purpose when I was working with Gennadi and Alex. That avenue is closed to me now. But athletes are trained to look to the future, not the past, and in this case I don't have much choice. I devote myself to training with Denis through the winter and get back to peak fitness before the end of the season.

I make my comeback to competition at the national short course championships in September, and I'm ready to go full steam ahead after that. Back in the pool, I'm doing a training set using just my arms with big paddles on my hands when I feel a click in my right shoulder. It's sore afterwards but I don't think it's too serious initially. Hacky says I'm like a Formula One car – when all the parts are working perfectly, I'm unstoppable, but if one bolt gets out of alignment, the wheels fall off.

I start to rehab the shoulder on the Gold Coast because I like the club atmosphere with Denis, and his neurotic approach to training. That's the way I am too. We get on well and I enjoy the challenge of training with him. He's a unique individual with a huge amount of energy. Some days he might have 30 guys in the pool, but he never misses timing a split for any of us. He gives every bit of energy he has to his swimmers. Consequently, I'm the fittest I've ever been, apart from the shoulder issue.

I'm fit but I'm not fast, so I decide I need a more specialist sprint programme to take me to the next level. Initially I decide on Fydes' former coach, Brian Sutton, who's based in Sydney. I move there for a couple of months in October, but I soon realise it's not for me – Sutto and I have different approaches – so I turn to Ian Pope, who is now running Melbourne Vicentre and has done excellent work with Matt Welsh. Gi also joins Popey and we set up house in Melbourne.

Back home, my shoulder specialist Greg Hoy gives me more bad news. I've ripped one of my tendons off the bone and will need a shoulder reconstruction. I've watched Dan Kowalski go through two reconstructions and I know I have a long road to recovery ahead of me now. Shoulder injuries are the particular curse of swimmers because we generally have unusually flexible joints, which allow us to develop better swimming technique but also expose us to injury because of the strain we put on them. Petria is about to have her third shoulder reconstruction.

I'm still hopeful that I will be able to come back to the Australian team in 2003, but it doesn't turn out that way. Four months isn't long enough to get my shoulder back to where it needs to be so I miss the national trials, which rules me out of the World Championships in Barcelona.

I gather a good team around me to assist with my rehab. I begin working with specialist shoulder physio Lyn Watson, and both she and Dan recommend a physical trainer called Jeremy Oliver, who works with the Victorian Institute of Sport, to assist with my dryland rehab. I'll be doing a lot of dryland work as I won't be able to roll my shoulders over in the pool for months – possibly for an entire year.

For now, I'm restricted to kicking in the pool. I attack that with gusto, but I can't hide the fact that it's incredibly boring and repetitive, as well as frustrating because I'm watching my Australian teammates do all the work that I would love to be doing and can't.

Through that difficult period, it's the two Jeremys – Jeremy Oliver and Jeremy Carp – who keep me sane.

Jeremy Oliver makes my gym programme as interesting as possible. We gel really well. He's an ex-police detective from St Kilda who has retrained as a physiologist, which gives him a unique set of skills. He's personable and empathetic, but he's also tough. He makes me accountable for every session we do and it's impossible to shirk the work when he's doing the session with you and he's already run 20km to the gym that morning.

In our first session together, at the VIS gym in South Melbourne, he puts me through a spin cycling workout because I can't move my shoulder yet. That becomes a regular part of our rehab routine. As soon as I'm able, I start cycling on the road too as a way to build my fitness without putting pressure on my shoulders.

Through my accountant, I meet cyclist Mark Hindmarsh, who introduces me to some of the pro riders, Stuart O'Grady, Simon Gerrans and Cadel Evans. They invite me to join them on some of their rides and I agree. One of these is known famously as the 'Hell Ride', a Saturday morning ride that is open to all-comers. It's a 63km route out and back from Blackrock Beach on Port Phillip Bay, along the Nepean Highway and over Olivers Hill. It takes about 90 minutes and I experience a level of fatigue by the end that I've never felt in a swimming pool.

I quickly learn that the coffee afterwards is the main attraction of these group rides for the amateur riders, and I start to enjoy this entry into a new and diverse sporting community. I join the Jayco Flyers cycling club and ride regularly with a bunch of retired footballers, including Danny Frawley. We meet regularly at Café Racer and ride down Beach Road toward Frankston and back. It's as much a social as a sporting gathering. When I'm riding alone, I'm amused to see the surprised faces of passing motorists who recognise me and can't fathom why I'm on a bike and not in the pool. It's an interesting diversion, but cycling will never be my main game.

Jeremy Oliver also takes me out of the gym and into nature as much as possible. He believes in the power of the natural environment to reduce stress, especially for someone like me who's been institutionalised from a young age. Over time, he adds hiking and mountain climbing to our regular workout schedule to give me physical challenges that I can conquer when I can't attempt any in the pool.

My friend Jeremy Carp provides an escape from swimming when I need it. He's not in that world at all, so when I'm with him I don't have to talk about any of my injuries or setbacks. We just have fun. We met through our common friend, my lawyer John Gdanski, when we both attended a St Kilda game at Manuka Oval in Canberra in 2001. Many of my non-swimming friends are fellow Saints tragics. Jeremy happened to sit next to us at the game and we hit it off, discovering that in addition to our irrational love of the Saints, we both had Polish backgrounds. We stayed in touch afterwards and became firm friends when I moved back to Melbourne.

On the swimming front, it's been a constant grind for Gi and me, and that struggle dominates our lives. I'm still highly motivated to train and compete, but I'm being constantly frustrated by my physical setbacks. At the same time, she's winning titles but she's searching for ways to stay motivated for training. She hoped the fresh start with a new squad and coach in Melbourne might help, but it hasn't. She's supported me through the treadmill of surgeries and rehab, and my frustrations as my body keeps breaking down. I've tried to help her find the motivation to keep swimming, but I also envy the fact that she's fit and healthy and able to have the success in the pool that I still crave. That hasn't left room for much fun in our relationship. There's also a lot of public and media focus on us because we're both so recognisable now, and even more so because we're together. In the end, there's too much pressure and we split in early 2003.

Gi confirms that we have separated in a February 2023 interview with *The Age*:

> Michael and I had a great relationship and we had so much fun together, but it was really hard; there was no private life. The general public knew about everything; that's something that a normal relationship doesn't have to deal with. The hardest thing is swimming is a sport where you need so much other support in your life. You can't do it without that, and it's kind of hard enough to look after yourself without having to try to look after someone else

> as well ... We really both want to do well at the Olympics and ... I don't think there is room for another person in your life. I know that sounds so selfish and so awful, but it is a selfish sport.

It had been difficult for both of us. When you have these feelings for another athlete, you can't help being affected when they are flying or falling. It's hard to preserve your own nervous energy and avoid emotional fatigue, which is a problem when you are both trying to compete at the highest level at the same time. You want to support your partner so you can't be cold and unaffected by what's happening with them, but that comes at a cost and it inevitably shows in your own performance. Neither of us wants to compromise the other's swimming career, or our own, and reluctantly we agree to go our separate ways so we can focus on the Athens Olympics.

I'm finally close to full fitness by the end of August and I test the shoulder in a low-key club meet in Melbourne. I enter for the 100m freestyle, hoping that I can break 50 seconds in the short course (25m) pool – a modest ambition considering my best is 47.49 seconds. I've barely raced for two years, and it's been over two years since I've been fully fit, but the muscle memory comes back to me when I face the starter's gun. I clock 48.7 seconds, a time that would have won this year's national championships. Popey and I are delighted, and we start making plans for a return to international racing at the World Cup meeting at our home pool in Melbourne in November. I feel like this is my chance. My Australian teammates have just started training again after the World Championships. I've convinced Hawkey to relocate from Sydney and come to train with me so I know I'll have a great training partner. He's a typical sprinter, a bit brash, plenty of bravado and committed to swimming fast. He will give me the daily challenge I need to train to a high standard.

I feel like I am back on an even playing field with everyone who will be regaining fitness after their post-season breaks. Hope wells up inside me, but it collapses when the shoulder fails me again. I can't even roll my arm over in the pool. I've been positive and persistent in the face of every setback over the last two years, but now I feel like I've fallen back to the bottom of the mountain I must climb, and time is running out. I'm getting to the bottom of my well of resilience, but I've come too far to give up, so I just keep going with treatment and rehab in the hope that it comes good. The shoulder finally settles down just days before the World Cup meeting, and I'm good to go in my first international race for two years.

I elect to do the 50m freestyle only as a precaution. But it has a strong field, with Thorpey, Ash, Hawkey and Jason Lezak, so I don't have great expectations. I'm happy just to be there racing with my old mates. I can feel a lot of eyes on me as I line up for the 50m freestyle heats on the second morning of the meet. There's more tension than usual, given it's a low-key qualifying session, but even standing on the blocks is a victory and I feel joy and relief just being there. In that mood, I rip through my race and lift my head to look at my time – 21.86 seconds, a very unexpected personal best time that qualifies me fastest for the final. Then I notice the loud cheers and applause from the grandstand and the pool deck. It's mostly just the swimming community here for the preliminaries, so they know what I've been through to get here. I'm touched by their support. It feels good to be back in the fold. There have been times this year when I doubted I would be.

I don't back up as well in the final. I'm out of practice at conserving my nervous energy during the day and saving it for the race. Jason wins from Ash and I finish third, but coming from where I was, it's a very promising start.

I've come good just in time. The Athens Olympics are only nine months away and we have Olympic trials in four months. The shoulder is still temperamental, but I now have hope that I can get back on the team and go to my third Olympics. I've been tested, but I still believe I can win another Olympic gold medal.

CHAPTER 14

Athens or Bust

Athens hosted the first modern Olympic Games in 1896 and bid to host the 1996 Centenary Games but was overlooked in favour of Atlanta. It lost again to Sydney for 2000 but finally succeeded for 2004. Despite its long candidacy, the home of the Olympics is beset by problems in its preparations to host the Games: construction delays, cost over-runs and general disorganisation. At one stage, the International Olympic Committee threatens to remove the Games altogether, but the Athens organising committee battles on. The media are focused on these trials and tribulations, but no matter what this Games will be like on the organisation front, we athletes want to be there.

Popey and I take a conservative approach as I dip my toe back into competition in early 2004. We don't have time for another setback, so we have to be cautious with the shoulder. It's not in my nature to be patient – I'm more the bull-at-a-gate type – but two years in a cycle of 'surgery, rehab, repeat' has taught me some patience and I stick rigidly to the schedule we've laid out.

I only swim freestyle at the Victorian titles in January, leaving a return to butterfly until my shoulder is more stable in late February, just a month before the Olympic trials. I line up to race at the AIS meet as my final hit-out before the trials and the media interest takes me by surprise. I've been out of the picture for almost three years now, and my 100m butterfly world record has been broken in my absence, but I'm inundated with media requests. After so long on the sidelines, I find the attention flattering but also exhausting, and I don't race that well. I'm going to have to swim the selection trials on hope rather than certainty.

Popey decides to take me underground for the final lead-up to the trials. I keep my head down and stay away from the media while I focus on getting myself ready. I don't even train at the Sydney Olympic Pool in the days before the competition begins. Popey also gives me some cover, telling the media I will be ready. He says, 'He spent 12 months just kicking, and he continued to persevere after two years out. It shows something about his character that he still has his dream of winning a gold medal at the Olympic Games.'

I've always got my confidence from racing, but this time I'm going to have to find it somewhere else because there's been precious little chance for me to face the gun in the last three years. But my desire to shine on the international stage still burns hot, so I'm going to give it everything I have. There's a dramatic start to the trials when Thorpey overbalances on the starting blocks and falls into the water before his 400m freestyle heat. Technically, it's a false start and he should be disqualified, so that is what the referee does. That means he is out of the event and can't qualify to swim it at the Olympics, despite being the reigning Olympic and world champion and world record-holder. Everyone starts to lose their minds over what Thorpey will later describe as his 'Oops' moment. In his absence, Hacky and Thorpey's former training partner Craig Stevens take the two spots for the Olympics, and huge public pressure falls on Craig to give up his spot for Thorpey – which he eventually decides to do, on the grounds that it is best for the national team. And Thorpey can't forget that he still has to qualify for the team, which he does by winning the 200m freestyle on the third night of the trials.

Thorpey and Ash are now Australia's dominant 100m freestylers. Thorpey got himself on the podium for the first time at last year's World Championships in Barcelona, finishing third behind Alex and Pieter, so he's now one of the very best in the world, but our 4 x 100m freestyle relay has suffered in my absence, missing the medals in Barcelona.

Don has retired as national head coach, but he weighs in to give me a boost as I prepare to compete. 'We need him; Australia needs him swimming fast,' he says. Unfortunately, wishing and hoping is no substitute for solid training and race practice, and I can't put together my best race in the 100m freestyle final. I only just scrape onto the team as a relay swimmer, courtesy of an equal fifth-place finish. I also swim the heats and the semi-final of the 100m butterfly, and make the final, but it becomes obvious that I don't have the conditioning to do three high-quality 100m races. We've barely done any butterfly in training to protect my shoulder, and it shows. I'm fading out in the last 20m each time, so I withdraw before the final.

I'm now a bit player in the Australian team, selected for the 4 x 100m freestyle relay only, but I'm also the only man on the team who's qualified for a third Olympics, and I know from experience that if I can find better form between now and August, I might be able to fight my way into the 4 x 200m freestyle team as well. It's not what I had hoped for, but it's still far better than I've experienced over the last three years.

Just after that, I get another healthy dose of perspective. Through a friend of a friend, Professor Andrew Kornberg, who is involved with the charity Brainwave Australia, I'm invited to tour the Royal Children's Hospital in Melbourne, particularly the ward catering for children with brain injuries and neurological disorders. I meet the children and their families. It's confronting and heart-rending to hear their stories. I'm emotionally affected by it, so I sign up to become Brainwave's national ambassador.

With a lighter competition programme for the Olympics, I also have time for some other things in the lead-up to the Games, including posing for photography magazine *Not Only Black + White*'s traditional Olympic edition. They first asked me to do it before the 2000 Olympics, but it's a nude photoshoot and I was too shy at that stage. But now I have a bit more life experience and I realise I'm not going to have a perfectly honed body forever, so this time I say yes.

When I get to the shoot, they tell me one of their ideas is to do a full-frontal photograph of me lying on a bed of dead fish, with three strategically placed mackerel guarding my modesty. It's all a bit smelly and slimy but it is in the name of art so I can't back out now. The overall experience proves to be surprisingly liberating. Later they tell me that one of the photos of me has been chosen for the cover.

Feeling somewhat over-exposed, I head to the United States with Thorpey and Hacky for a three-week high-altitude training camp in Flagstaff, Arizona, in May and June. I get much fitter swimming with Thorpey for three weeks. But Hacky, with his legendary lung capacity, struggles to get in enough of the thin air. He can't hit the pace goals that he and Denis expect in training and that drives them both mad. After a week and a half, they abandon the camp and go home to prepare in a familiar environment.

We meet up again at our pre-Olympic training camp in Sindelfingen in Germany, where I'm assigned to Denis's group as Popey isn't on the team. The Australian team has been coming here for the last three years, but it's all new to me. I'm rooming with Hacky so we quickly settle into a comfortable routine. I'm deep into my taper so my swimming sessions are now very short, whereas Hacky is still doing endless laps. That's the fate of the distance swimmer, to be still working hard while the sprinters are lying around getting a suntan.

I'm feeling more confident about my preparation now and I go to the head coach, Leigh Nugent, and request a 200m freestyle time trial so I can bid for a place in the 4 x 200m freestyle relay team. It's scheduled for Athens the day before the relay. I also try to rally the troops for the 4 x 100m freestyle relay, but it doesn't feel like it's coming together the way it did in Sydney.

Athens' scrambled preparation to host the Games is obvious when we arrive at the Olympic Village, which still looks like a construction zone. There's no vegetation at all and banners have been strategically placed in front of piles of rubble. The contrast between Sydney and Athens is striking in several ways. In Sydney, I was at the centre of the Australian team, but now I'm on the fringe, with few commitments beyond preparing myself for what could be one day only of racing if I can't force my way onto the 4 x 200m relay team. My 27th birthday is on the day of the Opening Ceremony, but again we watch the ceremony from the village.

The men's freestyle sprint relay has been moved to Day 2 of the Athens programme, which means I'm a spectator on the first night as Thorpey wins an emotional 400m freestyle gold medal, having been gifted the spot by his friend and Athens roommate Craig Stevens. It's our female sprinters who are really firing now. The combination of new world record-holder Libby Lenton, Alice Mills, Petria Thomas and Jodie Henry breaks the world record to win the Australian team's second gold medal of the night.

The men's 4 x 100m freestyle relay starts the next morning, but the coaches have shown faith in me, electing to save me for the final team rather than making me swim for a spot in the heats. Thorpey is also rested, which leaves

Ash, our talented rookie Eamon Sullivan, Jono Van Hazel and Todd Pearson to qualify us for the final. Unfortunately, Ash has lost his form and gets us off to a slow start and we only just scrape through in seventh place. That means we will have an outside lane for the final, away from the medal contest in the centre lanes. Eamon and Todd are the fastest of the heats team, so they will join Thorpey and me in the final team.

The South Africans have swum a blinder to set the pace in the preliminaries and are favoured to win the gold medal. I line up beside the South African speedster Roland Schoeman and the new American superstar Michael Phelps to open our account and produce my best 100m for three years (49.37 seconds), putting us in fourth place at the first change.

We still have a chance at a medal, but we don't have the firepower of the South Africans or Americans and by the time Thorpey hits the water there's far too much for him to do to drag us onto the podium. We finish sixth as the South Africans break our world record from Sydney to win the gold.

It's a disappointing outcome, but it will give me an extra swim in Athens. I've set the second-fastest time of the four of us and earned myself another swim in the heats of the 4 x 100m medley relay. That gives me confidence for my 200m time trial the next day. I now have a shot at winning my way onto all three relays, which is far more than I could have hoped for a few months ago.

The 200m time trials are scheduled after the morning competition session, and my task is simple. I have to swim faster than one of the guys who's rostered for the 4 x 200m relay team to force my way in. It's a perfect opportunity for me. I've always been good at time trialling – I like the mental challenge of having to produce your best without the stimulus of other competitors, so I know how to get into the right mindset for a race against the clock. I set myself to the task, blocking out everything to complete those four laps as fast as I can, fuelled by the knowledge that this is my only shot of winning an Olympic gold medal at these Games.

The time comes up, just under 1 minute 48 seconds, and I know I've done enough. I look up into the empty grandstand and somehow Mum and Dad and AIS chief executive John Boultbee have found their way in to watch and are cheering me on. Once again, the coaches have seen enough to put me straight into the final team along with Thorpey and Hacky. My mates Todd Pearson and Antony Matkovich, along with Craig Stevens and newcomer Nick Sprenger, will be the qualifying team. Pat Murphy is the unlucky one who misses out.

Hacky and I are rooming together again. He's had a rough week so far. He's been touched out by Thorpey for the gold in the 400m and just missed the medals in the 200m. He's absolutely fired up for the relay.

The boys do the business in the heats and we prepare for the final. Hacky will do the opening leg, followed by me, Nick and Thorpey. We knew we could win this race in Sydney, but the Americans now pose a serious threat to us.

A new generation of swimmers has emerged there, led by Michael Phelps and Ryan Lochte. Add in Peter Vanderkaay and Klete Keller, and they have the ability to win. Our guys finished first (Thorpey) and fifth (Hacky) in the individual 200m final, while theirs finished third (Phelps) and fourth (Keller). They have made no secret of their ambition to knock us off, and we will need to be at the top of our game to keep our title.

There has been huge hype around 19-year-old Phelps at this meet. He's come in with a chance of equalling Mark Spitz's record of seven gold medals at one Games, but the US loss in the 4 x 100m freestyle relay, and his bronze in the 200m, have put paid to that possibility. Still, he's on fire – he's won the 400m individual medley on the first night and he adds the 200m butterfly gold medal just an hour before the relay. The Americans elect to lead with him, so he will take on Hacky. I will race Lochte, Nick will be up against Vanderkaay and Thorpey will anchor against Keller.

Behind the blocks, I feel at peace – which is an unusual experience for me. In hindsight, I took these opportunities for granted in Sydney, but the last four years have taught me how rare and special the chance to win an Olympic gold medal is, and I'm grateful to have another opportunity.

It doesn't start well. Phelps puts a second into Hacky on the first leg and gives the US team a handy lead. I limit the losses against Lochte, but Nick, in his first big international final, can't hold on to Vanderkaay, leaving Thorpey to make up almost two seconds on Keller. It's too much of an ask, even for the best anchorman we've ever had. Thorpey makes up the deficit on the first 100m and tries to hold on, but Keller is fresher and kicks away on the third length. As ever, Thorpey surges at him down the last lap but he can't quite get there, not even with the fastest split in history.

The United States wins the gold by 0.13 of a second, in 7:07.33, which is nearly three seconds outside our world record, but that's cold comfort right now. Hacky has his head in his hands. He's convinced he's failed us and starts beating himself up – he'll still be doing that years later, but all three of us needed to set that race up better to give Thorpey the chance to swim Keller down.

I remember Gary Hall's sportsmanship in Sydney and go immediately to congratulate our conquerors as they celebrate. It's disappointing that we couldn't get it done – for the first and only time after a race, Hacky goes out to the warm-down pool and cries – but my sense of gratitude persists as I stand on the Olympic podium for the sixth time in three Games, with two of my best mates.

On the final day of the swimming competition, I have one more duty: to anchor the 4 x 100m medley relay team to qualify for the final. Welshy (backstroke) will lead off, followed by Jim Piper (breaststroke), Piney (butterfly) and me. We think this team is strong enough to qualify for the final, where Skippy and Thorpey will replace Piney and me, but some of the guys are a bit off their game after a long week of competition and we miss the final by one place. I put in a pretty good 48.66-seconds split but it's not enough. It's galling, but we're done.

The final session is always a big one for the Australian team because of the 1500m freestyle, the event in which we've won the most Olympic gold medals in our history. Hacky's in good form but he's started to get ill in the last few days – that's a perennial danger for him because he trains so hard and he doesn't know when to back off.

The Americans have basically put a bounty on his head, offering a $1 million bonus to any US swimmer who can win the 1500m gold medal and break Hacky's world record. But he's our ironman and he doesn't buckle, even when he's challenged by the new US hope Larsen Jensen and Briton David Davies over the closing laps. He fights them off to win the gold medal and beats his chest in celebration. It's another lionhearted performance, and my own heart swells in pride for my roommate and friend.

The Australian women's team is having the kind of Games we men had in Sydney and they finish their campaign with victory in the 4 x 100m medley relay, which gives Gi and Leisel Jones their first Olympic gold medals, and Jodie and Petria their third of the week. I'm very happy for them and for the whole team. It's been a much less pressured environment than it was in Sydney, and the Australian team has done even better, with six gold medals – a record for an offshore Games. Thorpey's now the most successful Australian athlete ever, with five gold medals.

My one silver medal is as meaningful as any medal I have ever won, because I have been to hell and back to win it.

The second week of the Games is much more relaxed for swimmers. We watch other teams compete, explore the Athens nightlife and enjoy the environment in a way that we couldn't in Sydney.

One day I'm in the village and I bump into our table tennis player, Dave Zalcberg, who is at his first Olympics and is showing his family around. It turns out that his family also originates from Poland and has washed up in Melbourne. Our families stay in touch and we become good friends as he completes his medical degree and becomes an anaesthetist. There's so much human potential in an Olympic Village, and not all of it ends up being directed toward sport.

CHAPTER 15

End Game

It takes a village to raise an Olympian, and my team has gone to the ends of the earth to get me from a swimmer with a non-functional shoulder to an Olympic medallist in 15 months. I'm very conscious of the people around me who helped me get here. I know I wouldn't have been able to do it without them and I want to recognise the extraordinary work they have done to aid my recovery. When I catch up with Popey back in Melbourne, I spontaneously place the medal around his neck and tell him how much he has contributed to me winning it. He's clearly touched and I decide to make the same gesture with all those who have given so much to support me. I repeat my own personal medal ceremony with Jeremy and Lyn, and my physio Helen Walker. They've all contributed enormously to my performance in Athens.

Athens was the launching pad I needed to get back into the top echelon of the sport. No Australian male swimmer has gone to more than three Olympic Games, and the vast majority don't get that far, but the desire is still there. I know I have enough internal motivation to get me through to Beijing in 2008.

Surprisingly, there's still a lot of corporate interest in me, despite my lean performances since 2000.

Before Athens, I made the difficult decision to find a new manager. Woody had been great for me, but now he's managing a lot of swimmers because of his success with Susie and me. The stable includes both younger up-and-coming stars and legends who have made their mark. I don't feel like I fit in anymore, so I look for new management.

I end up signing with Justin Cohen at Octagon, who has some new ideas for how best to use me. He lands a deal for me to be the face of Myer menswear for the Spring Racing Carnival, which falls perfectly into my post-Olympic break. I love fashion and they want me on the catwalk for a series of lunches.

One of them is the Victorian Racing Club's Women's Luncheon and for that show I am paired with a female model, Lindy Rama. We hit it off and pretty soon we are dating. We come from different worlds, and sport and fashion aren't always compatible, but we're keen to make it work. I find out later that Lindy is actually a Balinese Princess, the niece of the King of Denpasar. She was raised in Tasmania by her Australian mother after her parents divorced.

After my break, I go back to training with Popey in late 2004, but my body keeps letting me down. Every time I think

I'm about to get a clear run, something intervenes. The shoulder has never really come good and it flares up regularly, so I can't train the way I did early in my career. After three years of this, it's starting to get me down. I've always been very conscientious with training, I've never been one to miss training sessions or have late nights that might impact on my performance the next day, but now I'm slipping.

It's disheartening when you are competing for spots with swimmers who have never been able to challenge you before, and you're losing to them. One way to push those thoughts away is not to give myself time to think, so when I'm not training I throw myself into my commercial commitments and my social life with Lindy and my Melbourne friends.

I've bought a house in St Kilda and it's a classic bachelor pad. I still have the La-Z-Boy chairs for gaming, there's a big jacuzzi in the backyard and I have a children's python called Mitch.

I never shirk training but I am burning the candle at both ends. Instinctively I know I need other interests and non-swimming friends in my life to offset the setbacks and disappointments I've had to endure in recent years. I'm always hopeful that I can get my body right and rediscover the form I had in the lead-up to the Sydney Olympics, but I'm hedging my bets by making sure my name and face are seen at public events where Melbourne's movers and shakers gather. I'm very aware that my brand is the key to a business career once my swimming days are done.

I finally get a run of decent training in the lead-up to the 2005 Australian trials where, in Thorpey's absence,

I win the 100m freestyle and 100m butterfly to claim those spots at the World Championships in Canada mid-year. But I'm nursing my shoulder right through the preparation for Montreal.

My frustration at my stop-start progress boils up at a high-altitude training camp in Thredbo. I'm watching my training partners hammer out a big session, and remembering when I used to do the same, but I'm reduced to doing only part of the session to protect my troublesome joint. I half-hear something my housemate, backstroker Ray Hass, says in the pool, and I jump to the conclusion he's talking about me and then jump down his throat. Training can be emotional – in fact, it should be if you are doing it right. You need to bring all your passion and desire to the pool to perform at the highest level each day, but I usually direct that emotion inwards. It's not like me to lash out at others.

At the same time, my life has become even more complicated. Lindy and I have gotten engaged and she's pregnant with our first child. She gives me a choice – it's the baby or the pet python – so Mitch goes off to a wildlife park and my bachelor pad gets a makeover for family life.

I head to Montreal not quite sure of my prospects and that's the way I swim. We win the bronze medal in the 4 x 100m freestyle relay, but the writing is on the wall. My lead-off swim is poor by my standards and I don't take any confidence into the individual 100m freestyle. I do a slightly better job there, but I don't make the final and that really hurts. I feel like I'm watching the races go by me, rather than being in them. I've only had that sensation once before, when I was trying to nurse my broken ankle through the 100m butterfly final in Fukuoka. I've already opted out of the 100m butterfly here to protect the shoulder, then we miss the medals in the medley relay, thus ending what's been a miserable experience for me. All I've got to fall back on is bravado. 'Look, I still want to be swimming for my country so I'm not going anywhere,' I tell the media.

On the way home to Australia, Lindy and I do a stopover in Los Angeles for some R&R, along with Eamon's coach Grant Stoelwinder and his partner Leon, a costume designer. On a shopping trip, I buy a T-shirt from Urban Outfitters that has a drawing of a lion, my old talisman, on the front. The idea comes into my head that it would make a great tattoo. We're walking down Sunset Boulevard a few days later when we spot a tattoo shop. I walk in and get that image of the lion imprinted on my right shoulder. It's a reminder to me to be brave.

Back home, I keep pushing, knowing that my hometown of Melbourne will host the Commonwealth Games in March 2006. The trials are only five months away, but it's tough going for me to get there. At 30, Hawkey has decided to retire after the Commonwealth Games so we both have a lot riding on this. Even though we are good friends, things sometimes get heated between us on the pool deck. There are days when he is whipping my arse in training, which would never have happened back in the day, and I feel humiliated by that. One afternoon, I lash out at him after the session and we almost end up in a fistfight, pushing and grabbing at each other on the pool deck. We see some sense and go our separate ways before it gets too crazy, but we don't talk to each other for a day or two until we cool off.

There are good reasons why Hawkey is outperforming me in training, and they are not all related to my chronic shoulder pain. I'm desperate to perform, but I'm also afraid that I will fail again. The desire and the fear are wrestling inside me. Subconsciously, I start sabotaging myself by going out more, attending more events, sometimes prioritising my social life – which I have never done in the past. Going out in the evening costs me the sleep I need to be fresh for the next day's training, but sometimes I do it anyway. It helps me to forget about swimming when it isn't going well.

Despite my inner turmoil, I do okay at the Commonwealth Games trials, swimming over the top of Eamon to finish second behind Thorpey in the 100m freestyle, although neither of us is near our best. I also take out the double in the 50m and 100m butterfly events.

I'm most pleased to see Hawkey clinch a spot in the 4 x 100m freestyle relay. He's primarily a 50m specialist but he's contributed a lot to that relay over the years and it's good to see him finally get the chance to swim it, especially as he's decided to retire after the Games.

Lindy and I have a lot going on in early 2006. Our daughter Stella is born in January, just before the Commonwealth Games. Lindy goes into labour during the night while we're at home in St Kilda. We head to the hospital and alert our parents, who arrive a couple of hours later. Stella arrives safely but it is a difficult birth for Lindy and she experiences several bouts of post-natal haemorrhaging that have us back in the emergency room. Between Stella's arrival and Lindy's health concerns, I still need to find time to prepare for a home Commonwealth Games, but it's a difficult juggling act. Lindy gets up for Stella during the night so I can sleep, while I take the morning shift. When I need to leave home to join the Australian team, my parents and her mother and stepfather come through to support them.

Thing aren't going all that smoothly with the swimming team either. Thorpey goes down with severe bronchitis in the weeks before the Games and is forced to withdraw from the team. Hacky is already out after having shoulder surgery last November and Skippy has retired after missing selection, so our men's team is seriously under-strength for a home Games.

Nothing seems to go right for us during the Games. I'm rooming with Hawkey and on the day of the 4 x 100m freestyle relay, he takes a shower before we head to the pool. He comes out complaining that he feels hot. His heart is racing and a red rash has bloomed all over his body. We go to the team doctor, who says he's had an allergic reaction, possibly to shampoo or shower gel.

The doc doesn't want Hawkey to swim, but he's desperate to be part of the relay. It's his one chance to swim it for Australia. He begs the doctor for any remedy that will get him to the starting blocks. The doctor reluctantly agrees to give him a shot of adrenaline to calm the reaction but advises he could be at risk of having a heart attack during the race if he overexerts himself.

Hawkey ends up needing two shots to counteract his allergic reaction and is put under observation in the medical centre, but he's determined to swim. Meanwhile, it's time for the rest of us to go to the pool and warm up. Once again, we're a man down on arrival for the 4 x 100m freestyle relay.

Hawkey joins us in time for the race, but we can see he's not himself. He seems both wired and calm at the same time. His normal way of racing the 100m is to go out as fast as he can and hold on as well as he can, but with the doctor's warning about stressing his heart ringing in his ears, he goes out slower than he ever has in his life. I lead off the team but we're never better than third, and Ash guides us home to the bronze medal so at least Hawkey will have something to show for his trouble.

We're in the middle of the competition when Lindy's stepfather Michael calls to tell me they have had to take her to hospital. My urge is to leave the village and join them, but he reassures me that Lindy and Stella are in safe hands and she is being well cared for. I'm anxious for them, and I feel torn between my family and my teammates. I stay with the team, but I get regular updates. I'm relieved when she's discharged from hospital quite quickly, but the Games turns into a meet of near-misses for me. I get touched out by New Guinean Ryan Pini for gold in the 100m butterfly and take bronze in the 50m butterfly.

That's the trend right across our men's team. By the last session of the Games, we haven't won a single gold medal. We finally break through to win the medley relay on the final night to save us from complete embarrassment. By contrast, the women's team is soaring. With Libby and Leisel leading, they win 16 gold medals.

The whole Games feels surreal to me. Because we are in Melbourne, competing in the pool where I normally train, everything has been too familiar – not as special as a Games should be – so I don't feel the excitement I should.

Maybe that's because of everything else going on in my life. Lindy's father is also ill in Bali. We make a mercy dash to the island after the Games finish, but we're too late. He dies just hours before we arrive and I never get to meet him. We pay our respects as he lies in state, but we don't stay for the funeral ceremonies as we need to get back to Melbourne for our wedding.

Father Bob Maguire, a South Melbourne identity famous for his social justice advocacy, marries us in St Joan of Arc Church at Brighton in April 2006. We walk down the aisle together, with Lindy carrying Stella in her arms, watched by our families, and our swimming and fashion families. Thorpey, Hacky, Hawkey and Piney are all in attendance, as is Nicole Livingstone. Our reception is at the Prince Hotel on Fitzroy St. It's a fun night with 120 of our nearest and dearest. Hawkey and my friend Jeremy Carp serve as my best men and make hilarious speeches.

New Idea photographs our wedding and puts it on the magazine cover, with a feature spread inside. I tell the magazine, 'Lindy is mesmerising. All my friends and family know I have been completely taken by her since we met, so it's nice our love is now formalised and we can celebrate.

In our eyes we have been married for a long time, but today we cemented it and it feels fantastic.'

My personal life is on a high, but my swimming life is not. I'm still struggling with my body. I know my injuries are preventing me from doing enough training to perform at my best (45km a week compared with 70km when I was with Gennadi), but I can't face retirement.

I'm still hoping for a miraculous recovery that will enable me to get to the Beijing Olympics in 2008. I want to become the first Australian to compete at four Games, and the 2007 World Championships are being held at home in Melbourne, which is another incentive.

I finally get a break in the middle of 2006 and string together a couple of months of good training. I go to Perth to train with Eamon Sullivan and his coach Grant Stoelwinder for a few weeks in the hope that I can break out of this cycle of frustration. Eamon is the next-generation sprint hope and we've formed a good friendship. At one stage, he tells me that he was one of the basket carriers at the World Championships in Perth and he wanted my autograph, but he missed me walking by, so he asked my dad if he could help. The next day I came back and found him and gave him an autographed cap. I don't remember it but he does, which has given us a solid basis for friendship.

We've also bonded over our various injuries. Whereas mine have come late in my career, Eamon's have come early. In 2005, he stayed at my place in Melbourne to recover from hip surgery. I like training with him and Stolly. They do the work, but they make it fun.

I also do a training camp in Cyprus with Pieter and Jacco, and I reconnect with my old manager Rob Woodhouse. I'm in a better headspace as the national trials approach in December. 'It's dawned on me that this is the last chance I will get to swim in front of my home crowd at a major meet, because Beijing is where I have drawn the line,' I say to the media.

I know Thorpey has also been struggling for motivation but none of us are prepared when he announces his retirement from the sport in November 2006, aged just 24. Most of my contemporaries have now stopped swimming, apart from Piney who is a year older than me and appears intent on continuing until he's 40. It's a shock to know I'll never be on a team with Thorpey again. It's hard to avoid the signs that things are coming to an end for me too, but for now I refuse to acknowledge that.

It's nine years since the World Championships in Perth and I'm still searching for some magic that will help restore me to what I was then, but I haven't found it. I only just qualify for the World Championships team, again through the 4 x 100m freestyle relay.

Anna's wedding in January 2007 provides a much-needed ray of sunshine. She marries Andrew Eagle in St Joan of Arc Church, Brighton (the same one I was married in), and their reception is at the grand old mansion Rippon Lea. After a happy day with the family, I get back to the grind in the pool.

I'm hopeful that my proven record as a performer on the world stage will give me other opportunities to push my claims to swim in other relays at the World Championships, as it did in Athens. But in Melbourne it becomes apparent that the Australian coaching team is focused on the next generation for Beijing. I don't swim fast enough in the heats of the 4 x 100m freestyle to earn selection for the final team. I'm also allocated the butterfly leg in the heats of the 4 x 100m medley relay, but that will be the extent of my involvement.

Libby Lenton is the star of the Australian team now – she wins five gold medals that week to break my Perth record. At our team meeting on the penultimate day of the championships, Libby speaks beautifully about what it means to be part of this team. I'm inspired by her words and I ask our head coach Alan Thompson whether I can speak at our meeting the next day, which is the final day of the championships.

I have my last race in the morning, in the medley relay heats. I think I'm ready to speak when I stand up in front of my teammates, but I'm not. I struggle to get my words out as I talk about what it has meant to me to be part of the team for 12 years, to see so many other swimmers come and go in that time and to be at the World Championships less than a kilometre from my home.

Then these words come out of my mouth: 'I think this might be my last team.' I haven't planned to say this, the thought wasn't even in my conscious mind, but the truth of it hits me like a sledgehammer and I'm overwhelmed by emotion. It bursts inside me and I cry in front of my teammates. Afterwards, the team managers are concerned for my wellbeing. They give me special dispensation to sign off the team early, directly after the final session. They warn me that I won't be able to attend any more team functions after I leave.

I watch the final session from the grandstand, in almost exactly the same place where I once stood to watch Anna play tennis when we were kids. I feel some nostalgia for that time. Ironically, I win my seventh and last World Championships gold medal from the grandstand. I've helped the medley relay team qualify for the final in the morning heats, so I'm officially part of the winning team when they go on to claim the gold in the final. Waves of emotion roll through me as I sign off from the team and head home.

I'm not thinking rationally and, despite the warning that I'm no longer part of the team, I decide to attend the swimmers' post-championships function later that night. I was the one who organised that party and I justify it to myself that I have a right to be there. But by attending, I'm breaking our team rules. Thommo calls me to a meeting the next day. As I drive in, Woody (who is back on board as my manager) calls me and tears strips off me for my behaviour. I'm expecting more of the same from Thommo, but he says simply that he's disappointed with my actions and informs me that there will be a disciplinary hearing with Swimming Australia for breaking the team code. As I leave, I can't even recognise myself. I've never been a rule-breaker, but the realisation that my swimming career may be over has thrown me completely.

I take my normal post-championships break but when it comes time to go back to training, I'm still too scattered to focus on it. I train sporadically while I try to figure out what comes next. As I wrestle with my thoughts, I talk to my usual confidantes – including Thorpey, given his recent experience. He says that if I think it's the right time to retire, then it probably is. But I can't decide whether I should stop now or press on for Beijing. I seriously consider relocating to the United States for a year and training with Gary Hall's Race Club in Florida. I need to break out of the rut I am in, and I can't see how I can do that by continuing to train in Melbourne. But I have other responsibilities to consider. I'm married with a child, and I don't see how moving to Florida for a year would work for Lindy and Stella.

While I'm in this quandary, I attend the Swimming Australia disciplinary hearing, where I point to my previous good behaviour and current situation as mitigating circumstances. The disciplinary panel sanctions me with a fine of $500 and a suspended three-month ban. It's another nail in my coffin.

I still have the desire to compete, but I can't see a way forward that will allow me to swim at the highest level, so reluctantly, after two months of agonising, I conclude that it's time to retire from the sport.

At a press conference in Melbourne, I announce my decision with a heavy heart, saying: 'I want to go to the Olympics and try to win gold medals and break world records for my country, but I don't feel I've got that in me anymore. I probably could have pushed myself for another year just to qualify and be the only one to go to four Olympics in Australia, but I felt like I wouldn't have done it for the right reasons.' I tell the media that ultimately, I couldn't justify the emotional and physical cost of continuing to myself and my family. But every comment is tinged with regret. I really don't want to go out this way.

PART 2
REINVENTION

CHAPTER 16

How to Succeed in Business

While my former teammates put their heads down and prepare for the Olympic year, I immerse myself in another project – a skincare line for men.

Given my father's entrepreneurial attitude and my own lack of any formal tertiary qualifications, it seems obvious to me that I'm going to have to carve out a new career by starting my own business. Based on my long relationships with Speedo and Myer, I originally planned to launch a fashion line after I retired. However, two skincare brands approached me in 2006 about an ambassadorial role, which made me look at that industry. I did some research and discovered that the skincare market was growing at 40 per cent a year, which provided further food for thought.

Then there was my personal experience with skincare. Swimmers are always slathering on moisturiser because they spend so much time in the water, often in chlorine, and they are frequently outdoors where they are subject to sun exposure, which really dries out your skin. But I've noticed that there are few specific skincare products for men, and none are designed by an Australian man for Australian men. It feels like there is a gap in the market.

I intend to call the brand Milk & Co. Milk is a play on words, as it is Klim spelled backward. Back in the day, before the Sydney Olympics, Thorpey and Kieren both had sponsorships with milk companies, and I always thought I would get one based on my name. It didn't happen then but the idea stayed with me. Milk also has a clean, pure image, and it's an everyday product, so it fits perfectly with what we're trying to do. We're pretty advanced in developing the products, brand and marketing. Even during the World Championships, I had my roommates testing products and bottle shapes and colours to figure out which ones worked best and were most attractive to men.

We settle on a bottle shape that feels like a whiskey glass in your hand. We want to make the products seem familiar and accessible for men who have never had much of a skincare routine.

When we started out on this project, I had no idea how much work it would take to bring all the facets of the business together to make it successful. But once it becomes my primary focus, I take the same approach that I did to swimming. I work as hard as I can and gather a good team around me, surrounding myself with trusted experts. I'm not that financially literate – Mum and Dad and my management company have managed my money throughout my career – so I need advice there too. But ultimately

I have to make the decisions, and without any real business experience I have to trust my gut.

Initially, we focus on three products – a moisturiser, body wash and face wash – and we start talking to Myer about launching the brand through their stores. I throw myself into the project. It doesn't give me time to think about swimming, which is both good and bad.

A lot of professional athletes go through an identity crisis when they stop competing and I feel that too. I've seen myself as a swimmer since I was a kid. I was making Australian junior teams from the age of 13 and I've spent 12 years on the Australian senior team. Training filled most of my waking hours for most of my life and allowed very little time for anything else. It's hard to know who I am without swimming. The demands of launching a business more than fill the hours that used to be dedicated to training, but that's only part of it. I still have to forge a new identity for myself that doesn't rely on me being a swimmer. I feel as if I've stepped off the road without a map.

The Global Financial Crisis (GFC) also hits in 2007, which makes the future even more unpredictable for a fledgling business. I've financed our start-up with part of the proceeds from selling a shop that I had bought as an investment on Clarendon St in South Melbourne. The rest has been earmarked for the property development of a piece of land near our family home in Brighton. Dad spotted it and I bought it with the plan to subdivide and build two houses, one for my family to live in and the other to sell for profit. But we are still in the planning phase when interest rates start to accelerate and property prices slump.

It's a rude introduction to the financial world. Now there's real pressure on me to make Milk & Co a success. I'm loath to compromise on the quality of our products, so I'm squeezing my margins. At the same time, I'm learning about the complexity of supply chains and shipping and barcodes and developing reliable links to supply our products to wholesalers and retail.

Our son Rocco is born in May 2008, so we now have two children under three to raise in the middle of all this mayhem.

We launch Milk & Co into Myer in August 2008, just before the Beijing Olympics, to take advantage of my heightened profile around Games time and give the brand its best chance of success. We do create some good buzz, and we have found a niche in the market at a time when the 'metrosexual' man is becoming a trend, but it turns out that Australian men don't go into department stores to buy skincare products. They shop in supermarkets and chemists, places where they can duck in and out. Skincare is a new concept for most of them, and they just want a practical solution rather than a luxury brand.

We've also made a bit of an error with the initial packaging, which is cream-coloured and doesn't pop on the shelf. Sales are okay through the first year or so, and we launch a baby range that does well, but the brand is not taking off in a way that is profitable yet. At one stage, we have all of our family and friends packing boxes in our garage to get the product out to our suppliers.

However, we're ambitious for the brand so we buy a stall at a major international trade show, Cosmoprof in Hong Kong, in November 2008 to show our products to the world's distributors and retailers. But we're still babes in the wood and we realise that the samples we have sent will not arrive in Hong Kong in time, which shapes up as a marketing disaster.

We organise for some 20-litre bottles of liquids and creams to be sent to our hotel. Dad, Anna, Lindy and I arrive in Hong Kong and set up a production line in our hotel rooms to decant the products into the empty sample bottles the night before the show opens. By the next day, no-one will know we're not quite the professional operation that we seem. We get some good leads and contacts from the show so we also go to the next Cosmoprof in Bologna, Italy, in May 2009.

I contact my old swimming friend Massi Rosolino, who won the 200m individual medley at the Sydney Olympics and finished second behind Thorpey in the 400m, and later trained with my squad under Ian Pope in Melbourne. I tell him I'm going to be in Italy to exhibit our new brand, and he promises to come and visit us. There are over 2000 exhibitors in Bologna, so it's hard to stand out from the crowd, but it's a lot easier when one of Italy's sporting heroes comes to call. Massi is a bigger name in Italy than I am in Australia, and he attracts plenty of attention as he walks through the exhibit hall to our stand.

But there comes a point when I have to admit I don't really know what I'm doing. I'm energetic and committed. I'm good at outsourcing, PR and branding, but I have no business background. I've been too proud to ask for advice in the past, but there's now a lot at stake for me, my family, our staff and everyone who's relying on us to provide products. I'm introduced to a business development expert called Alan Miltz. His advice is invaluable as he teaches me how to analyse the business, understand the financials and establish a stable foundation. He has an incredible knowledge of the pitfalls that await start-ups and entrepreneurs, and crucially, how to avoid them.

He introduces me to Julie Milnes, the former head of fashion brand Metalicus, who I hire as our general manager. From there, we build a small team of experts to help our brand soar. Alan and Julie introduce me to Brian Hamersfeld, the son of Metalicus founder Melma Hamersfeld and co-founder of Bloom Cosmetics, who becomes another key adviser and confidante, as does David Briskin, who co-founded Mimco, the fashion accessories company in Melbourne. I engage my former swimming teammate Ryan Mitchell, who has become a business development consultant, to help us get more clarity on the brand. Alan and Ryno aren't shy about asking me the hard questions I've been avoiding. They want to know about the long-term vision and strategy of the brand, which forces me to come up with answers. I've been making a lot of decisions on gut instinct and intuition, but that can only take you so far. I need to analyse what we are doing and set our future course based on hard facts, not my instincts. Alan and Brian both advise me that we can't be everything to everyone and that if we are in a niche, we have to own it.

The Italian Cosmoprof trip pays off the following year when the huge Boots pharmacy chain agrees to stock Milk & Co products in its UK stores. By then we have decided to pivot to the mass market rather than chasing the prestige end to compete with international brands with much deeper pockets than us.

Multinationals like L'Oreal, Gillette and Nivea also dominate the mass market, but we offer a high-quality brand that is designed specifically for Australian men. We review the price point and reposition our products as 'mass-tige' (as opposed to prestige). I begin the process of selling it into supermarkets and pharmacies. I find that my name can always get me that first meeting, but then it's up to me to impress the distributors or retailers with the product.

I knock on the door of every major retailer in the country. I become a real hustler at trade fairs, handing out samples and talking to potential buyers about the products. I get some knockbacks, but I also get enough wins to keep going. Coles is the first supermarket to come on board, followed by Woolworths. We finally have some financial stability and we move into a small office in South Yarra. We expand into international markets, supplying retailers including Sephora in Singapore and Boshiwa in China. We have good growth now, but we still have some challenges managing our cash flow.

We're still being punished by the GFC. At one stage, I'm paying $20,000 a month in loan repayments and only just keeping my head above water. The property bubble has burst so the profit from the Brighton subdivide that I'd envisaged investing into Milk & Co has vanished. I sell the second property to get some debt relief, but by then most of the money I've put away from my swimming career has gone.

At about the same time, at a school function, our general manager Julie Milne meets another parent who works in private equity and they get talking. This guy recommends a company called Blue Sky. It's a private equity firm founded by Mark Sowerby in Queensland that looks for alternative investment opportunities. We think it could be the answer for us and Mark and his colleague Alex McNab come to Melbourne to meet me. Somehow I pass their 'no dickheads' test and they agree to invest $2 million in Milk & Co for a 30 per cent stake in the business.

I've thrown most of my energy into building the business since I retired, but I still need to stay active because fitness has always been a big part of my life. I box and cycle regularly, I work with a personal trainer and I crave physical challenges. I sign up to do the 2007 season of *Dancing With the Stars*, although I'm eliminated early – it turns out dancing requires a different type of rhythm from swimming. I get more into cycling and end up doing some road races, and I do Mark Webber's adventure race in Tasmania. The desire to take on physical challenges is one I can't shake.

CHAPTER 17

Comeback

In late 2010, three and a half years after my retirement, rumours start to circulate through the swimming community that Thorpey is considering a comeback. I send him a text message at the start of February 2011 saying, 'If you come back, I might as well.' I'm only half-joking. At 33, I've been slowly getting back to training with coach Rohan Taylor in the last three months, building up to about 60 per cent of a full training schedule, but I still don't know whether my shoulders will stand up to the load once we push to 100 per cent.

The next day, greeted by tremendous fanfare, Thorpey announces his comeback for the London Olympics. I'm reluctant to make my own announcement until I'm more certain, but that decision is taken out of my hands when a newspaper reporter gets wind of the news two weeks later. I end up announcing my comeback on a comedy radio show, with a dozen television cameras crammed into the studio. 'I am going to have a crack,' I say. 'I have no expectations.

I don't know if my body can handle it, or if my wife can handle it or my children. I don't know how far I can go. To get to the trials would be fantastic and to get to the Olympics would be amazing. In the true Aussie spirit, I am going to have a go.'

If I look at it rationally, it's madness for me to take on this challenge. We're still building Milk and Co, Lindy is pregnant with our third child, we're building our dream house in Brighton and I'm immersed in the design process. Dad and I disagree about the house design. He advises me to keep costs down and not to overcapitalise, but I have my heart set on a hi-spec home with an eight-star energy rating. He regards my approach as extravagant, but I won't listen to him. There's a lot going on even without training twice a day, but elite sport is about passion more than rationality and I feel the need to get back in.

I confess to the media that, despite my busy life, I'm still missing something: 'It's not an easy decision. It's a life-changing decision because I have a successful business, I have a family and our third child is due in June. But I am really inspired by the young swimmers around today. Another thing that really inspired me is that my kids haven't seen me swim at elite level.'

Both Thorpey and I are keen to get the band back together in the 4 x 100m freestyle relay. We realise the individual events may have passed us by, but we both love that relay and we think we can contribute to its success in London. We can see a young sprinter called James Magnussen coming through in Sydney and Eamon is still around, along with

Matt Targett, so there's the nucleus of a really competitive team and I want to be part of it.

We seem to have tapped into the zeitgeist, as Skippy Huegill and Libby Lenton have also announced comebacks for London. Skippy's comeback has been so dramatic and successful that he has won the 100m butterfly at the Delhi Commonwealth Games in 2010.

Rohan tells the media of my prospects: 'The first part was to give him a routine and the next step is to increase his workload and he's committed to doing that. At the moment, it's "watch this space". Even if he just creates competition for the young guys, it will be good for the sport.'

I'd talked to Jeremy Oliver first about the possibility of a comeback, and he connected me with Rohan, head coach at Nunawading Swimming Club, one of the biggest and best-resourced clubs in the country. The moment I raised the prospect of a comeback with them, they said 'we're in'. I've known Rohan for more than 12 years and I like him. I also feel the need for a fresh approach. I'm not a young swimmer anymore and I need a more collaborative coach–swimmer relationship, which Rohan is happy to provide. The rest of his male swimmers, guys like Ash Delaney and Travis Mahoney, are at the start of their international careers, so it's a good environment for me. I can tap into their youthful enthusiasm and they can learn from my experience. Rohan is particularly keen for them to see the attention to detail that I bring to training and racing.

In May 2011, we go to Sierra Nevada in Spain for a high-altitude training camp, but my shoulder plays up and I'm back to kicking only in the pool for the first part. When my shoulder settles and I can do more normal work, I find I'm not recovering from the training the way I used to. I can feel a distinct difference between the reactions of my 23-year-old body and those of my 33-year-old body. I'm happy to have the Australian team's head of sports science Bernard Savage there to provide extra guidance and support.

I'm back in Melbourne in June for the birth of our daughter Frankie, a little sister for Stella and Rocco. We now have three children under six and our family is complete. We bring Frankie home to our new house in Brighton.

It's a joyous but busy time. I manage to increase my swimming workload steadily through the year, and in October attend another three-week altitude training camp in Sierra Nevada. It's an opportunity to get myself back to an elite level of fitness. We introduce anaerobic sprints at this camp. Given that it's hard to breathe anyway, why not cut out breathing altogether. But our oxygen debt is so big at the end of each effort that we have to suck on tanks of 100 per cent oxygen to recover. Our strength and conditioning guru Jeremy Oliver is there as well. On a 'rest day' from the pool, he gathers us together and writes the word 'London' on a large bag packed with 20kg of water. He also has a selection of medicine balls and announces that we will be carrying these weights up the steep slope of a nearby mountain, and that the bag cannot touch the ground before we reach the top. At first it's not too hard, but over time and repetition, at altitude, the bag gets heavier and heavier. We each want to put it down, but Jeremy keeps at us, goading us by asking if we're intending to put 'London' down. We can't admit that defeat, so we strain and stumble to the top.

By the end of the camp, I'm feeling fit and strong. So far, my shoulders are holding up to the workload and it's going as smoothly as it can. The plan is to test the waters in a race directly after we arrive back in Australia. I'm entered for a low-key club meet at Nunawading, but my neck plays up on the flight home and I have to delay for a week until it recovers.

Seven days later, I stand behind the starting blocks at MSAC trying to remember my racing routine. I'm so excited when I dive in that I spin my wheels a bit on the first lap, and that leads to some fatigue. There's a timing malfunction when I hit the touchpad, but later I'm timed unofficially at 49.88 seconds for the 100m freestyle, which is a respectable start.

From there, I join the national team sprint camp in Sydney so I can acquaint myself with the new generation of sprinters. James Magnussen, 20, is now the world champion after dominating the 100m freestyle this year, and James Roberts, also 20, has emerged as a world-class competitor. Add in Eamon and Matt Targett, and there is unprecedented depth in the sprints domestically. There's going to be plenty of competition for those six spots in the Olympic relay, but I'm still hopeful.

I'm brought down to earth a bit when I attend the Queensland titles in December and finish seventh fastest in the preliminaries, clocking 50.44 seconds, while Magnussen sets the standard, winning in 48.64 seconds. I'm nearly two seconds off the pace at this stage. I make some progress at the Victorian and NSW titles in early 2012, but I will need a substantial jump in performance if I'm going to challenge for a place on the Australian team at the Olympic trials in Adelaide in March.

I arrive in Adelaide feeling hopeful but realistic. I know I'm an underdog now. The new generation has set the bar under 48 seconds, beyond my very best. I'm in good shape physically, I'm lean and strong, but I don't feel as fresh as I'd like to be. In the old days, I would get a big boost from my taper before competition, but I don't have that this time, perhaps because I've had to modify my training programme so much to accommodate my shoulder soreness.

I swim the fastest I have since I announced my comeback, but it's not enough. I don't reach the final eight in either the 100m freestyle or 100m butterfly. In my absence, the sport has moved on and I'm no longer competitive at the highest level. At least I'm certain this time when I announce my second retirement from the sport. I felt a lot of angst the first time I quit: I was still focused on winning and medals, and the lack of success late in my career hurt me. This time I've enjoyed the ride and rediscovered my appreciation for the sport as a whole, not just when I'm on the podium. I feel at peace as I step away from the pool.

CHAPTER 18

Headwinds

For 18 months, I've had to be selfish to get my training in, and my family has had to make sacrifices for me. We take the kids to Bali for an extended holiday so we can reconnect. The initial plan is for six months. I've been there three weeks when I have to return to Melbourne for a Milk & Co board meeting.

In return for the investment of $2 million, Blue Sky has demanded we clean up our structures and operations by defining roles and introducing a higher level of accountability. It's invaluable advice and helps me build a team with the appropriate expertise in all facets of the business, from online orders to customer service. The demand for accountability includes Blue Sky having a position on our board, so I need to attend those meetings. We also put in place weekly staff meetings where we talk holistically about the business, and each staff member outlines their objectives for the next week.

Too quickly, my life becomes a juggling act between the business in Melbourne and my family in Bali. I end up spending half my time in Melbourne and half in Bali, where the family is thriving. Lindy clearly loves living there and the kids are settled into a local international school. I still need that endorphin rush that I used to get from swimming and racing, so I take up surfing and quickly fall in love with it. Life is easier there than in Melbourne and, given that I'm doing so much travelling, I don't feel I can uproot my family. We've lived for a total of only ten months in the dream house at Brighton that took so much angst to build.

Instead, I end up doing upwards of 20 return trips between Melbourne and Bali each year, trying to serve the needs of my family and those of the business. I don't really understand why, but I'm hell-bent on the business being a success. Perhaps it comes down to the fact that my name is on our products, my face is on all our marketing and I can't let it fail, but it comes at the cost of family life. I tell myself it's a sacrifice now that will secure a better future for all of us.

My comeback brings a couple of side-benefits. It has boosted my profile again, which is good for the business, and it has forced me to take stock of the very social lifestyle I fell into after I retired the first time. I realise that I've been partying too hard and drinking too much, and I need to be more disciplined. I cut the things out of my life that weren't serving me well and I am determined not to backslide now that I'm no longer a professional athlete.

My routine becomes taking an overnight plane from Bali to Melbourne on Sunday night every two weeks, then heading straight to the Milk office, arriving at 8 am on Monday morning. We have a management meeting each Monday. I'm really happy with the team we have now. It's still a pretty lean operation, but each person has their specialty.

I co-opt my old friend Paul Byrne, the former Speedo marketing manager who has also worked for Adidas and Levi Strauss, who becomes our chief financial officer. We create a team of people who really love working for us and are committed to the brand. That's reflected in our customer service and in the shelf space we can secure with retailers.

When I'm in Melbourne, I live in the Olsen Hotel in Chapel St, South Yarra, which is walking distance from the office. If I'm there on Friday night, I join my friend Tory Trewhitt for a run after work. Sometimes we get carried away and run 25km.

The business is going well enough that we can support others. We become a sponsor of World Series Swims, which brings together two of my loves. It's a natural fit as we promote both water safety and a healthy lifestyle. I promote and compete in their open water races where possible, as do some of the Milk and Blue Sky staff. Mark is also an avid swimmer, and over time I feel I've gained a mentor and friend for life. He's training to swim the English Channel to raise money for the Starlight Foundation, of which he's a founding board member, so when he comes to Melbourne, we swim the bay together. He makes a successful Channel crossing from England to France on 8 August 2015, swimming for 14 hours 24 minutes, and raises $1.2 million for the Starlight Foundation.

Inevitably, my long absences start to take a toll on my marriage. I can see the cracks appearing, but I can't seem to close them. There are forces dragging us in different directions and we can't find a way back to each other. In February 2016, we announce our separation. Divorce is always messy, especially when kids are involved. But if there's one thing we agree on, it's that the main priority is making sure our three kids are happy and secure. We reach an agreement that we will both continue to live in Bali and the kids will spend alternate weeks with each of us. I find a house close by so there's not too much disruption for the family. To my relief, the kids settle into this new routine well. I spend one week with them in Bali and the other week in Melbourne.

Professionally, I refocus on Milk & Co. We get another big win when Chemist Warehouse agrees to stock our products. My proposal to owner Mario Verrocchi is for them to take our entire line and to launch a men's fragrance off the back of it. I like the team there very much. Their passion and pride in their business is very much in sync with my own. Despite the fact that they are now one of Australia's biggest retailers, they still run their company like it's a small family business. They agree to stock Milk & Co and our men's range, which we are rebranding as Klim by Michael Klim. Our market research has found that the Milk name is too feminine to appeal to a lot of men. Then we embark on the research and development required to launch the fragrance. R&D is my favourite part of the business. I love developing a new product and launching it into the world, which we do with our first fragrance Aqua Beyond, and then a second, Deep Blue.

A company like Chemist Warehouse relies on fast turnover, so whenever our sales rates dip, I'm quickly onto the phone to assure them we will justify our shelf space. One thing I've learned over the past nine years is that there is no smooth sailing in business. There are always headwinds and you can't let things slide.

In mid-2016, I'm on a global tour to launch our new Klim by Michael Klim branding and campaign. I've done the United States, China, Malaysia, the United Kingdom, Denmark and now I'm in Paris, about to fly to Mumbai for the Indian launch. In my free time, I go to the Eiffel Tower and do a handstand in front of the landmark as a fun photo for Instagram.

I'm meeting Anna in Mumbai and I'm looking forward to it. But as I settle into my seat on the plane, I realise I can't see the screen in front of me properly – it's like a curtain is being drawn across my sight. By the time I arrive in Mumbai, all I can see through my right eye is a grey cloud and I'm panicking about what's happening. I manage to get myself to the hotel, where I wait anxiously for Anna to arrive. Then we contact our local distributor, who organises a visit to an eye clinic the next morning – to see an ophthalmologist who appears to be the Fred Hollows of India in terms of providing free medical care to the poor. He tells me I have a detached retina and will need surgery in the next four days or risk permanent damage to my sight.

That gives us just enough time to do our launch the next day and get on a plane to Melbourne, where I have surgery to reattach the retina. But it doesn't hold: the retina detaches twice more before the end of the year and, while the third surgery is successful, by then I have lost part of my vision in that eye. I've been short-sighted for most of my life, which really made me protective of my vision, and now I'm struggling to cope with having a blind spot on my right side, which affects my depth perception. The kids soon realise that if they sneak up on me from the right side, I won't see them and they can startle me any time they like.

In the middle of the eye saga, I need to fulfil a commitment to Chivas Regal, with which I have a three-year partnership agreement. When I was a swimmer, I shied away from alcohol-related promotion because I didn't think it was right for me. But it does make sense as part of my business career, especially as the campaign that Chivas wants me to front is about promoting ethical and sustainable entrepreneurship, with the slogan 'Win the Right Way'.

The collaboration kicked off in 2015 and the first advertisement featured the Milk & Co staff, including Lindy, which made it a bit awkward when we announced our separation a few months later. I've also filmed an ad with another Chivas ambassador, Chris Evans – better known as Captain America – and I've helped launch Chivas's million-dollar competition to find the world's best social entrepreneurs, called The Venture. I was on the judging panel in the first year to find the Australian winner of the competition, and this year they have asked me to MC the event in Sydney.

I've been doing public speaking and appearances for two decades now, but as the day approaches, I realise that I'm unusually nervous because of my diminished sight. When I'm speaking about myself, I'm happy to ad lib, but on this occasion I can't. I need to do a specific introduction to this event, so I need to read the messaging from cue cards. I practise it over and over beforehand, but I'm still freaking out when I walk out on the stage to welcome everyone and I freeze. I'm seeing spots in front of my eyes so I can't read the cards and I can't remember what they say. I'm stumbling and fumbling over my words. It's excruciatingly embarrassing, particularly as the room is full of entrepreneurs and go-getters, as well as Chivas executives. I can feel the energy going out of the room as I keep losing track of where I am. After the first segment, I go off stage and take a swig of the sponsor's product in the hope it might help. Eventually I relax enough to start finding some rhythm, but the whole thing feels like a car crash. The Chivas people are surprisingly understanding afterwards, and we continue with our partnership for another two years, but they don't ask me to MC a function again.

All in all, 2016 is a difficult year. After my divorce is finalised, I try to begin dating again. I start a new relationship but we struggle to make it work.

After the health scare, on top of my personal problems I immerse myself in physical training as a means of regaining control of my life. There is a desire to get myself as fit as possible, but it is also an escape from another failing relationship. I'm turning 40, so there could be a bit of a mid-life crisis happening. I start training super hard, combining gym sessions, CrossFit and running to an insane level that is, ironically, not healthy for me at all.

In contrast to my personal life, my professional life is thriving. Milk & Co is now on the shelves in 3000 stores in Australia and selling well in Asia – where Australian products have a good reputation for being pure and healthy. We are doing good business in India, South Korea, Malaysia and Singapore, which creates a new opportunity. I'm approached by an Australian–Chinese syndicate wanting to invest in my company. I've been thinking about the next step, and the opportunity to sell comes at the right time. Lindy and I both have new partners, but we are still entangled financially, which is not ideal for either of us. The buyout gives Lindy the chance to exit the company, and Blue Sky also takes the opportunity to recoup on its investment. Apart from my eye problem, I'm starting to have some other health issues and it seems like a good time to simplify my life.

We reach a deal in early 2017 whereby I will sell them 90 per cent of the company, stay on as a salaried general manager and retain 10 per cent of the shares. It's hard to put my baby in someone else's hands, but it's also a relief. My left ankle is playing up badly. It's often sore and swollen, and the joint is so loose that it's prone to dislocation. My lower back is also giving me problems.

At first, the business continues much as it has. The new owners, operating under Aubrands Pty Ltd, come down to Melbourne occasionally and they have grand plans for international expansion. I also know they want to reduce costs by outsourcing. On one visit in 2018, I come back to the office after Friday staff drinks to find them packing up. They inform me that they are moving the company headquarters to Chatswood in Sydney. That's when I come to a hard realisation that the company is no longer my baby and material changes can be made without my approval.

I've expected changes, but I assumed I would be consulted before decisions were made. However, I don't want to leave the business I created. I'm proud of all we've achieved so far, and I am confident it can flourish in the right hands.

It's not that difficult for me to relocate from Melbourne to Sydney, so I continue in my role as general manager. The rest of our long-term staff choose to leave rather than relocate and new staff are employed in Sydney. It's no longer my team and I find myself increasingly isolated by this new direction, which is focused almost entirely on the export market, and particularly China. The Australian business is not their priority.

At the same time, my health continues to deteriorate. I can't keep up the hectic work and travel schedule that I've grown accustomed to. In late 2018, I have arthroscopic surgery on my ankle to clean out any debris. After the ankle surgery, my orthopaedic surgeon, Martin Sullivan, says, 'I will see you soon.' The surgery has been a temporary fix, not a solution. He thinks the ankle will need further work before long.

I also have chronic pain in my back and sciatic nerve problems, including a sensation of hot water being poured down the back of my legs. I undergo a lumbar puncture to explore its causes. Separately, I'm getting increasing cramps in my muscles and pain in my joints. I can also see that I'm losing muscle in my thighs and I've started to feel weakness and numbness in my legs and feet, which is affecting my balance when I move suddenly. I've always been a bit clumsy, but not like this. There's clearly something wrong and I work with my long-term GP in Melbourne, Gary Zimmerman, to explore what's happening. Over the years, I've spent a lot of time in Gary's medical rooms, so he knows me well and has steered me through many challenges, but this may be the biggest of them all. We embark on a battery of tests and scans to try to figure this out.

CHAPTER 19

Fear and Falling

My medical team is still investigating when I set off for a week in Los Angeles in mid-2019. I've committed to helping Gary Hall and Brett Hawke run a swimming camp in Torrance, California. I've run swimming clinics with various former teammates and swimming friends regularly over the years. After he retired, Hawkey established himself as a leading sprint coach at Auburn University in Alabama, where the world 50m and 100m freestyle record-holder Cesar Cielo of Brazil was his star swimmer. Gary coached himself and other world-class sprinters late in his career, so they both run an excellent clinic.

I like passing on my knowledge to new generations, just as it was passed on to me by my former coaches. Running a week-long clinic like this takes a lot of energy, but when I arrive in California, I feel extremely fatigued. I blame jetlag and drag myself through the first few days of the camp, but by the final day I can't even get out of bed. My dodgy ankle has also been bothering me throughout and now I can't stand on it – it won't hold my weight. I call Hawkey and tell him that I won't be able to attend the final day. I also need to get back to the kids in Bali, so I rest up for 24 hours, hobble to the airport in agony and get on a plane home.

A few weeks later, I'm back on my feet to some extent, limping around with the aid of tape and painkillers. One night I'm seeking distraction from my woes, and I decide to go to the beach club Mrs Sippy, managed by my close friend, former water polo player Ryan Crowe. My friends from the band Sneaky Sound System are playing a gig there.

One of the many good things about Bali is that most people come through here eventually, including a lot of my friends and my favourite bands. I arrive at the venue, not planning to stay long. I step up to the bar to order a drink, but before I do, I catch the eye of Connie Mitchell, Sneaky's lead singer, across the room and she waves a bottle of tequila at me, gesturing me over.

When I get there, she is pouring shots for a group of people and she introduces me to her friend Michelle Owen, a DJ and artist who is also doing some gigs at beach clubs in Bali. I'm not looking for a relationship, but the first thing that strikes me about Michelle is that she doesn't look like any other woman I've met. She has an understated elegance but wild hair, which gives her a unique look. We start talking to each other and basically never stop.

There's an instant attraction between us and the more we talk, the more fascinated we become with each other.

We have so many friends in common that it's amazing we've never met before. One of them, Stephen Pavlovic, is one of Australia's most well-known music entrepreneurs. We were both previously nominated for GQ Entrepreneur of the Year and have remained close friends ever since.

Michelle and I quickly discover our common loves for travel, art, Bali, music and the water. Both of us realised what we wanted to do at a young age and went for it – me with swimming and Michelle with music. I already feel like we've known each other forever. When the band goes on stage to start playing, we are left as an accidental couple, so we dance together. At one stage, I realise I'm swaying, so I tell her it's not because I'm drunk, but because I have an issue with my legs that affects my balance. For the first time in a long while, I feel light-hearted. After the gig, we go to dinner with the Sneaky crew, by which point we're as giddy as teenagers.

The others start teasing us, but we don't care. We only have eyes for each other. We're basically inseparable until Michelle goes home to Sydney a few days later, and there's no question about us continuing to see each other there. We talk every day until I get back to Sydney. This is a complicated time for me, but one thing is simple: I've fallen for Michelle and I want to spend as much time with her as I can.

Meanwhile, I continue to explore diagnostic and treatment options, which involve another swathe of tests, MRIs, nerve conduction studies and muscle biopsies. As I lie there in scanner after scanner, I can't believe the part of me that forms such a large chunk of my identity – my strength, my athleticism – is being taken away from me and I can't do anything to stop it.

Over two years, I start to see severe muscle wastage in my legs and I'm no longer able to stand unaided. Some days, my legs give way and I collapse on the floor. I can no longer feel my feet touching the ground as I hobble around with a walking stick.

I'm still trying to meet my work commitments, which include a fair bit of travelling. I'm alone in the Kuala Lumpur Airport one day when I lose all sensation in my legs and collapse to the floor. I just have to wait until I regain feeling below my hips. I call Michelle in tears to tell her what's happening. Just hearing her voice soothes me, but there's not much more she nor anyone else can do. It takes half an hour before my legs work again and I can make my way out of the airport, but it feels like hours. It's the scariest experience of my life.

One thing all the medical experts agree on is that I am going to need surgery on my ankle and back to relieve my pain and to exclude the old injuries as causes of my neurological symptoms. I'm scheduled for ankle fusion surgery in November 2019, with the back operation to follow once I've recovered from the first procedure.

In the meantime, I begin intravenous immunoglobulin (IVIG) therapy and a course of steroids to reduce the effects of the inflammatory condition that is attacking my immune system. I'm told there are other treatments – such as plasma replacement therapy – but they have limited proven success rates.

Michelle stays with me on this daunting journey through the medical system. We've been together only a few months but I know she's right for me, so I invite her to a family gathering for my mother's birthday, which Anna is hosting in November. Meeting my family for the first time is possibly more than she bargained for. My parents are there as well as my kids, Lindy and her new husband, Adam Ellis. It's a pretty unique extended family gathering, but it doesn't scare her off and my family takes to her as quickly as I did. I know they like her because they keep telling me: 'She's a good one … don't mess this up.'

By the end of 2019, there's still no answer on the nerve issues and I'm losing patience with the specialists in Melbourne, so my old friend and Athens Olympic teammate Dave Zalcberg, now an anaesthetist at Royal Prince Alfred Hospital in Sydney, recommends that I consult Dr Judith Spies, a noted neurologist at his hospital. I make an appointment and am immediately impressed by her dynamism and commitment to identifying what is causing my decline.

The RPAH team works through the potential culprits for my nerve problems. They conclude that I have an auto-immune disorder, but they haven't identified which one. They start with the most severe disorders, raising terrifying incurable possibilities like multiple sclerosis and motor neurone disease, which would put me in a wheelchair at first, then an early grave.

In January 2020, I have the cast taken off my ankle, my leg emerging one centimetre shorter on my left side, then return to Bali to recover with my family. I'm still in the early stages of my recovery when the first reports reach us from China that a coronavirus mutation has been discovered in Wuhan and many people are dying from infection. For the moment, it all seems a long way away – but that changes fast.

I'm due to return to Sydney for regular treatment, but in March, travel restrictions are imposed and borders start to close. The World Health Organization declares a global pandemic and when the Australian border shuts on 20 March, I'm faced with an agonising choice – either stay in Bali, where I don't have access to proper treatment, or leave for Sydney and be separated from my children for an undetermined period.

I choose my children before myself. They are all under 15 and they need me. That leaves Michelle with a big decision to make. We have been seeing each other for six months and are facing an unknown period of separation. She's visiting me in Bali when it becomes apparent that the Australian border is about to shut. I ask her to stay with me.

Her work is drying up in Sydney as social events grind to a halt, so she has no real commitments there in the coming months, but this proposal still requires a leap into the unknown on her part. Luckily for me, she closes her eyes and jumps. Neither of us know exactly how momentous that decision will be, or how long it will be before we can return.

Without the infusion treatment I was receiving in Sydney, my health deteriorates drastically. I develop crippling back pain as the result of a degenerative disc. I start falling over and I can't climb stairs unaided. If I stand up, I have to lean on Michelle or the kids to stay upright, but often I am lying in bed all day because the bedroom is upstairs and my back pain is unbearable. By June I can only get around with the aid of crutches or a walking stick. I can't ride my bike because I don't trust my legs or my balance. When people see me and ask about my obvious lack of mobility, I use a slow recovery from my ankle surgery as cover. I'm not ready to admit what's happening to me yet – not to others and not to myself.

I'm not in touch with reality at all. At the same time as I'm watching my legs waste away and I can't get out of bed without help, I am simultaneously planning an ocean swim around the island of Bali to raise money for charity. I start using alcohol to pass the time in lockdown and to numb my fears and my emotions. When Michelle has a glass of wine, I polish off the bottle.

I'm desperate to halt my physical decline so I take a course of steroids, one of the few treatments that are available locally, in the hope that this will ease my symptoms. But it is a false hope and I experience rebound side-effects that make my symptoms worse, both physically and emotionally. I have vision loss and mood swings, experience weight gain and start to get rigors, shivering uncontrollably because my body can't control its temperature.

I've tried my best to protect the kids from my situation, but it's become impossible to hide because I'm in bed so much and when I get up, I'm falling all the time. I can see that they are afraid for me. I know I have to get back to

Sydney for treatment, but I don't want to be separated from them when there's no guarantee that I will be able to return in the near future. They are old enough to know that I may be stuck in Australia, so we are all anxious and fearful.

The crunch comes one day when I am in the villa with Michelle and the kids, and I fall heavily when I try to walk up the stairs. The kids find me on the floor, which is distressing for them. I realise that it's better for all of us if I get back to Sydney to have the spinal surgery I've been putting off and the nerve treatment I need.

Michelle and I travel to Sydney in late June and do a two-week quarantine in a hotel. I then undergo the back operation to decompress the nerves in my spine. We're in surprisingly high spirits in quarantine. It's the closest we've gotten to a honeymoon period in our relationship.

I am released to the Wolper Rehabilitation Hospital for two weeks of rehabilitation, but I hate everything about it from the minute the ambulance drops me off. Somehow, I haven't realised that I would be in constant pain and need full-time care for weeks after the operation, but I definitely don't want to be here. Most of the patients are decades older than me and are recovering from hip or knee replacement surgery. I'm confronted by a palliative care wing on the ground floor. This isn't for me and I don't want to stay. I ring Anna and tell her I'm leaving. We argue on the phone, and she insists I stay. When Michelle arrives, I fight with her as well.

I still see myself as a young, fit man. I can't possibly be in the right place. But I stay because there really isn't any alternative. I can't ask Michelle to become my full-time carer less than a year into our relationship. If I want to go home, I need to get myself fit enough to manage without round-the-clock nursing care. I commit to completing my daily rehab, which includes water therapy. The therapy pool seems to taunt me, reminding me of who I used to be.

When I am finally released to the Adina Apartments in Bondi, I resume an aggressive course of IVIG, the treatment that seems most effective in addressing my symptoms. But the medical drama doesn't end there. As a result of my loss of sensation, I end up with pressure sores on my bunions and develop cellulitis. The infection spreads up my leg and does not respond to antibiotic treatment. Then my other ankle and foot turn blue and become cold to the touch. From the knees down, my legs look like they belong to a dead man, not a live 44-year-old Olympian.

At first the doctors think I may have developed a blood clot, then they decide it was a weird allergic reaction to some of my medication. I start to get headaches and fevers. I develop pressure behind my eye. It feels like my body is literally falling apart. I'm bouncing in and out of the emergency department at Royal Prince Alfred Hospital far too often.

As my system goes haywire, I finally receive a diagnosis for what ails me. It's an autoimmune disorder I've never heard of: Chronic Inflammatory Demyelinating Polyneuropathy (CIDP). It's almost as hard to say as it is to endure. It's a neurological disorder that targets the body's nerves. Myelin is the nerve sheath, and when the sheath is damaged it can't transmit signals from the brain effectively to the nerves.

The messages aren't getting through. Polyneuropathy means it affects the extremities of the body. In my case, it is primarily my feet and legs that are compromised.

At least I know what is happening to me now and that's something of a relief – not only to me, but to Michelle and my family. It gives us a focus, but there aren't that many good therapy options because its progress is unpredictable. About 30 per cent of people end up in a wheelchair, about 30 per cent make a full recovery, the rest are somewhere on the spectrum between, and there's no known cure. And the doctors can't tell me what has caused it – all they can say is that my body is attacking itself as a reaction to being under stress.

I need to wear special shoes, each of which attaches to a brace (ankle-foot orthosis) around my shin to prevent my feet from dragging on the ground and tripping me up. I can't go outside without a walking stick and my physical ability is now so limited that I must calculate how many steps I have to take and how many stairs I must climb and work out whether I can do it. My whole world has changed.

Then there's the terror of being seen by someone who recognises me. I'm now using my back surgery as the excuse for my immobility when I'm in public, but that can't last forever, especially as my physique is changing dramatically due to muscle wastage. I'm incredibly self-conscious about my condition, I don't want anyone to see me like this and when I think about the future it looks completely bleak.

I'm in this state when I hear that Gennadi has died suddenly in Switzerland. It appears that he suffered a stroke.

His daughter Sasha texts me. My primary concern is for her and her mother, Inna, but it's also a loss for me at a time when I am least equipped to bear it.

When I left home at 16, Gennadi became my guide – not only in swimming, but in life. I'd only been in Australia for five years when I moved to the AIS. He showed me not only how to be an elite swimmer, but how to be a man. His never-ending quest for innovation and improvement was a powerful example to me, which I followed in swimming and then took into my business career. I don't know what I would have done without him, and I don't think Australia would have made the sprint revival it has made in the last 30 years without him either. Freestyle sprinting was in the doldrums when he arrived. He gave us direction and confidence that Australia could still produce world-class sprinters and that legacy continues today.

Just three months later, Don Talbot is gone too. Without Don, Gennadi would never have come to Australia, and I may never have reached the heights I did as an athlete. Both men changed my life and I'm grateful to them. I could really use their guidance now.

Between these two deaths, we hit the 20th anniversary of the Sydney Olympic Games in September, which revives media interest in the Sydney Olympic team. Our relay team is in high demand. We're invited to launch a new Marvel superheroes video game in Sydney, which is followed by a series of media interviews. I'm far from being a superhero now and I'm anxious about doing the media round but it would raise questions if I didn't attend, so I pull myself together and prepare to step into the spotlight. Fydes and Thorpey will do most of these interviews with me (Ash can't leave Queensland due to travel restrictions), which means I have to tell them what is happening with my health, even though I'm not ready to tell the world. They are both incredibly supportive and they watch out for me as we complete our media commitments the next day. Fydes offers to walk in front of me when we enter a room, so I can surreptitiously grab his belt for support if I feel I am losing my balance.

The anniversary is a temporary distraction, but it doesn't drag me out of my general despondency. I have so many dark days that I'm struggling to see the light at all. I can't see myself recovering well enough to regain the physical prowess that makes up a large part of my identity. It's a prospect that I find enormously confronting.

For as long as I can remember, I've been an athlete. Even after I stopped swimming, I continued to use my physicality to empower me psychologically. I've taken every opportunity to push myself to extremes, challenging my body to achieve the unachievable. Each success drove me to push even harder the next time, but now I'm going to have to find the mental strength first and use that to overcome my physical limitations, and I don't know how. My mental health is spiralling down with these dark thoughts. I feel like I've completely lost myself.

After five long months, my physical condition stabilises enough for me to return to Bali. We have an early Christmas lunch with my family and then prepare to fly home. To my embarrassment, I need to be taken through Sydney Airport in a wheelchair. I can't walk the distance required to board the plane. I can sense that people have recognised me, but I keep my head down and think about the end goal – which is to see my kids. This is the longest I've ever spent apart from them. It's wonderful to see them, but it doesn't arrest my slide into depression. It brings home to me how limited I am now in what I can do with them.

CHAPTER 20

Taking Control

I'm going through the motions of following a rehab plan – swimming, physiotherapy, meditation – but I'm not committed to it in the way I would normally be. I struggle just to get out of bed each morning. I've never lacked motivation before, but I keep wondering what the point is when I can't even wriggle my toes. One thing I am doing is self-medicating, with painkillers and alcohol, even though the doctors have warned me that alcohol will have an adverse effect on my condition.

I've known about my diagnosis for six months now, but I still haven't told the kids. I know they will have questions, chiefly 'When will you get better?' and I can't answer them. We've used my ankle and back surgery to explain why I can no longer go surfing with them, or play tennis, or do any of the physical activities we used to love. Eventually, those excuses won't wash anymore. They know something is not right, and Michelle and my family believe it's time to be honest with them. When I tell them, they take it surprisingly well. I tell them I don't know when I'll be better, or even whether I'll be better. That breaks my heart. But they respond to my new reality with a maturity and sensitivity that make me proud of them.

Once the kids know, I begin to tell my friends. I'm overwhelmed by the love and support I receive, which puts me in a better headspace temporarily, but it doesn't last.

Through all this turmoil, I have not been able to give much energy to Milk & Co, and once the pandemic hits we start having production and distribution issues that prevent us from restocking retailers in Australia. Slowly but surely, our products are disappearing from the shelves. The whole situation is unstable and for the first time I'm unsure of the future of the business I started 12 years earlier.

I have a bigger fight on my hands now. But it's still a shock when the new owners send me an email terminating my employment in January 2021. I am willing to leave, as it's no longer the company I loved. We enter an extended negotiation on my severance package, which at one stage threatens to end up in the Federal Court and remains unresolved for more than two years.

My body continues to find new and inventive ways to betray me. In May, I go back into hospital in Sydney at the Chris O'Brien Lifehouse, to have a golf ball-sized cyst removed from my larynx. Luckily it is benign, which is the first good medical news I've had for a long time.

The pandemic also disrupts Klim Swim in Melbourne. Mum, Dad and Anna are running the learn-to-swim business out of the Richmond AFL Club pool and the Wesley College pool, but Melbourne has become the most locked-down city in the world, and it is impossible to maintain the schools. We keep getting shut down every time a new wave of coronavirus hits and most of our instructors decide to find more secure employment or go back to government-subsidised study. Mum and Dad are now over 70 and Anna is bearing most of the daily load, while raising three sons. When our lease expires at the Richmond club, we close down the business, both there and at Wesley College.

I'm starting to wonder what else can go wrong in this perfect storm. In some ways, the world really is conspiring against me because the lockdowns and travel restrictions make it easier for me to hide away. Without the discipline of work and public appearances, there's nothing to force me to get my act together and show my face. At the moment, Michelle is my lifeline and this is not what she signed up for. I'm not the man she fell in love with at all. I'm angry, needy and self-pitying, and focused entirely on what I've lost rather than what I have.

Michelle and Anna suggest we start up a Klim Swim Academy in Bali. Without Milk & Co, and the clinics and speaking engagements that have dried up during the pandemic, I'm at a loose end professionally and I've taken a financial hit. The last thing I need is to worry about money or have too much time on my hands.

I haven't done much day-to-day coaching, but I do love giving clinics to young swimmers and helping them improve, and Bali is a great place for a high-quality swimming school, as there is pool access and warm weather all year round. We approach the Finns Recreation Club, where I've been a member and ambassador for more than a decade, with a proposal to start a learn-to-swim school and pre-elite training squad. They jump at it.

I would normally go hard on promotion of a new business venture, but in the current situation I'm more cautious because I'm not sure how much I'll be up to physically. However, Michelle and Anna (from afar) share the workload and we hire good staff and allow our academy to grow organically, which it does surprisingly quickly. We soon set up a second operation at the Australian International School.

I now have more purpose and financial stability, but I'm still struggling to adjust to my physical circumstances. I'm grumpy and unsociable most of the time. I'm not looking after myself properly and I've become a bit of a recluse. I'm also self-conscious about my lack of mobility. I don't want to see the looks on people's faces when they notice my condition or have to explain what's happening. I don't want them to feel sorry for me while I'm busy feeling sorry for myself. I've been one of the fittest people on the planet, I've continued to look after myself physically, I've always tried to do the right thing, so why have I been chosen for this fate? I don't deserve it. I feel like I'm being punished for something I didn't do, and I don't think anyone understands how difficult this is for me. I'm also taking it out on Michelle, making it difficult for her to help me. I know it's not her fault, but she's the one who's there.

Things are no better when my family visits from Melbourne for Easter in 2022. They are disturbed to see me so disengaged, as if I've checked out on life. They can see I'm not interested in anything and they are alarmed by how much I'm drinking to numb my feelings and avoid my new reality. They know this is not me.

With Michelle, they stage a quiet intervention. There's no drama or shouting. It's the calmness and sorrow with which they express their concern that gets through to me. I can finally see how much everyone close to me – especially Michelle and the kids – is being affected by my mental state. My attitude is more alarming to them than my disability.

I admit I'm not coping with my situation and I need help, not just physically but emotionally. I realise I need to take some control of my life or I am in danger of losing much more than I have already.

I'm not the only former swimmer to face big personal challenges. I reach out to Thorpey, who has publicly discussed his mental health struggles, and is now Chair of the AIS Athlete Wellbeing Advisory Committee. He recommends that I contact the AIS Mental Health Referral Network, a group of psychologists and mental health clinicians who specialise in addressing the stresses of high-performance sport. They connect me with Lyndel Abbott, the Australian Olympic Team psychologist. I feel comfortable with her because she understands athletes. She agrees to help me find a way through this.

It is Lyndel who suggests I am feeling grief for the ability I have lost. I haven't considered that before, but it fits.

I've experienced denial, anger, bargaining and depression, but I'm a long way from acceptance. She sees that I am masking a lot of my emotions and helps me work through them. She also encourages me to be more open with Michelle and my family about what I'm feeling. She gives me some coping mechanisms. One is to give myself one hour a day to feel sorry and angry and frustrated and whatever emotion comes into my mind, but then to move on with the rest of my life. That gives me licence to grieve, but it also helps me to stop wallowing.

Lyndel also delves deeper into the impact this condition is having on my identity, ego and sense of self-worth, and the triggers that are sending me off the rails. It's not a short process: it takes months, and many more incidents that demonstrate I'm not coping, which are followed by lots of difficult conversations with Lyndel, Michelle, my family and my friends. Eventually, I begin to understand myself better and feel more in control and become more positive about the life I still have. However, it takes longer still before I can give up the crutch that alcohol has become in my life.

I'm building up my inner strength and resilience, but my physical strength continues to drain away. I've lost almost all my calf muscles, and most of the muscle tone in my legs. I'm fitted with more special ankle-foot orthotics (AFOs) to support me when I'm walking. I'm having frequent massages to keep the circulation moving in my legs. The process of putting on all these aids is time-consuming and annoying.

As part of taking charge of my life, I read widely about autoimmune diseases. There is research that suggests a change of diet may help with my symptoms, so I go through a process of elimination. When I switch to a carnivore diet, I can feel the positive impact almost immediately. I lose weight and I have more energy. I try to maintain a more balanced diet, but I mostly eat meat. It might not work for everyone, but it works for me. I know from my sports days that even small changes to your lifestyle can make a big difference to the outcome.

As I get a bit stronger mentally, I realise that I have to reveal my condition to the public if I'm to stop hiding from the world. The travel restrictions have eased, so I'm flying to Sydney every six weeks for treatment, and inevitably people see me coming or going through the airport and into and out of the hospital. It's time to tell everyone my secret. The only question is how.

I don't want to call a press conference, I'm too vulnerable for that. I need a more controlled environment for this news. I've met Lisa Wilkinson from Channel 10's *The Project* at various events and seen her work. She strikes me as an empathetic interviewer who will tell my story the right way, so my management company TLA contacts her to set up an interview.

I do the interview in my parents' house in Melbourne, with Michelle by my side as she has been for every step on this traumatic journey. When Lisa asks me what my condition is, I stumble over the name – it's a tongue-twister even when you aren't nervous. I tell Lisa about the moment when I couldn't walk in Kuala Lumpur Airport, my failing mobility and the fact that the mental toughness I had as an elite athlete has been no help to me in facing this new reality. Because my identity is based on my physicality, it has been harder for me to accept my new disability because it's such a contrast to my former athleticism. I say that Michelle has been my rock through this ordeal. She has stuck by me even though I've been a difficult person to be around.

Lisa also does short interviews with my parents and my kids about the impact of my diagnosis. My dad breaks down in tears, but vows that this will make us stronger as a family. My daughter Stella also gets quite emotional, and I plead with the crew to cut that footage, which they do. We finish on a positive note when I tell Lisa I am swimming every second day as part of my rehab: 'It used to be my happy place, and it is again,' I say. Afterwards, I feel relieved that I'm no longer carrying the burden of this big secret.

The interview airs on *The Sunday Project* on 10 July 2022 and the response is overwhelming. In the days that follow, I receive over a thousand emails and messages. A handful are obvious scams, but most are from people reaching out to offer help or tell me their own stories, some of having CIDP, others of facing their own challenges in life. My swimming community also responds. Teammates who I haven't talked to lately get back in touch, offering every bit of support they can. Swimming Victoria asks me to be an ambassador for its Performance Pathways development programme. I'm extremely touched. It feels as if Australia has wrapped its arms around me.

But it turns out that while I'm well enough to announce my situation, I'm still not well enough to deal with it and

I have a mental health relapse afterwards. I seek more professional help to quit drinking and improve my mental wellbeing.

However, going public is an important step for me in reawakening my elite mindset. As I struggled to accept the changes to my life brought by this neural disorder, I lost my way and forgot the lessons I had learned as an elite athlete. Now I need to find that mental strength again – to fight against the effects of the disease and work toward a normal life, or as close to it as I can get. It helps that I no longer need to hide from anyone because I can focus on my treatment and rehab.

As my attitude improves, everything else turns around. Professionally, I start to attract new offers and opportunities, including a consulting role with Firbank Grammar School in Melbourne. Klim Swim in Bali is growing steadily. It's labour-intensive, but I'm motivated to make it work.

Without the pandemic travel restrictions, I am able to follow the full protocol prescribed by my neurologist, Dr Judith Spies, and the team at the Royal Prince Alfred Hospital, which enables me to see improvement in my everyday function and mobility. I travel back and forth every six weeks for treatment in Australia, both for the IVIG treatment and for check-ups and tests with my medical team. It is a relentless process to manage my current condition and the long-term effects of my previous injuries.

I start thinking about my treatment and recovery in the same way I once thought about my swimming career. I apply the same discipline and attention to detail that I did as an elite athlete. The difference is that the goal then was to be the best in the world, and there was an end-date to the preparation. Now the goal is to get as close as possible to normal function so I can continue living my life. Knowing that this will be a daily mission for the rest of my life makes it tougher mentally, but I try to remember that this is the only way I will be able to do at least some of the things I love with my family and friends.

I try to stay positive, but my morale is severely tested. I have constant stiffness in my legs, limited mobility and low energy levels. Even with my orthotics, I still fall down occasionally, which is humiliating. For my own safety, I need to use a walking stick in public. This disease has pushed me to the limits of my endurance like nothing else in my life. I've had to accept that I may never surf again, that I may never run again. But there are still many great things I *can* do. I buy a paddle board, which gets me back on the ocean and out there with the kids. And I can still swim. At times I've gone away from swimming and toward more social types of exercise, but the pool is once again my solace. These days, I swim better than I walk.

Some of my training now is in mental visualisation, to make sure my mind is fit to face the daily challenges ahead. I do breathing exercises and meditate regularly to calm my thoughts and help me sleep at night. I practise mindfulness to help me appreciate what I still have, rather than grieve for what I have lost. I have a wonderful support network – a close and loving family, great kids, a beautiful partner and amazing friends. I do a lot of that mental processing while

I am swimming. When I do my rehab, I make sure I'm in the moment and fully focused on the part of my body that I'm working on. I don't go through the motions anymore; I am very purposeful and aware of what I'm trying to achieve with each action.

I'm on a much better path both mentally and physically, which is when I realise that the trauma of the past two or three years has taken a huge toll on Michelle. While I can now focus on the future and plan for what's in store, it's not so easy for her. She also has emotional scars from our journey to hell and back, and she's still triggered from time to time. She's afraid I'll revert to the type of person I was after my diagnosis. Neither of us want to see that person ever again. Michelle put her life and businesses (Almost Real and Snaaps) on hold for me and now she needs to rediscover herself after all we have had to endure. This brings home to me how much my health and wellbeing impacts my loved ones. I have to keep working on being my best self.

My new attitude, and the improvement in my physical condition, make it possible for me to fulfil my professional commitments to my swimming schools in Bali, as well as a schedule of swimming clinics and corporate engagements internationally, and to resume a semblance of my previous life with the kids in Bali. That means a lot.

CHAPTER 21
Surfacing

During the COVID-19 lockdown in April 2020, the International Swimming Hall of Fame announced that I had been chosen as one of that year's inductees, but because of the pandemic the organisers were forced to cancel the ceremony in October. They contact me again in early 2022 to invite me to attend this year's ceremony, which will take place the following November.

I'm to be inducted alongside a host of legends of the aquatic sports, including fellow Australians Jon Sieben, diver Matthew Mitcham and coach Ursula Carlile. I'm surprised by how much it means to be recognised in this way. Despite all my medals and world records, I still have a lingering sense of under-achievement as a swimmer. I feel the absence of an individual Olympic gold medal like a hole in my heart. It still hurts to this day.

It's gratifying to be recognised among the sport's greatest athletes. I invite my parents and Michelle to come with me to the ceremony in Fort Lauderdale, Florida, where the Hall of Fame is based. Unfortunately, it's not possible to take my kids on this trip.

When I walk into the function room, with my walking stick, I spot some of my childhood idols in attendance, including Rowdy Gaines, Greg Louganis and Mary T. Meagher. It's a surreal experience. Jono Sieben is also there. I was in awe of him when I was a kid, and I'm touched when he proudly introduces me to his family.

There's an amazing array of swimming greats and I feel humbled just to be in their presence. It's only then that I understand the enormity of the honour being given to me. When it's time for me to be inducted, I'm introduced as a swimmer 'who will forever be remembered as a great underwater kicker, a great relay swimmer and a great leader of Australian swimming'.

I've prepared a speech, but at the last moment I abandon it. When I'm moved by an experience, I generally just speak from the heart: 'For someone who didn't quite get that individual gold at the Olympic Games, it's a great honour to stand here with [20] world records and a number of World Championships and to feel that I was able to contribute in the fashion I wanted to the Australian team.'

I take the opportunity to thank my parents publicly for the sacrifices they made so I could succeed. I can see that this moment means as much to them as it means to me. Then I'm presented with a red sash, which symbolises my induction to the Hall of Fame. Later, Jono and I do laps of the ISHOF pool together as our own private celebration.

While I've revealed my condition to an Australian audience, the news has not spread to all parts of the international swimming community. When I walk into the ceremony using a walking stick, my lack of mobility is obvious to all. Dara Torres, who is hosting the awards, asks me what is wrong before the ceremony begins.

Afterwards, I'm contacted by 1996 Olympic sprint champion Amy Van Dyken, who is paralysed from the waist down after a car accident. She has heard about my illness and offers me her support. Small kindnesses like this mean the world to me. I'm also glad that Michelle is here to experience this event, as it's her first real introduction to the swimming world. She's had to travel a hard road with me, so it's nice for her to see another side of my life.

My swimming family has been amazing throughout this ordeal. I can't count the number of phone calls and messages I've received from former teammates, coaches and swimmers around the world, sometimes providing ideas and information and offering help, other times just checking in to see if I'm okay. Daniel has offered me the keys to his apartment in Darlinghurst to make my stays in Sydney more comfortable. Matt Abood has lent me his car so I can get to my treatments, Hacky has organised some corporate talks for me to assist with my finances. Thorpey, Simon Cowley, Simon Hinsley, Tim LaForest, Fydes and Skippy regularly check in on me. Hawkey has helped me spread the CIDP message through his community, and we have since embarked on a world tour of clinics, passing our knowledge to the next generation. Adam Pine has also joined the Klim Swim team and supports our camps and clinics. I'm overwhelmed by the support I have received from everyone, and enormously appreciative of their care and thoughtfulness.

My most recent formal contact with the Australian swimming team was in 2016, when I was invited to visit the Australian team training camp at Auburn University ahead of the Rio Olympics. It was great to be with them in that crucial period and offer my support and any words of wisdom I had. I remember doing a breathing exercise with them and talking to them about the power of breathing and being in the moment. I told them that the biggest thing that could hold them back was a lack of self-belief, so above all they had to believe.

I went on to Rio as an Omega Ambassador and was thrilled to see the then 18-year-old Kyle Chalmers stand up and win the Olympic gold medal in the 100m freestyle, the first Australian to win the event since Mike Wenden in 1968, almost half a century before. Kyle and I have formed a good bond and I'm in awe of his consistent excellence, despite his own health challenges, as he approaches his third Olympic Games in Paris.

It's a joy for me to see the Australian swimming team back where it belongs: on top of the world.

In the lead-up to the 2023 World Championships in Fukuoka, Rohan Taylor, now the Australian head coach, invites me to address the team. I can't do it in person because I'm in Bali and it isn't easy for me to travel anymore, but I send a video in which I tell them that the 21 years since we went to the 2001 World Athletics Championships in Fukuoka have passed 'in the blink of an eye', so it is important to make the most of an opportunity that may not come again.

I advise them to set no limits or boundaries on what they can achieve at the championships because I never expected to win seven medals in Perth. I tell them to cherish their teammates because those connections can last forever, and that I am still proud to be an Aussie Dolphin (Swimmer No. 459). At the end of my address, I exhort them to 'enjoy the experience and get after it'.

I am delighted when the team builds on its success at the Tokyo Olympics by reproducing our historic achievement from 2001 and beating the US team to the top of the gold medal tally. The Dolphins finish the 2023 championships with 13 gold medals, including both the men's and women's 100m freestyle titles. Cam McEvoy makes an extraordinary comeback to win the 50m freestyle, Kyle claims the 100m crown, Mollie O'Callaghan wins the 100m and 200m freestyle double and breaks the 200m freestyle world record, leading all three relays to victory, and Kaylee McKeown sweeps the women's backstroke events.

It's a brilliant team performance, and some of the younger swimmers in that team may still be around to experience a home Olympic Games in Brisbane in 2032. Kaylee will be 31 then, Mollie 28 (prime years for a sprinter) and the new world 400m freestyle champion Sam Short will also be 28. A younger generation waits in the wings, some not even teenagers, who will be on that team in Brisbane.

If I could give them some guidance, I would fall back on the lessons my first coach Gene Jackson taught me, which still resonate: 'Listen to the lion' and remember that 'It's nice to be important, but it's more important to be nice'.

As the Brisbane Games approach, some of the leading athletes will become huge stars to the Australian public, as some of us did ahead of Sydney. It's important to stay grounded and not let your head be turned by all the people who are telling you how wonderful you are. Listen to the people who were there before you were famous because they have your best interests at heart.

And know that it's the journey that will give you the most satisfaction, not the ending. A quote from Rudyard Kipling's poem 'If' stands above the entry to Centre Court at Wimbledon:

> If you can meet with Triumph and Disaster
> And treat those two impostors just the same

These are lines for every athlete to live by. It's how you deal with glory and defeat, rather than the fact of them, that ultimately counts.

I won't lie. There is enormous pressure to perform at a home Games. But you can prepare for it by focusing on your training and the process of competing and doing every little thing to the best of your ability. That will give you confidence. Try not to look ahead – stay in the moment. Work toward achieving that optimal balance between arousal and relaxation when you race.

And a word to swimming families and friends. The one thing you can do above all to help your swimmer cope with the stress of Olympic competition is to make sure they know you love them, whether or not they win gold or make the Olympic team. They need to know that their family will be there for them no matter what happens in the pool. Don't talk about their performance unless they want to talk about it. They need your support, not your advice or judgement. Leave coaching to the coaches. Be their lifeline to normality, not another source of expectation. When the stakes are high, fears and self-doubts rise to the surface in almost every athlete, even those who may seem bulletproof. As I said at the beginning, swimmers are never more alone than when they are on the starting blocks. Knowing that they have the unqualified love and support of their families makes a world of difference.

The landscape of sport has changed enormously over the last 20 years: the way governing bodies are structured, the way the media operates and the rise of social media all present new challenges. There are more distractions for athletes, but there are also more opportunities to create a brand and channels through which to express themselves.

There is no doubt that the Australian high-performance system is working well under Rohan Taylor's leadership. You don't get the results the national team has seen in recent years without that, but success can disguise weaknesses in the system, which should be addressed if the national team is to continue to soar.

The high turnover in leadership at Swimming Australia in recent years is worrying because it creates a grave risk of losing institutional wisdom and the deep knowledge of the organisation and the sport that is needed for it to flourish. The sport needs leaders who are fully immersed in swimming and have a long-term vision for the future if the Australian team is to deliver on its potential in 2032.

There has been a trend over the last decade or more toward favouring corporate expertise over sporting expertise in national governing bodies and we need to be careful to make sure the balance between commercial skills and specific sporting knowledge is not tipped too far to the corporate side, because while there are commonalities, sport is different from business.

I hear concerning reports about a lack of coordination and collaboration between Swimming Australia, the state associations and the peak coaching body, SWIM Coaches and Teachers Australia, which means the system isn't working as effectively as it could be. The investment in high performance needs to be matched by investment in and attention to the grassroots, particularly around coaching. Queensland is currently providing the bulk of the national team which means the bigger states are under-performing and we aren't maximising our potential in that area.

The talent keeps coming through the system. However, the right guidance and support are needed for outstanding junior swimmers to make the leap to the world's elite. Every link in the chain must be strong for Australian swimming to make the most of the opportunity that lies ahead of us. This work can only be led by Swimming Australia and it needs to be done immediately. The 2032 Olympics will be here before we know it. I'm confident that the new CEO of Swimming Australia, my old manager Rob Woodhouse, will address these issues.

I still feel quite connected to the Australian swimming team. Being a member of that team was one of the great privileges of my life and I'm immensely grateful that I was part of it for 13 years. In an ideal world, I would have had one more year and one more Olympics, but people who keep pursuing big goals inevitably have to cope with disappointment.

I have my own swimming team now. As head coach, I take my academy squad to meets and championships in Indonesia and go through the highs and lows of competition with them. My sister Anna and brother-in-law Andrew have become swimming parents. Their three boys – Sebastian, Xavier and Jack – are all good swimmers. We watched proudly as Xavier won the 13 years 100m and 200m breaststroke at the Victorian Championships in December 2023. It feels as if we are completing a circle.

CHAPTER 22

The Future

In my life, I've been a son, an immigrant, an athlete, an Olympian, a celebrity, an entrepreneur, a corporate speaker, a husband, a father, a partner, an invalid and a coach. I've broken world records, and I've won and lost gold medals. I've made and lost a lot of money. I've made good decisions and bad decisions. I've put each failure behind me and forged on to chase success. For much of my life, that was my way. Whether it was in sport or business, I was a human steamroller – I just kept moving forward. But it took an illness that threatened to put me permanently in a wheelchair to teach me what was truly important in life.

For a while, the future was a terrifying place, but it isn't now. I've reached a place of acceptance of my situation, which has allowed me to let go of some of the destructive thoughts and emotions I had when my body was deteriorating so alarmingly. I know the road ahead won't be easy, but I can look forward with hope.

I have found a purposeful rehab routine that is improving my health and functionality, thanks to my physiotherapist Hamish Dickie, who lives just down the road in Bali when he's not travelling as an official physiotherapist on the LIV Golf tour. Three times a week, I wake up at 4.45 am to do my gym programme. I liaise daily with Hamish, and we adjust the sessions to ensure I don't fall back into old habits and push myself too hard. I have a simple home gym that includes a Swiss ball, an assault bike, kettle bells and free weights. I use a TENS (transcutaneous electrical nerve stimulation) machine and blood flow-restriction belts to stimulate the nerves in my legs. I'm trying to grow back some of the muscle I've lost. With the electrodes stuck to my body while I work out, I feel like I'm back in the AIS lab.

After my workout, I have an ice bath. I immerse myself for three or four minutes to reduce inflammation, stimulate my immune system and aid recovery. I've turned that into a family activity, so Michelle and the kids often do an ice bath too. Hamish makes me accountable for my training, just as Gennadi used to do. He regularly benchmarks my improvement, which I'm glad to say is significant in most areas. I'm definitely more mobile, and I have more control over my body than I did 18 months ago, which means I've been able to create a lifestyle I can enjoy.

On other days, I keep active with more standard gym sessions or swimming, or some activity with the kids – mostly paddling or snorkelling. About once a month, I have an infusion of vitamins and electrolytes to keep me as healthy as possible.

I've been in the water all my life, but for the first half it was mostly following the black line in swimming pools and swimming fast was my primary objective. It wasn't until we moved to Bali in 2012 that I really fell in love with the ocean and began to fully appreciate the restorative power of the water. Most of the expats in Bali are surfers and that encouraged me to learn how to surf. I was surprised by how much I loved it. I also started doing more open water swimming through my involvement with World Series Swims.

Wherever I travelled in the world, I took the opportunity to swim in the sea and I hope to continue that. On land, gravity has become my opponent, but in the water I am free. One of the reasons why Michelle and I connected so quickly and strongly was our mutual love of the water and we still enjoy that together.

The Klim Swim Academy is going from strength to strength. We opened a third centre at the Australian International School in Jakarta in February, 2024. Bali is a desirable destination, particularly for Australians, and I've had a host of leading swimmers and coaches visit since I opened the Klim Swim Academy – including Kyle Chalmers, Matthew Temple and Isaac Cooper from the current Australian team, internationals Florent Manaudou, Ricardo Busquets and Michael Andrew, and my old teammates Adam Pine and Andrew Lauterstein. I'd love to see an elite training centre set up here with a quality 50m pool. I think it could become a regional hub because it offers perfect training conditions all year round.

I still have hard days, but if I feel low or flat, I just accept it and know tomorrow is a new day. I am not as self-conscious in public about my mobility issues, but I can't pretend I'm not aware of the reactions when people see me using a walking stick. With Michelle's encouragement, I make an effort to go out in public and continue doing the activities my body still allows. We went to a Foo Fighters concert in Melbourne recently. Simple outings like that mean the world to me.

One of the hardest things for me to accept is how my kids see me now. I loved being competitive in sport, business and life, and pushing myself to extremes. I liked the idea of being some kind of superhero to my kids. But I've realised they don't need a superhero; they want a father. They would like me to be able to shoot hoops, dance to music or surf with them like I used to, but what they really want is for me to be there for them, and that I can do.

In my early days as a father, I thought my primary responsibility was as a provider, to make sure the kids had the security of a good home and their physical needs were met. In hindsight, I neglected the nurturing side of being a father. I was trying to do everything at once – a swimming career, a business career, a family life. I was very much present when I was with them, but I was away a lot. I thought it was the big things that mattered, but now I know it's the little things, like turning up to their milestone moments and appreciating their individuality and their achievements. I provided a four-bedroom villa for the family, but some of our best times are when we are hanging out together in one room. What kids really need is stability, to know they are loved and safe. This only became apparent to me once I got sick and had to slow down.

Where once I looked after my kids, now they often look after me, especially when we leave home. They take turns offering their shoulders for me to lean on to keep my balance. We make light of it together, but I know this is taking a toll on them. They are worried about me, and that's not how it should be. As a parent, it grieves me that they have been exposed to this situation at such young ages. It's my job to protect them, not theirs to support me.

It was extremely difficult for my parents and sister to watch my deterioration from a distance without being able to help me due to the COVID-19 restrictions. But it has brought our family closer together, even when we are apart. We are a bigger extended family now because Michelle's parents, Denise and Tony, have also shared our load and supported us through the darkest days.

Michelle had to do all the heavy lifting through the worst of times, and she has not faltered for a single step on this challenging journey. I can only imagine how testing this period has been for her. Our relationship was still relatively new when she left her family, friends and home behind in Sydney, stepping into the unknown to be with me and the kids in Bali. She didn't realise she would become a full-time carer, and I know she felt isolated and abandoned when I could not see past my own misery. I was not nice to her at my lowest points and I'm grateful she stuck with me. She's been a tower of strength in hard times.

This has been a transformative time for all of us, but especially for me.

For many years, I dreamed of personal glory, but now my dream is to establish the Klim Foundation to support research into CIDP and help other sufferers. When I was trying to find information about this disorder, I realised there was no central place where sufferers could find help, advice, recommendations and community, so Michelle and I are creating a foundation that will provide a place to go for those diagnosed with CIDP, where they can find a directory of services, resources and experts to assist them. I also want to be able to put funds into coordinating research and medical trials so we can treat sufferers more effectively in future.

My inspiration for this is my long-term relationship with the Melbourne charity Brainwave Australia, which supports children and families with brain injuries and neurological conditions. I've been their ambassador for almost 20 years, and I've seen the difference they make in people's lives. What they do for children, I want to do for adults with neurological disorders. Our motto will be 'Championing life with CIDP'. I'm putting everything I've learned through sport and business into this new project to make a difference.

There's a lot of work still to be done to understand this disease, and my profile puts me in a unique position to raise awareness and funds.

That's why I accept an offer to become the face of a Red Cross Lifeblood campaign to encourage Australians to donate plasma as well as blood. Donated plasma has become my lifeblood. Every six weeks, I receive an infusion of six bottles of plasma. Ten donors are required to fill each bottle, which means I'm dependent on the generosity of 60 people for each treatment. Without it, I know my physical condition would deteriorate rapidly, as it did when I was unable to return to Sydney for the infusions during the COVID-19 lockdowns.

Awareness is so important. One in three people will need blood products as treatment in their lifetime, but at the start of the campaign only one in 300 people donates blood or plasma. We need to boost those donor numbers.

Six weeks later, Lifeblood reports that the campaign has been a great success. Donations and awareness are at record levels. I am over the moon to have been able to assist in generating awareness and encouraging Aussies to donate blood and plasma.

Once, I thought that you had to be someone like Bob Geldof or Elton John or Greta Thunberg to make a difference to the world, but now I realise that I can also have an impact. The level of fame I have makes me more approachable than those huge international stars, which gives me an opportunity to touch people's lives.

I've always had an all-or-nothing attitude. I wanted to do things 100 per cent or not at all. I always pushed everything I did to the extreme, and it has taken me a long time to discover that while this works for elite sport, it's not a sustainable approach to life. Now I have a better appreciation of the need for balance.

I use the 'Wheel of Wellbeing' as a tool. It encourages people to keep a balance across eight aspects of life: physical, mental, emotional, relational, recreational, environmental, spiritual and financial. The theory is that if one or two spokes become the primary focus, that puts the whole wheel out of balance. The wheel works best when you pay attention to every part of your life.

When I was a teenager, I thought success was about personal achievement and public recognition and materialistic concerns – the gold sports car, the gold chain, the expensive watch. Now I think it's about personal growth, making a difference in other people's lives and finding peace. Some of Bali's spirituality has rubbed off on me.

So am I at peace with myself? I have my good days ... and bad days. It's a work in progress, but I've always had a strong work ethic. Life's a journey, and mine still has a long way to go.

For the Record

Olympic Games

6 Medals: 2 Gold, 3 Silver, 1 Bronze

Atlanta 1996: Bronze, 4 x 100m medley relay

Sydney 2000: Gold, 4 x 100m and 4 x 200m freestyle relay. Silver 4 x 100m medley relay and 100m butterfly

Athens 2004: Silver, 4 x 200m freestyle relay

World Championships

11 Medals: 7 Gold, 2 Silver, 2 Bronze

Perth 1998: Gold, 200m freestyle, 100m butterfly, 4 x 200m freestyle, 4 x 100m medley. Silver, 100m freestyle, 4 x 100m freestyle. Bronze, 50m freestyle.

Fukuoka 2001: Gold, 4 x 100m freestyle, 4 x 200m freestyle

Montreal 2005: Bronze, 4 x 100m freestyle

Melbourne 2007: Gold, 4 x 100m medley

World Championships (Short Course)

15 Medals: 5 Gold, 5 Silver, 5 Bronze

Rio 1995: Gold, 4 x 200m freestyle. Silver, 4 x 100m freestyle, 4 x 100m medley. Bronze, 200m freestyle, 100m butterfly.

Gothenburg 1997: Gold, 4 x 200m freestyle, 4 x 100m medley. Bronze, 100m freestyle, 100m butterfly, 4 x 100m freestyle.

Hong Kong 1999: Gold, 4 x 100m freestyle, 4 x 100m medley. Silver, 100m freestyle, 200m freestyle, 100m butterfly.

Commonwealth Games

11 Medals: 5 Gold, 3 Silver, 3 Bronze

Kuala Lumpur 1998: Gold, 100m freestyle, 4 x 100m freestyle, 4 x 200m freestyle, 4 x 100m medley relay. Silver, 200m freestyle. Bronze, 50m freestyle, 100m butterfly.

Melbourne 2006: Gold, 4 x 100m medley. Silver, 100m butterfly, 4 x 100m freestyle. Bronze, 50m butterfly.

Pan Pacific Championships

12 Medals: 6 Gold, 6 Silver

Atlanta 1995: Silver, 4 x 100m freestyle.

Fukuoka 1997: Gold, 100m freestyle, 200m freestyle. Silver, 100m butterfly, 4 x 100m freestyle, 4 x 200m freestyle, 4 x 100m medley.

Sydney 1999: Gold, 100m freestyle, 100m butterfly, 4 x 100m freestyle, 4 x 200m freestyle. Silver, 200m freestyle.

FINA World Cup

61 Medals: 33 Gold, 15 Silver, 13 Bronze

World Records

20

Long Course

100m freestyle (1)

100m butterfly (3)

4 x 100m freestyle (1)

4 x 200m freestyle (4)

Short Course

50m butterfly (2)

100m butterfly (3)

4 x 200m freestyle (3)

4 x 100m medley (3)

Other Major Awards

1995 Australian Swimming Rookie of the Year

1997 Australian Swimmer of the Year

1997 Swimming World Male Swimmer of the Year

1998 Male Swimmer of the FINA World Championships

1998 Male Athlete of the Year – Australian Sports Awards

1998 Australian Swimmer of the Year

1998 AIS Athlete of the Year

1999 AIS Athlete of the Year

2001 Order of Australia Medal

2001 Inducted into AIS 'Best of the Best'

2022 Inducted into the International Swimming Hall of Fame

Secrets to Success

When I retired from swimming, I wanted to find other passions in my life and my business career has certainly been one of them. I really enjoy passing on to other entrepreneurs what I've learned about running a successful business, and I do so regularly through podcasts and corporate speaking engagements.

I started from nothing and built a company in Milk & Co that I'm really proud of to this day. In the process, I realised that many of the lessons I learned as an elite swimmer were transferable to my business career. I also learned quite a few more along the way. For anyone who is pursuing a career in sport or business, here are the key principles I follow.

Intention/the Why/Passion

Having a clear sense of purpose or a reason to do something simplifies the decision-making process. Making most decisions based on the 'why' usually puts us on the right path. Sacrifices, discipline, perseverance and time management all become a byproduct of our intentions.

Team/Leadership

Surround yourself with like-minded people with similar values and experts in their chosen fields. In life, there are many opportunities to lead, and learning how to do that is crucial to a successful team.

Relationship and Communication

Building and maintaining relationships with staff, coaches, teammates and support staff, and communicating effectively with them, are vital aspects of both sport and business.

Knowledge

Strive to learn more about yourself and others. Being inquisitive is a key to evolution in sport or business. The more knowledge we possess, the better decisions we can make.

Innovation

In sport and in business, standing still is the same as going backward. It's important to continue exploring new ways to innovate. Utilise the resources around you and think outside of the box.

Focus and Concentration

To achieve at an elite level in any field requires high levels of focus and concentration. Being able to focus on the task at hand and maintain concentration are controllable skills that can be developed over time.

Preparation and Planning

Proper preparation for meetings, training sessions, competitions and other aspects of sport and business can lead to more consistent performance.

Response to Adversity

How a person responds to challenges, failures or setbacks is within their control. Learning from mistakes and viewing challenges as opportunities for growth are key.

Self-Talk and Mental Strategies

The internal dialogue in which you engage as an athlete or entrepreneur, and the mental strategies you employ to deal with pressure or anxiety, are within your control and can be refined.

Acknowledgements

For many years I resisted writing a memoir, and now I know why. It's a much bigger project than I anticipated when I said yes to my publisher Hachette in early 2023.

My chief collaborator in this task has been sports journalist Nicole Jeffery. Nicole and I go way back. She first interviewed me when I was 16 and had just moved to the Australian Institute of Sport, and she was a constant throughout my swimming career as she reported on the Australian team, both at home and overseas. So I was in safe hands with Nicole. I'm not sure that anyone else could have wrangled my story into such good shape. For most of my life, I've focused on the future rather than the past, so it wasn't easy to tap back into some of my memories, and sometimes it felt a bit like being on the psychiatrist's couch. Thanks to Nicole for her persistent and (mostly) gentle delving into my history.

I also want to pay tribute to my partner Michelle Owen.

Michelle and I met as my health was deteriorating and we had virtually no honeymoon period before we were plunged into the worst of times. Michelle's steadfast love has been my lifeline at my lowest points and has guided me back to a place of wellbeing. She has enhanced my life in every way. She is a constant inspiration through her individuality, her love for my children, and her creativity in life and business. I love you, Michelle.

In some ways, this book is a long love letter to my children, Stella, Rocco, and my youngest Frankie, who may not remember a time when Daddy didn't need her help to stand up straight.

It is also an expression of gratitude for the life that my parents, Ewa and Wojtek, worked so hard to give me, the lifelong support I have had from my sister Anna, and the incredible generosity I have experienced from my partner, friends and teammates.

When my memory failed me, they were there to remind us of stories, facts and details that have greatly enhanced the telling of my story. My parents and sister dug into our collective memory bank to recall the early years, and provide background on the journey that led us to Australia and enabled our family to thrive in Melbourne.

My former teammates, and lifelong friends, Ian Thorpe, Grant Hackett, Chris Fydler, Daniel Kowalski, Brett Hawke and Adam Pine gave generously of their time to help out an old mate, as did my former rival, now friend, Gary Hall.

Sadly, two of my biggest coaching influences Gennadi Touretski and Don Talbot were no longer around to consult, but Jim Fowlie, Ian Pope, Rohan Taylor and Alan Thompson contributed their recollections, as did the former Australian team media manager Ian Hanson and my long-standing manager Rob Woodhouse.

My friend Jeremy Carp and trainer Jeremy Oliver came into my life when I needed them and have been stalwart supporters, in this as in all things.

I would also like to thank my managers at TLA, Tony Box, Jack Elliott and Shannon Beck; my publisher at Hachette, Scott Henderson, who first brought this project to my publicist George Moskos; and editors Annie Zhang and Sue Jarvis, for guiding us through this process, providing reassurance when needed, and making the book better.

My life, and this memoir, would be poorer without all of these contributions.